Library 2.0 Initiatives in Academic Libraries

Laura B. Cohen, editor

http://acrl.ala.org/L2Initiatives/

Association of College and Research Libraries
A division of the American Library Association
Chicago 2007

The paper used in this publication meets the minimum requirements of American National Standard for Information Sciences–Permanence of Paper for Printed Library Materials, ANSI Z39.48-1992. ∞

Library of Congress Cataloging-in-Publication Data

Library 2.0 initiatives in academic libraries / Laura B. Cohen, editor.
p. cm.
ISBN 978-0-8389-8452-9 (pbk. : alk. paper)
1. Academic libraries--Information technology--Case studies. I. Cohen, Laura B.

Z675.U5L48 2007
025.5'24--dc22
2007041401

Printed in the United States of America.

11 10 09 08 07 5 4 3 2 1

Table of Contents

Introduction

Laura B. Cohen

This book presents case studies of Library 2.0 initiatives in academic libraries. These initiatives, taking place in three countries, range from the accomplishments of individual librarians to projects that involve significant staff collaboration. The beneficiaries of these initiatives are similarly wide-ranging, from students in a single course to university-wide populations and beyond.

This scope is intentional. It is possible, and in fact desirable, to develop Library 2.0 projects on many levels. The pursuit of these projects will depend on a number of factors, including library and campus needs, individual and group initiative, administrator support, funding, technical infrastructure, and skills available on staff. Partnership opportunities can also bring projects to life. The cases presented in this publication drive home the fact that the necessary conditions for undertaking successful Library 2.0 initiatives can be quite varied.

Library 2.0 Concepts

In order to fully understand the nature of these initiatives, it is important to grasp the concept of Library 2.0. It is generally agreed that the term emerged in 2005 through discussions on blogs and at the California-based Internet Librarian conference that fall. While there has been debate about the exact parameters of Library 2.0, a consensus has developed around the basics of the concept.

Library 2.0 is a response to Web 2.0, the revolution in the way people create, edit, search, evaluate, organize, and share information. In contrast to the surfing-based environment of Web 1.0, Web 2.0 is characterized by networked communities on which users contribute content, interact, and collaborate.

Facebook, Del.icio.us, Flickr, YouTube, Digg, and Wikipedia are well-known examples of the user-driven, participatory, personalized world of Web 2.0.

Library 2.0 is an endeavor to incorporate this culture into the culture of libraries. Through the use of 2.0 tools and with a 2.0 mindset, librarians provide services, undertake instruction, and enhance access to collections and other useful content, all in a way that seeks to meet user needs and respond to user feedback. Breaking down barriers between librarians and users is a primary goal of this library transformation.

The guiding principles of Library 2.0 for academic librarians may be summarized as a collection of concepts. As with many things related to the Web, there is fluidity in the ways in which these concepts may be interpreted.

Web 2.0 as a model. Library 2.0 emulates Web 2.0 as a promotion of user participation in community-based environments. Accordingly, libraries become socialized institutions. Active participation on the part of users is seen as essential to the process of research and learning. Libraries *make collections available via open, personalized, interactive services that encourage such activities as content creation, editing, commenting, annotating, bookmarking, rating, and tagging by users. Librarians use social software, such as IM chat clients, to communicate interactively with users. As a result, networked library spaces become community spaces. Librarians also host research spaces that enhance the findability of their collections with features found in the 2.0 world, for example faceted browsing, relevancy ranking, subject or tag clouds, and various social options. Bringing content into li-*

brary spaces from the wider Web is an additional goal, often with the use of RSS feeds.

Assessment drives nimble change. Library 2.0 encourages assessment as an impetus for the creation and refinement of library services. In so doing, librarians become informed about the ways in which users participate in their information culture and how this participation shapes their needs and expectations for library services. This viewpoint recognizes that libraries are an important player in the information culture of the world. Because of the rapid changes in the world's information culture, routine assessment contributes to the continual adaptability of library services.

The long tail. The long tail is a concept attributed to Chris Anderson and first appeared in his 2004 article in *Wired* (Anderson). In this piece, Anderson proposed that niche markets drive the entertainment industry. In libraries, reference services and interlibrary loan are excellent examples of the long tail. These services cater to a steady aggregation of niche markets which accumulates to a larger market share than that represented by the smaller market of identical requests. In the world of Library 2.0, the long tail is relevant to the development of collections as well as technological and service innovations. The endeavor to serve the range of user needs and expectations in a networked social environment is one of the central concepts of Library 2.0

Promotion of social scholarship. Social scholarship is an open process that utilizes Web 2.0 tools to foster the sharing of research interests and publications. Social scholars employ collaborative tools to publish, ruminate about, comment on, annotate, store, tag, bookmark, and rate content related to research. For example, wikis host scholarly publications that optimize collaborative authorship and track ongoing revisions. Blogs are used to relay observations about a research area and to invite comments. New models of journal publishing offer social features that create a community of interaction around articles. Librarians can play an important

role in social scholarship by promoting the use of social tools in the scholarly endeavor. Whenever possible, librarians host or collaborate on hosting Web platforms that foster a 2.0 way of scholarship. They incorporate social tools into information literacy courses to create engaged, user-driven learning environments and to train users to become social scholars. They also train students to find and use content in non-traditional sources including RSS feeds, blogs, social bookmarking sites, and online communities.

Radical trust. User input is a hallmark of Web 2.0. Many 2.0 sites consist exclusively of such contributions. On other types of sites, users can contribute comments, ratings, tags, or annotations to existing content. The notion of radical trust asserts that users make these contributions in good faith. In the library context, users are invited to play an integral role in the transformation of libraries into participatory institutions. *Librarians* can open their Web spaces to various types of user input, for example contributions to topical resource pages or maintenance of help documentation. They can maintain blogs about public services and encourage user comments and suggestions. They can invite user ratings and discussion of featured content. Students can train librarians to use Web 2.0 tools and suggest ways in which these tools can enhance library services. They can serve as consultants on committees, or act as rovers to provide peer assistance to other users. While librarians are dedicated to serving their constituents, the library's constituents also contribute to the endeavors of librarians. The value of the communication flows in both directions.

Librarians cede control. As libraries move to develop services in collaboration with users and to open Web spaces to user contributions, librarians give up a measure of control over their environment. For example, a tagging option in online catalogs demonstrates the value of user-generated subject access alongside precoordinated subject headings. Through these types of activities, librarians and their users forge a new kind of partnership.

Taking the library to users. Over the past several years, the growth of the Web has created a significant expansion of library use that accommodates remote users. Web 2.0 has accelerated this trend as users set up profiles on community spaces, upload content to photo or video sharing sites, save bookmarks on social reference sites, maintain blogs with external providers, and use research materials not associated with the library. Library 2.0 advocates for a librarian presence in the Web 2.0 spaces where their users may be found. Librarians can push their own content, offer research services, answer questions, develop resource lists, and carry out other professional activities in the community spaces where their users congregate. Academic libraries can enhance their presence within the campus portal or course management system to provide resources and services at the point of need. The creation of physical spaces that enhance 2.0 ways of teaching, research, and learning is also a part of a Library 2.0 scenario.

Component applications. Librarians take their cue from Web 2.0 and construct online spaces managed by interoperable, scalable components, e.g., content management systems, Application Programming Interfaces, Web services, widgets, mashups, XML formats, and so on. This mix and match scenario allows librarians to offer feature-rich sites using components that are often freely-available, open source applications. For example, a spell checking service can be added to an online catalog, a chat widget embedded on a Web page, and links to targeted research tools pushed to a course management system via RSS feeds.

Perpetual beta. In creating component applications, librarians take an experimental, risk-taking approach. They do not attempt perfection when releasing a new application. Rather, they understand that any product will undergo enhancements as a result of user feedback, experience with the project, new skills and insights, developments in technology, examples from other libraries, and so on. This scenario encourages expedited development, flexibility, and an openness to ongoing improvement.

Ultimately, the notion of Library 2.0 can be seen as a transcendent belief system that is a jumping-off point for ongoing flexibility in a world in which the information culture is rapidly changing. In this view, libraries evolve wisely and nimbly to meet users' evolving needs as their information culture shapes these needs. The culture may be Web 2.0 or other future developments. Timeless adaptability is key.

Format of this Publication

Library 2.0 Initiatives in Academic Libraries is a hybrid monograph/wiki publication. This monograph presents twelve case studies. Each case introduces the topic and describes the rationale for pursuing the project. The Library 2.0 principles embodied in the case are also discussed. The case study is then presented. In some chapters, multiple initiatives comprise the study. Plans for future developments conclude each chapter. The authorial voices in these cases are varied by design, and often reflect the individual or group experiences that saw these projects through.

The wiki, hosted by the Association of College and Research Libraries, presents project updates for each of the cases for at least two years subsequent to this monograph's publication. The wiki is located at http://acrl.ala.org/L2Initiatives/. The updates can be tracked on the wiki site or by RSS feed.

This combination of publishing formats is meant to extend the useful life of the case studies. A printed monograph is a static publication that is only updated when a new edition is produced. The production of a new edition is subject to a variety of considerations. These include the sales potential of such a publication and the willingness of authors to rewrite their chapters. A book of case studies does not routinely lend itself to this type of republication. There is also the issue of lead time. Case study updates – potentially numerous, varied, and evolving through time – are optimally useful if published in a timely manner.

A regularly-updated wiki is particularly appropriate to the case studies presented in this volume. Many of the cases are early stage projects. All are evolving. In the spirit of perpetual beta, any initiative that follows the principles of Library 2.0 will undergo change. The wiki updates will keep readers informed as these projects develop.

In true Library 2.0 fashion, the use of a wiki to update the case studies is an experiment in open-ended networked publishing. This is a novelty in the professional library literature. The method of maintaining the wiki updates has been left to the authors' discretion. Readers can assess the development of best practices as this publishing format matures.

The Case Studies

The case studies describe several emerging practices of Library 2.0. These include the varied uses of networked social software and open data formats to facilitate scholarly communication and to add value to and distribute library resources and services. Other cases describe 2.0 ways of pedagogy, the provision of services in physical and online spaces where students congregate, online catalog enhancements, and the creation of feature-rich interfaces for accessing digital research collections.

In Chapter 1, "Discovering Places to Serve Patrons in the Long Tail," five authors from the University of Nevada, Las Vegas University Libraries, discuss how their institution has employed the long tail approach to services and conducted routine assessment activities in order to define the physical and virtual environments to best serve its patrons. Patrick Griffis, Kristin Costello, Darcy Del Bosque, Cory Lampert, and Eva Stowers describe a long tail approach that provides services by experimenting with a multitude of low-risk initiatives that can extend the library to users in diverse settings rather than focusing on a few large-scale initiatives designed to reach a concentrated set of users. Initiatives presented in this case include virtual reference, a Wikipedia page about the library,

a library presence on MySpace, a variety of blogs, use of RSS feeds to distribute library information, a library presence in the campus portal and course management system, and provision of a librarian's services on a branch campus. This case outlines the University Libraries' endeavors to extend its presence through the testing and evaluation of innovative services which are fostered through an internal participatory environment.

In Chapter 2, Kathryn Greenhill, Margaret Jones, and Jean McKay of Murdoch University Library in Australia describe their discovery that they had already implemented several programs that could be considered Library 2.0. In their case, "Chat, Commons, and Collaboration: Inadvertently Library 2.0 in Western Australia," they note that participative, egalitarian, and interdisciplinary aspects of Library 2.0 were already ingrained in their library's culture. The authors discuss their chat reference service, creation of a Learning Common, a collaborative project to learn about Library 2.0, creation of an Emerging Technologies Group, and experiments with a virtual library service in Second Life. The theme running throughout is that their University already held some of the core values of Library 2.0 and that these services flowed naturally from this background.

In Chapter 3, Kalee Sprague and Roy Lechich of Yale University Library describe an initiative to incorporate library resources and services into the diverse environments where readers and researchers conduct their daily intellectual lives, including course management systems, non-library portals, and personal information management tools. In their case "Yale: Taking the Library to Users in the Online University Environment," the authors discuss the library's efforts to embed library services and resources in Web browsers, Yale's uPortal portal application, and the Sakai course management system. Specific projects include: adding the library catalog to Open WorldCat, creating a browser search plugin, the production of library XML feeds for use in Sakai and uPortal, and the library's exploration of ways to provide federated search tools in the Sakai environment. The authors highlight their practical experiences identifying, developing, and implementing these projects.

In Chapter 4, "Delivering Targeted Library Resources into a Blackboard Framework," Richard Cox discusses the planning, development, and implementation of an application that pushes library content into the Blackboard Course Management system. Developed at the University Libraries, University of North Carolina at Greensboro, this tool is built around a number of technologies including SOAP Web services, ASP.NET, Java, AJAX, and Adobe Flex. Through use of this application, the library provides up-to-date links to databases and e-journals at the course level, thereby establishing a presence at a point of need. This application may be the first to integrate library content dynamically into Blackboard at this level and scale.

In Chapter 5, "Adapting an Open Source, Scholarly Web 2.0 System for Findability in Library Collections," Bethany Nowviski, Elizabeth Sadler, and Erik Hatcher examine solutions to the difficulty in creating a usable interface for digital library collections. The authors introduce NINES, an independent digital publishing initiative housed in the main research library at the University of Virginia. They describe the development of Collex, an open-source tool that enables Web 2.0-inspired interaction with federated online collections. Through an informal collaboration with NINES, the University of Virginia Library is adapting this scholar-driven social software system into Project Blacklight, a faceted OPAC with relevancy ranking. Blacklight is designed to address issues of findability in complex library catalogs. This case describes Collex and Blacklight and discusses these aligned projects in terms of the value of a technical partnership between libraries and the scholarly communities they serve, communities which are beginning to take an active interest (albeit from a different perspective) in interface design and access to digital collections.

In Chapter 6, "Push and Pull of the OPAC," Daniel Forsman describes the work done at Jönköping University Library in Sweden to implement technical solutions associated with Web 2.0. These include developing the OPAC as a Web resource rich in content and features and fully integrated with the library Web site. Emphasis is placed on the technical aspects of Web 2.0 rather than the social features often discussed in the literature. In his case, Forsman gives examples of spelling suggestions, dynamic help, search forwarding, linking to catalog content, and graphical and structural integration with his library's Web site, all implemented within the Ex Libris Aleph 500 system.

In Chapter 7, "UThink: Library Hosted Blogs for a University-Wide Community," Shane Nakerud of the University Libraries, University of Minnesota, Twin Cities Campus, describes UThink: Blogs at the University of Minnesota Libraries. UThink began in April 2004 and is now one of the largest, if not the largest, academic blogging sites in the United States. UThink began with these goals: to promote intellectual freedom, to help build communities of interest on campus, to investigate the connections between blogging and the traditional academic enterprise, and to help retain the cultural memory of the institution. This case discusses how well the University of Minnesota Libraries has met these goals through the UThink project. It also focuses on the project as a whole, from its inception to its current iteration. The future of the project is also discussed.

In Chapter 8, Gregory Bobish presents a case on his information literacy course blog developed at the University Libraries at the University at Albany. His case, titled "Discussing Student Engagement: An Information Literacy Course Blog," describes how student discussion in a one-credit information literacy course at the University Libraries at the University at Albany was flagging. In order to stimulate discussion and broaden participation, a course blog was developed. This blog functions both as a clearinghouse for course information and last-minute announcements as well as a forum for discussion. Most importantly for student engagement, students are required to comment on several information literacy-related blog postings as part of their homework. This not only means that every student has to process and respond to course material in writing, but also enables each student to see what his or her peers have to say and ensures that everyone is ready for class discussions. Students have been very receptive to the initiative, participating more often and in more depth than is required. Bobish notes that with each semester, new assignments and new technologies have increased the effectiveness of this flexible tool.

In Chapter 9, Susan Sharpless Smith, Erik Mitchell, and Caroline Numbers discuss a pilot program at Wake Forest University's Z. Smith Reynolds Library that was designed to revitalize information literacy instruction through the introduction of Library 2.0 concepts. Their case is entitled, "Building Library 2.0 into Information Literacy: A Case Study." The pilot explored new methods and technologies that can be used to engage students in a collaborative environment. The goal was to produce a class that is more relevant to how students learn through using current information issues, collaborative social software, and information management applications. The authors include a discussion of conventional information literacy program standards and educational theories that informed the framework of the pilot's structure.

In Chapter 10, "IMplementing IM @ Reference: The GW Experience," Deborah B. Gaspar and Sarah Palacios Wilhelm detail the development of the Instant Messaging (IM) Reference service at The George Washington University. The authors include a brief literature review exploring the characteristics of 21st century college students as well as the uses of IM. Information on software selection, including an examination of downloadable versus Web-based IM applications, is provided. The case also addresses staffing models, advertis-

ing, and training. Librarians at the University focused on the question: how do we serve students in their preferred medium of communication? When seeking information, students have many options available to them. The librarians wanted to shape reference services to place the library and credible information within the students' selected mode of communicating.

In Chapter 11, "Taking the Library to Users: Experimenting with Facebook as an Outreach Tool," Dawn Lawson of New York University Libraries describes her outreach effort as East Asian studies librarian using Facebook, a social networking Web site popular among undergraduates. After searching the site for students who had listed East Asian studies as one of their concentrations, Lawson sent messages to them within Facebook, introducing herself and inviting them to make use of library resources. Close to twenty percent of the students replied immediately, several with specific reference questions. Lawson describes many of the challenges she faced in her attempts to provide services within the Facebook environment. In addition to discussing the motivation, methodology, and results of the outreach project, she suggests various possibilities for future expansion of this type of activity.

In Chapter 12, Jason A. Clark of Montana State University Libraries, Bozeman, describes how Application Programming Interfaces and XML feeds have enhanced content for Montana State University digital library projects. His case is entitled, "YouTube University: Using XML, Web Services, and Online Video Services to Serve University and Library Video Content." The case study project, "TERRA: The Nature of Our World," is a working digital video library which leverages the user communities of blip.tv, iTunes, and FeedBurner to distribute its content. The site features a robust XML metadata architecture that enables podcasting and syndication of content. It also features social networking functionality with ratings and comments for each episode. The case considers: the advantages of leveraging popular online video sites to distribute content; employing the network infrastructure of these sites to serve large video files; how to use common XML formats for pushing content to users and retrieving content from remote Web sites; and finally, the advantages of opening up digital library sites to user communities through commenting, rating, and forum systems.

The library profession is in the early stages of coming to terms with Library 2.0. This compendium paints a picture of libraries in a state of exploration and experimentation. In the cases described in this book, Library 2.0 concepts are driving the provision of resources and services to meet critical new challenges for teaching, learning, and research. Whether on an institution-wide or individual level, these cases demonstrate that libraries are playing a key role in incorporating the rapidly-changing landscape of information culture into both physical and online spaces. In many ways, these Library 2.0 initiatives are positioning libraries as innovators on campus.

Library 2.0 Initiatives in Academic Libraries reinforces a consensus around Library 2.0 concepts and best practices. The case studies will be useful to librarians who wish to gain practical knowledge about the nature of Library 2.0 and the types of projects they might consider for their own institutions. As such, they can serve as a guide to action. This publication will also appeal to librarians engaged in these types of initiatives and are interested in similar projects taking place in other libraries. Undergraduate and graduate students in library and information science will also find value in this publication as they prepare for their careers.

The "Library Initiatives in Academic Libraries" Wiki can be found at http://acrl.ala.org/L2Initiatives/.

Acknowledgments

Library 2.0 Initiatives in Academic Libraries owes its existence to Kathryn Deiss, Content Strategist at ACRL. Kathryn is a visionary. She conceived of the topic, invited me to serve as editor, and above all, enthusiastically embraced my proposal to make this a hybrid book/wiki publication. She shepherded our project through all its phases. Kathryn is an editor's dream, and I'm very grateful for the opportunity to work with her.

Many thanks to the authors of these chapters. Their work confirms the serious effort, creativity, and teamwork it takes to move libraries into the 2.0 era. They are role models and inspirations. I especially appreciate their tolerance of not only my edits, but also Kathryn's. They were gracious throughout the process. Their participation in the wiki phase of this publication will contribute to new models of scholarly communication.

Thanks to Charles Fineman, Librarian for France, Italy, and Scandinavia at Harvard University, for his editorial assistance. I also appreciate the work of David Free, Marketing and Communications Specialist at ACRL, for his help in setting up the post-publication wiki. The book design and wiki logo are products of the talented Dawn Mueller, Production Editor at ACRL.

Notes

1. Anderson, Chris. The Long Tail. 2004. Wired 12 (October). http://www.wired.com/wired/archive/12.10/tail.html.

Discovering Places to Serve Patrons in the Long Tail

Patrick Griffis, Kristen Costello, Darcy Del Bosque, Cory Lampert, and Eva Stowers

Abstract

This chapter describes the efforts of the University of Nevada, Las Vegas (UNLV) University Libraries to employ the long tail approach to services and to conduct routine assessment activities in order to define the physical and virtual environments to best serve its patrons. The University Libraries has harnessed the long tail in providing services by experimenting with a multitude of low-risk initiatives that can extend the library to patrons in diverse settings rather than focusing on a few large-scale initiatives designed to reach a concentrated set of patrons.

In pursuing this approach, the University Libraries has focused more on expanding its virtual presence than its physical presence, as it already has an established physical presence on campus. This chapter outlines the University Libraries' initiative to extend its presence through the testing and evaluation of innovative services which are fostered through an internal participatory environment.

Introduction

The Long Tail and the UNLV University Libraries

A central tenant of Library 2.0 is taking the library to the user. This entails catering to niche markets to fulfill unique user needs. This is similar to a concept called the long tail, which is essentially an economic model that purposefully caters to niche markets. The concept of the long tail was first introduced by Chris Anderson in his October 2004 article in *Wired* Magazine. In this article, Anderson explains that businesses traditionally focused on selling popular items, because products cannot create a profit if they do not generate sufficient demand. As e-commerce allowed companies to sell to a wider base of customers, while at the same time reducing manufacturing costs, distribution fees, and the cost of maintaining a traditional store, it opened up the possibility of creating a profit from selling niche products to a small segment of the population. Anderson (2004) states, "The market for books that are not even sold in the average bookstore is larger than the market for those that are." This concept is not unfamiliar to libraries because collections are built to serve a wide patron base and many items are checked out very rarely or not at all. Marylaine Block was quoted in the OCLC Newsletter (Storey 2005) as saying, "Libraries have been in the Long Tail business for centuries. The only thing new about the Long Tail is that because of the Internet, the commercial world is just now discovering it."

Although the concept of the long tail was not new for collections, the vision of user services at the UNLV University Libraries articulated in its strategic plan began to mirror this concept. Rather than considering the distribution of items through the long tail, the Libraries began to think in terms of service locations. The focus on service locations has been motivated by an increasingly diverse set of interests and preferences regarding traditional library service offerings expressed by users in response to LibQual surveys and via comment boxes

Patrick Griffis, e-mail: patrick.griffis@unlv.edu; Kristen Costello, e-mail: kristen.costello@unlv.edu; Darcy Del Bosque, e-mail: darcy.delbosque@unlv.edu; Cory Lampert, e-mail: cory.lampert@unlv.edu; and Eva Stowers, e-mail: eva.stowers@unlv.edu, all from the University of Nevada, Las Vegas.

placed at library service desks. It became clear to University Libraries staff that their users wanted a variety of choices for library service offerings.

It also became clear that the user base reached by library services could be greatly expanded if small segments of users with unique needs could be reached through several innovative, low-cost initiatives such as a library presence in MySpace, WebCT, or Wikipedia,. In their article "Library 2.0: Service for the Next-generation Library" authors Michael E. Casey and Laura C. Savastinuk (2006) assert that "In the current library world… we are accustomed to focusing our services on those customers we already reach" and further claim that "…nonusers might be better served if librarians consider what's called the long tail." The authors propose that "going after the diverse long tail requires a combination of physical and virtual services, a move underway in many libraries."

If an academic library were truly to harness the long tail in pursuing the Library 2.0 initiative of taking the library to its patrons, it would need to create a presence wherever students and faculty spend their time both in the real world and the virtual world. Should academic libraries work primarily toward integration into emerging academic contexts or should they strive to integrate into emerging contexts of a more social character? The nature of Library 2.0 is one of rapid change and beta stages of production. How does an academic library, with a culture based on careful planning and assessment, adapt to such an environment?

The UNLV University Libraries has taken a proactive approach to the Library 2.0 environment by educating and empowering staff in the use of new technologies. Communication is fostered by open, cross-departmental forums in which staff creativity and innovation are encouraged. Staff members propose topics of interest and meet to discuss them. Web 2.0 tools, such as wikis and blogs, are used to communicate information and encourage dialogue after meetings. These discussions generate new ideas for projects which stimu-

late the evaluation of possible future services. As projects are proposed, designed, implemented, and assessed, they are subject to modification to increase success or may be discontinued in favor of new projects with more potential appeal.

The encouragement of staff to meet the long tail of unique user preferences for services has led to the initiation of such projects as blogging, instant messaging (IM), text messaging, wikis, enhanced digital collections, and use of social networking sites. Entrance into virtual settings encourages interaction with a more diverse patron base and integration into the course management system reflects efforts to provide personalization of library services. Virtual spaces are not the only areas that have been revisited. Librarians have also gained exposure in physical spaces outside the library, including faculty offices and satellite campuses. Many future projects are in development with proposals to investigate Web conferencing platforms, Web page widgets, and Webcams. These initiatives will continue to be evaluated to determine which environments are most beneficial for serving patrons in the era of Library 2.0.

UNLV University Libraries Strategic Plan

The University Libraries is an innovative and creative organization whose mission statement reflects the organization's commitment to embracing change while continuing to support the traditional role of the library. The statement, adopted in 2005, states that the University Libraries (2005) "supports the mission of the University to emerge as a premier metropolitan university, embracing the traditional values of higher education adapted for the global community in the 21st century." This mission statement reflects a dynamic approach to the future as well as a dedication to helping the academic community respond to change. The University of Nevada, Las Vegas is a young organization, celebrating its 50th anniversary in 2007. Its student body is heavily commuter based and has been rapidly growing over the last decade. As a result, the University Libraries has adopted strategic goals that are reflective of the rapidly changing nature of this distinctive educational community.

The user experience is the central focus of services at the University Libraries. The strategic plan (2005) affirms that the University Libraries seeks to provide "user-focused environments committed to identifying and delivering information resources and services that meet or exceed user expectations, regardless of user location." By insisting on highest service standards for patrons (both in the physical library buildings and virtually), the University Libraries acknowledges that as user expectations change and as services are extended to more niche groups, the University Libraries will refocus and adapt to continue to meet the full spectrum of information needs. Through exploring new ways to meet patrons in virtual and physical environments, social and academic contexts, and individual and community settings, the University Libraries has worked on a variety of recent projects which support this strategic goal.

The strategic plan addresses the changing nature of library collections, in addition to valuing user-focused services. The University Libraries' forward-thinking stance on providing information resources to support research and learning is demonstrated by the first strategic goal listed in the plan (2005), which states "Provide greater access to digital collections while continuing to build and improve access to collections in all formats to meet the research and teaching needs of the university." By acquiring and building physical and digital collections that are rich in useful content and by striving for the highest possible levels of access, the University Libraries has responded to the evolution of library collections. Web 2.0 trends contribute to new types of access, user-contributed content, and extremely flexible and multi-purpose information products, such as wikis, folksonomies, and tag clouds. Having a strategic plan that supports the development of new user services and

methods to deliver content encourages staff to invest time in examining the use of these tools for the future.

Evaluation and assessment are key areas both in the University Libraries strategic planning and in the iterative process of technology design. The University Libraries' goal to "plan and execute an evaluation plan for the University Libraries, and use the findings to make strategic decisions," reinforces the notion that library outcomes must continually be monitored, evaluated, and updated (2005). In practice, the University Libraries consistently works to attain this strategic goal by supporting communication and open decision-making throughout the institution. Staff time is allocated to evaluate projects, technology solutions are implemented to help monitor data, and managers foster an environment in which brainstorming and imagination are encouraged during the assessment process.

The Initiatives
2.0 Experiments for Staff
Strategic planning is informed by goals and evaluated by metrics that are established by individual divisions and departments. The University Libraries has created an integrated approach to encourage staff participation on a variety of levels. Throughout the organization, senior leadership encourages a culture of participation. When library-wide input is necessary, for instance in prioritizing initiatives, key staff lead information-sharing meetings or facilitate decision-making workshops where information and feedback is recorded and shared. The empowerment of staff to experiment and implement with no-cost new technologies supports experimentation and learning and has provided the platform for establishing new and innovative library 2.0 services for patrons.

Hot Topics Open Forum
The Hot Topics Open Forum is a key example of the way in which the University Libraries admin-

istration encourages staff participation in strategic planning. Charged by the University Libraries Dean, this group serves to "provide all staff with a mechanism to share ideas; encourage opportunities for cross department / division collaboration; create ways for staff with common interests to generate ideas for new projects; provide leadership opportunities; foster conversations that help staff keep current with external trends and issues; provide places to vet reports / progress from Cabinet, working groups, and committees; institutionalize cross divisional communication channels; involve people below department head" (UNLV University Libraries 2005). Established less than two years ago, the Hot Topics Open Forum is still experimenting with its structure. At the beginning of each fiscal year, a list of topics is chosen for the upcoming year. All interested staff attend Hot Topics meetings to discuss ideas and learn about various topics. With both the chair and chair-elect serving on Cabinet, a senior decision-making group in the University Libraries organization, the Hot Topics Open Forum provides opportunities for staff at all levels to suggest input and innovative ideas.

Last year, most of the proposed topics were related to technology. Topics covered included the future of catalogs, Web 2.0, and the next generation of the Web. University Libraries staff members continue to be enthusiastic to learn about new developments and to discover how technologies can be incorporated into the workplace in innovative ways. The group has enabled staff who may not be directly involved in technology decisions an arena in which to participate, experiment, and provide input.

Staff Wikis

One of the first Hot Topics Open Forum meetings of 2006 featured a discussion of Web 2.0 technologies currently used in libraries. A wiki was created for the Hot Topics Open Forum to encourage further exploration of this topic and experimentation with wiki technology. Although the University

Libraries Technologies Division had begun experimenting with MediaWiki, the implementation was not advanced enough to support the Hot Topics Open Forum. A wiki was created using the free hosting service PBwiki (http://pbwiki.com/) as suggested by a meeting attendee. The Hot Topic wiki hosts meeting minutes and supplemental reading lists and the talk feature can be used for nonsynchronous conversations. The wiki has provided all University Libraries' staff with opportunities to learn from the information posted, experiment with wiki technology, and discover useful applications for wikis throughout the University Libraries.

As people grew comfortable using wikis, several departments and committees requested internally hosted wikis for a variety of purposes. As wiki-mania ensued, the installation of MediaWiki was formalized and the internal staff Web site was changed into a wiki. Staff training sessions on creating and editing content in the staff wiki have been offered to staff on an ongoing basis by the University Libraries' Web Management Committee. Once staff had a chance to become proficient using wikis, benefits became clear and possible drawbacks were minimized. This experimentation with wikis is just one example of how an environment open to innovation and hands-on investigation can foster the adoption of new technologies in ways that benefit staff. Such an environment can also reduce staff fears prior to the public implementation of technology, since it allows staff to take risks and become comfortable using something new.

Benefits to patrons from the establishment of wikis are already beginning to surface via the creation of an internal Frequently Asked Questions (FAQ) Knowledge Base for staff to use as a resource for answering patron questions. Converting the staff Web site to a wiki format has facilitated the creation of the Knowledge Base by enabling staff throughout the Libraries to contribute knowledge and expertise without requiring staff to have Web editing expertise. This internal

Knowledge Base has benefited patrons by ensuring that they receive consistent answers to their questions about the University Libraries at different library service points. The Knowledge Base has also increased the confidence of staff members in answering patron questions at service desks and via phone, chat, and e-mail.

Staff Collaboration Tools

The Hot Topics Open Forum is just one way that staff members have been given opportunities to experiment and test new technologies in the organization. Any staff member can create a work-related blog for either internal communication or to provide updates on various topics to patrons. Internal interactions illustrate how librarians have embraced Web 2.0 technologies and principles for workflow. Throughout the library, staff in dispersed locations can connect in a moment via chat. The Web Management Committee uses the Lotus Notes Sametime instant messaging client to arrange on-the-fly meetings when committee members need to collaborate on decisions or let other members know about immediate issues. Documents, meeting minutes, policies and procedures are shared on the staff wiki. Several departments keep a Web-based Google Calendar to track meetings, absences, and upcoming events. In the digitization area of the library, staff members use Protopage (http://www.protopage.com/) to create Web pages for sharing information quickly and NetOffice (http://www.netoffice.com/) for managing group projects and progress on time-sensitive work.

Because digitization projects require a high level of collaboration, they are particularly well-suited to the Web 2.0 principle of decentralization. In fact, when working with staff in other library departments, in other units on campus, or with regional partners, many collaboration tools are essential to good communication and efficient completion of project work. This year, in response to the need for shared network space, UNLV's Office of Information Technology (OIT) created cross-departmental network space for sharing large digital files and associated project documents. The use of Web-based application interfaces allows project partners to contribute efficiently (i.e., creating metadata from dispersed locations) and for a central project manager to monitor progress and retain quality control. For scholarship, presentations, and publications (such as this chapter), authors are using Google Docs & Spreadsheets (http://docs.google.com/) to easily collect information and collaboratively write and publish.

2.0 Services for Patrons

Virtual Reference

One of the more traditional services in an academic library is reference and research assistance. The University Libraries, in common with many other academic libraries, has experienced a steady decline in visitors to the reference desk. It appeared obvious that if reference was to survive at our institution it needed to be offered in non-traditional ways.

IM reference is one of the earliest examples of Library 2.0 at the University Libraries. The evolution of the service from e-mail reference to a collaborative reference service to instant messaging demonstrates the way in which projects are developed, assessed and refined at the University Libraries. E-mail reference was first offered in 1998. However, as UNLV began offering more distance education classes, the University Libraries sought ways of extending reference services to off-campus students. Librarians investigated options for synchronous online reference in a desire "to meet or exceed user expectations, regardless of user location," a stated strategic goal (UNLV University Libraries 2005).

A library task force, formed in 2002, investigated collaborative reference tools. The task force evaluated two freeware options but determined that the software would be too difficult to implement. Instead, a recommendation was made to purchase a commercial product. Initially funding was denied, but two years later, library administration advocated the implementation of the QuestionPoint service and provided funding for it. This was installed in 2004. QuestionPoint was an attractive option because of its chat reference features and co-browsing functionality. Unfortunately, co-browsing was never implemented because the patron would have been required to download and install a plug-in. The University Libraries staff was not satisfied with the reliability of the QuestionPoint software. When it was time to renew the subscription, librarians looked for an alternative. As part of this process, the Remote Services Librarian surveyed students to determine their interest in using Instant Messaging (IM) for reference if it was offered. The results revealed an enthusiasm for IM, so University Libraries began the process of setting up an IM reference service. More can be read about the transition at http://blog.uwinnipeg.ca/schwagbag/archives/2005/06/iming_goes_live.html.

Currently, the Ask a Librarian link (http://www.library.unlv.edu/ask/) appears on almost every page of the University Libraries Web site as part of the standardized left menu column. A link to the Ask a Librarian page is embedded within many of the University Libraries subscribed databases. In the EBSCO databases the link appears below the citation, adjacent to the link provided by SFX, the link resolver in use at the University Libraries. Within CSA databases the link appears at the top of each page. The Ask a Librarian page offers the patron the choice of e-mail or IM, and provides links to subject librarian information as well as reference desk telephone numbers.

Although the University Libraries offers IM reference, IM software is not installed on library computers. However, students are able to download it or use Web-based IM logins. Patrons are often observed on library computers using IM for personal conversations. The free version of Trillian is installed on the reference staff computers so that staff can access messages from AOL, Yahoo!, and Hotmail clients.

During the day, IM reference is staffed by reference librarians from their offices. Shortly after the IM reference service was established, the Univer-

---

Figure 1. Ask a Librarian Web page

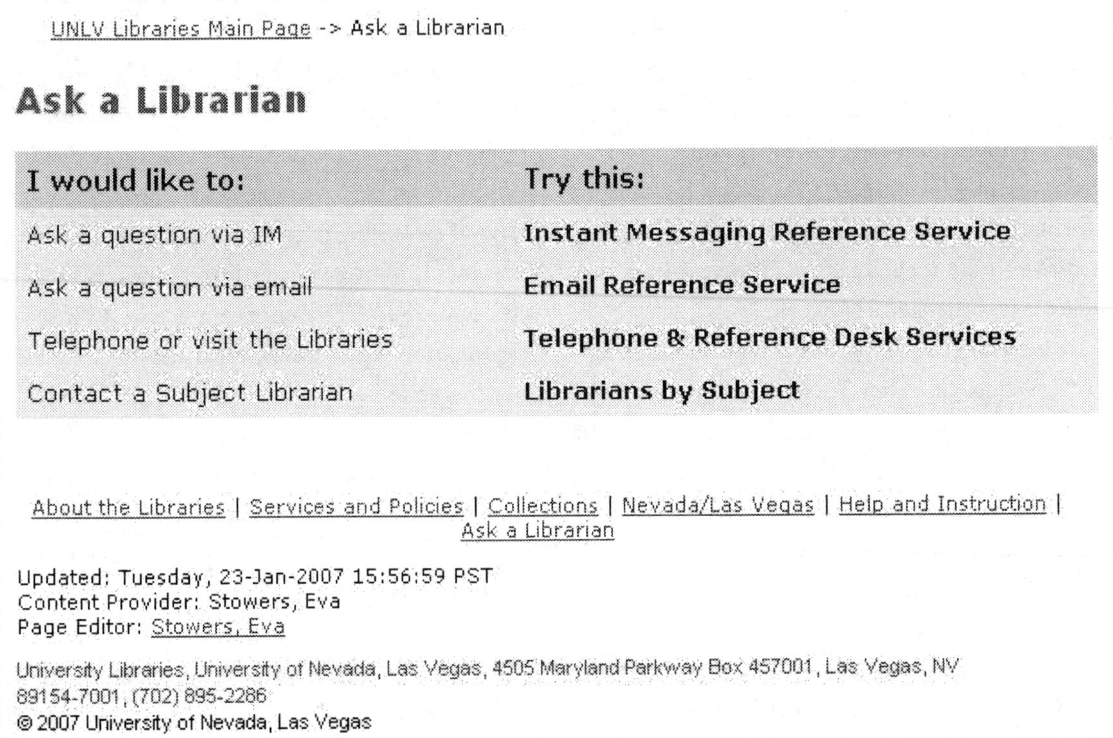

UNLV Libraries Main Page -> Ask a Librarian

Ask a Librarian

I would like to:	Try this:
Ask a question via IM	**Instant Messaging Reference Service**
Ask a question via email	**Email Reference Service**
Telephone or visit the Libraries	**Telephone & Reference Desk Services**
Contact a Subject Librarian	**Librarians by Subject**

About the Libraries | Services and Policies | Collections | Nevada/Las Vegas | Help and Instruction | Ask a Librarian

Updated: Tuesday, 23-Jan-2007 15:56:59 PST
Content Provider: Stowers, Eva
Page Editor: Stowers, Eva

University Libraries, University of Nevada, Las Vegas, 4505 Maryland Parkway Box 457001, Las Vegas, NV 89154-7001, (702) 895-2286
© 2007 University of Nevada, Las Vegas

sity Libraries hired a student to monitor IM reference usage between nine o'clock at night until midnight. The student sat at the Research and Information Desk near the on-duty librarian, who was ready to assist with questions beyond the student's level of expertise. However, low usage of IM reference during the evening hours led the University Libraries to discontinue using a student to monitor IM reference. Since the question levels are low, the on-duty reference librarian monitors IM reference in the evening from the reference desk. Statistics for the IM reference service are shown in the table below. The second half of 2006 showed a decline in usage from the second half of 2005, from 301 to 256, while the first half of 2007 showed almost identical usage as the previous six months. The University Libraries is committed to supporting IM reference and during the Fall 2007 semester will distribute cards with information about this and other reference services to students.

Table 1: Instant Messaging use statistics			
	2005	2006	2007
January		28	42
February		23	69
March		32	39
April		62	51
May	4	33	33
June	24	22	23
Half Year	28	200	257
July	29	22	
August	38	16	
September	57	55	
October	73	34	
November	85	76	
December	19	53	
Half Year	301	256	
Year	329	456	

Web Services Presence

Wikipedia

Adding Web 2.0 functionality to library Web services is a great start to creating an improved user experience, but the university and library Web sites may not be the primary places where patrons spend time or search for information. The University Libraries is currently experimenting with Wikipedia as a popular alternative information venue for promoting physical and virtual library resources. Lied Library, the main branch of the University Libraries, has a Wikipedia page (2007b) describing the library building and several of the technological innovations the library has undertaken. In addition to using Wikipedia to showcase these physical features, the library is also promoting digital library content. For instance, the recently launched *Showgirls* (http://www.library.unlv.edu/showgirls/) digital collection features digitized costume designs and photographs documenting the history of entertainment in Las Vegas. The *Showgirls* collection is one of several library-created digital collections that have been linked to from Wikipedia pages on related topics. The Showgirl Wikipedia page (2007c) contains a link under the "Showgirls in Popular Culture" heading referring users to the University Libraries *Showgirls* digital collection for additional resources. The Hoover Dam Wikipedia page (2007a) contains a link to the *Las Vegas and Water in the West* (http://www.library.unlv.edu/water/) digital collection under the External Links heading. Recent research has shown that adding links to digital collections in Wikipedia increases traffic to digital collections (Lally and Dunford 2007). Analysis of University Libraries' Web statistics document that visitors consistently find the University Libraries Web site and digital collections from Wikipedia links.

MySpace

The University Libraries MySpace page is an example of experimentation by one library staff member. After investigating other libraries with a MySpace presence, she created a page for the University Libraries (http://www.myspace.com/unlvlibraries) to reach students in a popular virtual location. MySpace is one of the first social spaces

Figure 2. Lied Library Wikipedia page

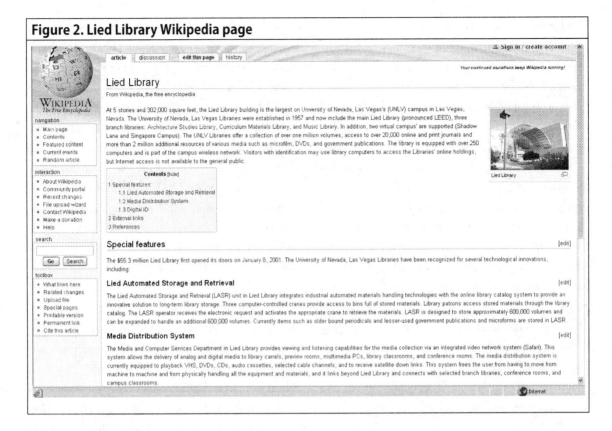

that the University Libraries has entered and the page is maintained with the rationale that reaching patrons in this social space is worth the minimal time and effort invested. The profile has been primarily used for advertising University Libraries events and services, but it also serves as a location for answering questions left in the comments or via e-mail and instant messaging. No formal marketing of the MySpace page has been undertaken, but the MySpace page has been used. During the fall semester of 2006, sixty-seven people navigated to the University Libraries Web site from the MySpace domain. If continued assessment reveals that patrons use library services in social spaces, more support for these projects will enable the social profiles maintained by the University Libraries to reach their potential for serving patrons.

Blogs

The first public blog at the University Libraries was created by the Medical Librarian using Blogger and was placed on the Web page created for a virtual

branch that supports the School of Dental Medicine (http://www.library.unlv.edu/shadowlane/). In May 2006, the University Libraries migrated to the Movable Type platform and the Medical Librarian replaced her original blog with a new one designed to provide information about health resources and intended to support all units in the Division of Health Sciences (http://blogs.library. unlv.edu/healthscience/). Shortly after the migration to the Movable Type platform, a presentation about blogs was provided by Library Technologies staff members to orient staff throughout the library on how blogs work and potential uses in libraries. At the conclusion of the blog presentation, staff members throughout the library were given the opportunity to request a blog to be set up by the Library Technologies Division. The result was a variety of blogs with some having internal staff uses and others used to push information out to patrons. The blogs are housed on a library server and are placed in one Web location called "Blogs @ UNLV Libraries" (http://blogs.library.unlv.edu/).

Several problems arose in the early stages of the Movable Type implementation. For an extended period of time, people were unable to post comments on the blogs, hampering the goal of two-way communication with patrons. The greatest setback occurred several months into the blog implementation when hardware failures caused the loss of all data. Because backups did not exist, users had to reenter all of their data. Not all blogs were recreated, possibly because their owners were discouraged or simply that momentum was lost. Currently, there is not a process in place at the UNLV University Libraries to provide training to aspiring bloggers.

Despite the setbacks, some librarians have continued to embrace the use of blogs. The Architecture Studies Library has an active public blog (http://blogs.library.unlv.edu/arch-studies/) that is used to advise patrons of new resources and upcoming events at the library. The Digitization Projects @ UNLV Libraries blog (http://blogs.library.unlv.edu/digital/) is an example of a blog that alerts staff to new developments and issues in digitization. Although it is intended as a staff tool, it is viewable by the public. The most visible University Libraries blog is the Library News blog (http://blogs.library.unlv.edu/newsblog/). Information from the Library News blog is fed to the University Libraries home page and is a quick way to alert visitors to new databases, maintenance issues, and library events.

Really Simple Syndication (RSS) Feeds

The UNLV University Libraries is using information feed technology, such as RSS, to announce library news as well as notifications of interest to individual patrons. RSS is an XML format for the syndication of Web content to which people can subscribe and then track through a feed reader. The Library News blog includes an RSS button.

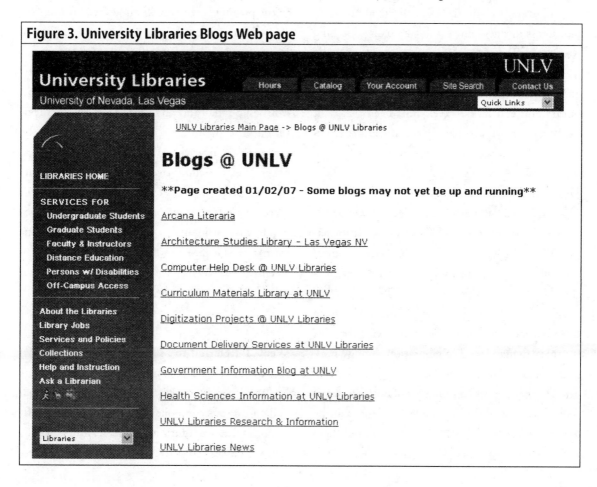

Figure 3. University Libraries Blogs Web page

Other UNLV Libraries' blogs include links that connect to XML code so that users can add the feed to their reader.

In addition, there is a new enhancement to UNLV Libraries' online catalog called "My Record Feed" which allows patrons to receive information about their library record from the online catalog to their feed reader. This includes materials ready for pickup, materials due soon, and new fines. As is the case for the UNLV Libraries' blogs, the patron subscribes to My Record Feed using a feed reader. However, unlike the UNLV Libraries' blogs, in which content is generated by an individual, the content provided to a subscriber from My Record Feed is generated automatically. The feed reader requests the latest version of the patron's record and generates a feed which the patron views. The feed contains a title and a link. If patrons are not logged into their record, they will be prompted to validate themselves before viewing the content. The University Libraries also alerts patrons to new items in the online catalog by using outgoing RSS feeds. The content of the feed is controlled by queries updated nightly. An example of new travel and tourism titles can be seen at http://innopac.library.unlv.edu/feeds/travel.xml. Feeds are an easy way to broadcast library-specific information without significant staff intervention.

University Web Portal

Not all Web 2.0 initiatives have been driven by the University Libraries. UNLV's Office of Information Technology Department embarked on a portal project several years ago with the active participation of the University Libraries. The project has been time-consuming because of the desire for a dynamic and useful end-product involving complex technical demands and collaboration among a multitude of departments. When finished, the UNLV portal will integrate components of both academic and social spaces. For example, students will be able to subscribe to RSS feeds that will tell them if they have library overdue fines or that indicate

their enrolled classes, as well as to news and cartoon feeds. The portal project adheres particularly well to Coombs *Pillars of Web 2.0* by providing remixable pieces of content that students can join together in ways that make the most sense for them (2007). The University Libraries has been an active participant in the project in an effort to raise awareness of students to the services the Libraries provides. By allowing patrons to take the information they want and incorporate it into spaces they already use, it is believed that students will be more likely to use what the University Libraries has to offer.

Currently, the portal is in beta stage and the University Libraries tab is under construction. When completed, the University Libraries tab will include search functions for the Libraries catalog, databases, and journal titles. Subject-specific information and library hours will also be available for students to add to their portal pages. Portal content will be created at the Libraries and pushed to the portal via RSS. RSS allows feed readers (in this case the portal) to subscribe to a stream of information and to display updates when changes occur. Since content will be hosted by the library, instead of being housed on portal servers, content can be updated and added more easily. Incorporation of feeds into the portal will also allow the University Libraries to feature content from another Web 2.0 initiative, the University Libraries blogs discussed earlier. Ideally, the portal will increase student usage of the University Libraries by allowing students to subscribe to only the information they are interested in and to access it in a centralized Web space they visit to take care of other needs.

WebCT

WebCT (referred to as WebCampus at UNLV) is the course management system used on campus for both hybrid courses (classes with both a virtual and on-campus component) and for exclusively off-campus Distance Education courses. Although both types of classes use WebCampus, each uses a differ-

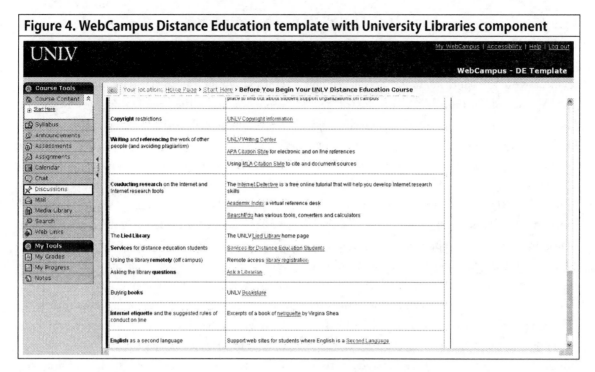

Figure 4. WebCampus Distance Education template with University Libraries component

ent template. Templates provide a standard design and set of tools which faculty can adapt to their course need without having to start with a blank slate. WebCampus is an academic space heavily used by students. The Office of Distance Education is responsible for the creation of the template used in all distance education courses. In hopes of encouraging the large segment of students using WebCT to find and use library resources, the University Libraries endeavored to find ways to be incorporated into distance education WebCT templates.

Several ideas were proposed to enhance service to students, including embedding tailored library content into specific courses. In the end, due to staffing issues and technical limitations, the less sophisticated choice of linking to the Libraries' Web site was chosen to integrate the University Libraries into Distance Education courses. A link to the University Libraries Services for Distance Education Web page (http://www.library.unlv.edu/services/distance.html) is now included prominently on the Distance Education WebCampus template. This gives the University Libraries high visibility in an academic space that students frequently use. Instead of leaving WebCampus to

access library services, students can click a link within the template to open library information in a new window. As with the RSS feeds used with the portal, the WebCampus link allows the University Libraries to retain control over content. When changes are needed, they can be made quickly and without intervention by technical staff in the Distance Education Department. This ensures that information remains timely and that news about technical problems and new services can be immediately posted.

To assess usage of the link, the University Libraries plans to track the number of times a student enters the University Libraries Web site from the WebCampus distance education link. This data will help the University Libraries to decide if alternative strategies should be considered for integrating into the Distance Education template. It will also aid in beginning the conversation about establishing University Libraries representation in the general WebCampus template.

Extending Library Service Points

Although the UNLV University Libraries has focused primarily on extending the library presence on virtual spaces, experimentation is also underway to extend the library presence in physical spaces beyond the library walls. The first attempt in this effort was an initiative to introduce library services in remote UNLV academic facilities. UNLV's School of Dental Medicine (SDM) and UNLV's Biotechnology Center are located on the Shadow Lane campus approximately seven miles from the main campus. The Shadow Lane campus does not have a physical library. The Medical Librarian, based at the main campus, interacts with Shadow Lane patrons primarily by e-mail and telephone. At the request of SDM faculty, she has experimented with holding regular office hours at the Shadow Lane campus. The students at Shadow Lane have no classes on Thursday afternoons, so she established office hours during this time period. This proved to be unsuccessful due to the fact that most students took advantage of the free time by leaving campus. Next she held office hours on a different day during lunch hours. Student visits increased, but they still were not frequent enough to warrant regular office hours on that campus. University Libraries continues to explore other physical spaces on campus that may be better suited to reaching out to students.

Assessment

Currently most University Libraries Web 2.0 initiatives have been assessed informally. In the near future, University Libraries plan to systematically assess projects and to ensure that resources are being best utilized to support patrons. The University Libraries has already begun to review Web site statistics using Urchin software. Urchin provides a range of statistics, including daily page views, referring sites from which users visit, and search terms that bring users to the site. Urchin statistics confirm that MySpace is getting use, that many users do not enter the Libraries Web site through the University's Distance Education page, and that many patrons are trying to find University Libraries' unique collections, such as the Howard Hughes collection.

The creation of an Assessment Librarian position and the recent establishment of a Web Usability working group will enhance the ability of the University Libraries to assess its Web 2.0 projects. As mentioned earlier, the University Libraries relies on staff collaboration to suggest and test Web 2.0 initiatives and many new initiatives have been started through this process. Assessment is the next step for several projects in order to ensure that projects with the most impact will be enhanced, while those with little benefit will be discontinued. The newly appointed Assessment Librarian created an Assessment Blog soon after the creation of her position, and this blog will serve as a resource for best practices in assessment. In the future, the University Libraries will need to move beyond raw data to determine how patrons are using new services and to discover what additional services they would like to see implemented. Brief surveys have already been conducted to discover what students know about Web 2.0 terms and to gauge reaction to a recent update of the library home page. However, more formal focus groups, usability testing, and surveys are needed to ensure that the University Libraries are deploying Web 2.0 practices in ways that students use and appreciate.

Future Plans

The University Libraries continues to monitor Web 2.0 developments and adopt them whenever possible. Several new projects are currently being developed for implementation in the upcoming year.

Virtual Reference

Virtual Reference at the University Libraries is under continual assessment and new technologies are being reviewed to determine if patron service can be enhanced. Usage of the IM reference service is beginning to decline. This is of critical concern as this service is highly staff intensive and requires significant time and energy to support. As mentioned earlier, this service has not been supported by marketing efforts to increase awareness of its availability. A marketing campaign for Virtual Reference is being planned for the fall semester of 2007. This campaign will include a coupon for a free USB flash drive within the University Coupon Book given out to students during orientation week. This coupon can be redeemed by students at library information desks where students will be given a wallet-sized card with information about how to get research help by phone, e-mail, and IM. The University Libraries will be able to track how many students have redeemed coupons and will monitor the impact of this campaign.

Another possible cause of the decline of IM service usage may be the increased use among college students of text messaging to communicate with their peers. The University Libraries Research and Information Department is planning to conduct a pilot project in the fall semester of 2007 to determine if students would use short message service (SMS), more commonly referred to as text messaging, for providing reference services. An analysis of LibQUAL survey results for the University Libraries indicate that students especially value face-to-face interaction with library staff. This may be another cause of the decline in use of IM reference service. The Research and Information Department plans to conduct a pilot project in the fall semester of 2007 to discover if students will be more inclined to use IM reference services if video chat is available. The department has purchased a few Webcams with headsets which are compatible with commonly used IM platforms such as Yahoo! Messenger and AIM. If the video chat feature proves popular, the pilot project will be developed further and other forms of video communication will be explored. Another possibility for the near future is embedding a chat widget, e.g., Meebo (http://www.meebome.com/) into library Web pages to allow students to enter their question directly into the Web page instead of using their IM client.

UNLV continues to develop distance education programs. At present, the University has a hotel administration program in Singapore and a nursing program in the Philippines. These provide the catalyst for the subject librarians to pursue new avenues for extending reference and instruction services to remote patrons. Webinar or Web conferencing software is being investigated for purchase in order to enhance the options for providing services to those students whose courses do not meet on campus.

Implications of virtual reference are also being explored for digital collections. By embedding an IM widget such as Meebo on the digital collections home page, guests could chat with library staff without having to create or log into an IM account. This could also facilitate e-commerce (which often involves extensive customer service) to improve the current inefficient, manual process used to request Special Collections reproductions. The need for increased staffing, the high volume of materials requested, and the necessity for careful licensing have put e-commerce/IM on hold.

Extending Library Service Points

Additional initiatives are underway for extending the library presence in campus facilities where students spend much of their time, for example the Student Union, the Student Recreation Center, and student dormitories. One initiative offers peer-to-peer research assistance to students by students, while another offers research assistance via mobile library cart. The peer coaches' initiative was developed by two librarians as a pilot program to address undergraduate student retention. Students are recruited and trained to serve as frontline research coaches to other students. In the fall semester of 2006, two students were selected from a pool of applicants and were trained extensively on how to use library research tools. By the spring semester of 2007, these two students began staffing reference desks at the main library. Students appeared to be comfortable approaching the student peer coaches for research help. This confirmed a suspicion amongst library staff that some students may be more comfortable asking for help from their peers than from library staff. The peer research coaches program will continue with the coaches holding consistent service hours within campus Residence Halls with the goal of building a clientele with a captive audience of undergraduate students. The initial deployment of the coaches to the Residence Halls will begin in the fall semester of 2007, and an evaluation of student use of this service will be conducted at the end of the semester.

Additionally in the fall semester of 2007, the University Libraries will investigate the possibility of deploying a mobile cart with a laptop computer to campus events and campus facilities with the intention of offering research help throughout campus. This potential service was inspired by the Reference a la Carte mobile research help service of the University Libraries at George Mason University (Coniglio). At the University Libraries, this service would most likely consist of a beverage cart with space for a laptop computer and an umbrella branded with the University Libraries logo. A key benefit of this service for the University Libraries would be the opportunities it would provide for determining campus facilities where students need and ask for research assistance.

LibX Toolbar

The LibX Toolbar is a Firefox extension that allows patrons to search the library catalog directly from their browser. LibX eliminates the need to enter any library space, but rather puts the library in the user's space when they need it. LibX (http://www.libx.org/) was created by Virginia Tech, but the open source software has been implemented at forty-seven libraries. Additionally it is currently being tested at eighty-five libraries, including the UNLV University Libraries.

LibX is another example of how an organization that is open to sharing and innovation can lead to enhancements for patrons. A UNLV instruction librarian discovered LibX and had a test version created. She shared this with the Web Services Li-

brarian, who distributed the download to several other librarians as they expressed interest in testing the product. Each of these librarians has begun utilizing LibX to see how it worked and if they thought it would be worthwhile to share with students, faculty, and staff. Once the testing is complete, it will be the experiences of these librarians that lead to the decision to implement this service or to discontinue its use. Google Desktop Gadgets are being tested in a similar way at this time.

Conclusion

The UNLV University Libraries has adapted to an environment of rapid change in the era of Library 2.0 by using a long tail approach that caters to students and faculty with a variety of unique needs. It has explored the long tail in extending the library presence to a variety of new virtual and physical locations rather than focusing on a few key domains. In pursuing the long tail approach to expanding services, library staff members have undertaken small projects which establish a basic library presence in a variety of new arenas with minimal time, effort, and financial resources rather than large scale projects requiring significant investments. This pursuit of projects has fostered a culture of innovation which is vital to the University Libraries for adapting to the Library 2.0 challenge of rapid change. This culture could not have been possible without higher levels of the organization supporting and encouraging all staff to embark on innovative and creative projects.

The encouragement of staff to meet the long tail of unique user preferences for services has led to the initiation of such projects as blogging, instant messaging (IM), text messaging, wikis, enhanced digital collections, and use of social networking sites. Entrance into virtual settings encourages interaction with a more diverse patron base and integration into the course management system reflects efforts to provide personalization of library services. Virtual spaces are not the only areas that have been revisited. Librarians have also gained exposure in physical spaces outside the library, including faculty offices and satellite campuses. Many future projects are in development with proposals to investigate Web conferencing platforms, Web page widgets, and Webcams. These initiatives will continue to be evaluated to determine which environments are most beneficial for serving patrons in the era of Library 2.0.

The low risk approach of exploration in a variety of new domains enables the University Libraries to conduct periodic simple assessments to determine the places within the long tail where the inclusion of a library presence adds value for students and faculty and increases their use of library services. Moreover, current service offerings can evolve in this environment to meet changing needs and services which will enable the UNLV University Libraries to retain relevance with users in the era of Library 2.0 and beyond. This forward-thinking and flexible investment in information technology, staff skill development, and organizational culture has enabled the University Libraries to adapt its services to meet the long tail range of user needs and expectations in a networked social environment.

References

Anderson, Chris. 2004. The long tail. *Wired* 12 (October). http://www.wired.com/wired/archive/12.10/tail.html.

Casey, Michael E. and Laura C. Savastinuk. 2006. Library 2.0: Service for the next-generation library. *Library Journal*, September 1. http://libraryjournal.com/article/CA6365200.html.

Coniglio, Jamie. 2007. Takin' it to the streets: Reference a la Carte. Poster presented at the 25th American Library Association Annual Conference, New Orleans.

Coombs, Karen A. Building a library Web site on the pillars of Web 2.0. *Computers in Libraries* 27 (January). http://www.infotoday.com/cilmag/jan07/Coombs.shtml.

Lally, Ann M. and Carolyn E. Dunford. 2007. Using Wikipedia to extend digital collections. *D-Lib Magazine* 13 (May/June). http://www.dlib.org/dlib/may07/lally/05lally.html.

Storey, Tom. 2005. The long tail and libraries. *OCLC Newsletter* 268 (April/May/June). http://www.oclc.org/news/publications/newsletters/oclc/2005/268/thelongtail.htm.

University of Nevada Las Vegas University Libraries. 2005. A strategic plan for the UNLV Libraries: 2005-2010. http://www.library.unlv.edu/about/strategic_goals.pdf.

Wikipedia. 2007a. Hoover Dam. http://en.wikipedia.org/wiki/Hoover_Dam (accessed October 16, 2007).

Wikipedia. 2007b. Lied Library. http://en.wikipedia.org/wiki/Lied_Library (accessed October 16, 2007).

Wikkpedia. 2007c. Showgirl. http://en.wikipedia.org/wiki/Showgirl (accessed October 16, 2007).

Chat, Commons, and Collaboration: Inadvertently Library 2.0 in Western Australia

Kathryn Greenhill, Margaret Jones, and Jean McKay

Abstract

When staff at Murdoch University Library (a small multi-campus academic library in Perth, Western Australia) first read about Library 2.0 in April 2006, we discovered that we had already implemented several programs that could be considered Library 2.0. Participative, egalitarian, and interdisciplinary aspects of Library 2.0 were already ingrained in our culture, as part of an institution initially viewed as an "alternative university".

We have provided a chat reference service since 2003. We have renovated two floors of the library to create a Learning Common. We have immersed ourselves in a collaborative project to learn about Library 2.0, created an Emerging Technologies Group, and are experimenting with a virtual library service in Second Life.

This chapter gives background about our library, and describes how we implemented our Library 2.0 services. We explain why we pursued these initiatives, some challenges they presented, and our future plans for them. The theme running throughout is that our University already held some of the core values of Library 2.0 and that these services flowed naturally from this background.

Introduction

In May 2007, Murdoch University Library began a series of workshops showing participants how to create and use an avatar in Second Life. University staff and students who took this class walked to the library PC lab by going through the first floor of our new Learning Common, past the large screen TVs, café style booths, and comfy couches. They passed service points for our First Year Experience Co-ordinator, the library reference desk, the Printing and Photocopying service, and our Student Learning service area. If participants were unsure of the session time, they could have gone online and opened a chat session with an Online Librarian.

This chapter describes what happened in Murdoch University Library to make possible the scene above. It gives background about our library and describes how we implemented our Library 2.0 services. Further, it explains some of the reasons for implementing these services and some challenges they presented.

Background

Murdoch University opened in 1975 as a "new" university - open to students who might not qualify for Perth's older established university, perhaps not having completed their secondary education or achieved results at the required level. Once admitted, students completed a course of study that included subjects outside their selected discipline. Interdisciplinarity was a guiding principle in both teaching and research. Offered units included subjects which were not typically available at that time, for example environmental studies, peace

Kathryn Greenhill, e-mail: k.greenhill@murdoch.edu.au; Margaret Jones, e-mail: margaret.jones@murdoch.edu.au; Jean McKay, e-mail: j.mckay@murdoch.edu.au, all at Murdoch University Library.

studies, and women's studies. Another distinguishing characteristic was the egalitarian approach to relationships between academic staff, general staff, and students- evident in the shared tavern and dining facilities. Murdoch acquired a reputation as the "alternative" university.

The Library followed the lead of the university as a whole. For example, Special Collections placed an emphasis on popular culture (including comics and fanzines, popular magazines, and posters) as well as women's studies (including the personal collection of a well-known local feminist, and collections of the local branch of the Women's Electoral Lobby, and the Abortion Law Reform Association). This section of the library remains a significant resource, and continues to grow.

Information literacy was central to services provided by the Library, and a required part of the Foundation Unit completed by every first year student. An automated test was introduced very early. As technology developed, this was replaced with online interactive instructional materials.

The Library was one of the first in Australia to introduce a home grown online integrated library management system. It was among the first to investigate the opportunities offered by the Internet, dedicating a Network Services Librarian to the task in the late 1980s.

Murdoch University Library currently has a staffing level of 55.4 equivalent full time staff, and serves a student population of 13, 217, studying on campus, off campus, and off shore.

We began as a library open to new technology and as part of a university stepping outside of traditional ways. Consequently, it is not surprising that in 2006 we found ourselves already embarked on the journey towards what we learnt was becoming known as Library 2.0.

The Initiatives

Below we describe five of our initiatives that fit the user-centred, technology-smart, participative ideas of Library 2.0. The services outlined are:

1) *Learning Common*. Two floors of the library were totally renovated to capitalize on the library's status as a central, social environment on campus.

2) *Online Librarian*. Live Online chat reference in collaboration with Macquarie University, evolving over four years to include authentication via Shibboleth.

3) *Discovering Your Second life*. A seminar and workshop series for the University community using the Library's plot of land within a Multi User Virtual Environment.

4) *MULTA*. A two month collaborative learning project designed as a hands-on introduction to new Web tools (blogs, wikis, RSS, forums, social tagging) for our library staff.

5) *Emerging Technology Group*. Weekly sessions about new technologies with a hands- on focus, plus experimental project work, aimed at library staff.

Learning Common

Murdoch University's 2003-2007 Strategic Plan incorporated a new objective: to create a Learning Common focused on the needs of first year university students. The Learning Common provides not just an attractive, comfortable, welcoming physical environment, but also a supportive learning environment where students can request assistance without feeling constrained.

Why a Learning Common?

Murdoch University is known for its excellence in teaching as well as in research. Surveys of student satisfaction with teaching consistently indicate high rates of satisfaction. The experience of first year students has been a high priority in recent years, with the objective of improving student experience at university, and ultimately improving outcomes and retention. One area of interest has been student engagement - with the university, their teachers, their units of study, and their peers.

With its diverse student population studying on campus, overseas, and through distance and open learning, Murdoch has placed great importance on flexible learning. The University provides unit information and a range of course materials online. It offers instruction on WebCT, and provides audio (and soon video) files of lectures. A range of other learning technologies are under investigation. A Learning Technologies Steering Group reviews new learning technologies, seeks funding for those chosen to trial or implement, and ensures that training and support is available. This group has representation from across the university, including academic staff, students, and staff in support areas such as the Library.

In this context, students need access to the Murdoch network and require skills in computer use. This access is already provided in the library. They also need a wider range of support. Some students need help identifying and selecting appropriate resources for their study. This is a library role. They may need assistance with learning skills, literacy and numeracy, essay writing, etc. This is the role of Student Learning staff from the University's Teaching & Learning Centre. The First Year Coordinator assists students with integrating into the university, meeting other students, understanding the administrative requirements of the university, and finding out about financial, social, and other supports available. Services from the Library, Teaching and Learning and the First Year Co-ordinator are all now centrally available in the new Learning Common.

Designing the Learning Common was a collaborative exercise. Initially a number of workshops were held with potential participants to identify what it might seek to achieve, given the range of services and support required by students. Subsequently, the University's designers were engaged and briefed on the concept in the context of the Library as a whole, including its research focus. The plan was to renovate two floors of the main library building on the University's original and largest campus.

The building consists of two wings connected by a wide, room-sized corridor (called the Link). The South Wing, with four floors and significant floor space, was designated as the research wing, containing most of the Library's printed collections, quiet space for individual study, and postgraduate study carrels.

Two floors of the North Wing, including the floor with the Library's main entrance plus the Link, were designated the Learning Common. The Learning Common now contains the Library's service desks, high use Reserve collection with study space, and reference collection. It also contains a printing and photocopying service point, a new café area opening out into Bush Court (the central gathering place of the University), and new offices for the First Year Experience Coordinator and staff from Student Learning. There are two computer laboratories for training and general use when not booked for teaching, and two tutorial rooms to support the work of Student Learning staff. There has been a threefold increase in the number of computer workstations available in the Library building.

A new objective was to provide more physical space for students to use their own laptops, anticipating that in the near future the number of students in the University's population with laptops would increase. In the meantime it was necessary to continue providing PC workstations. To accomplish this, the IT Service Desk was moved to the lower level of the North Wing. This wing has become a 24x7 computing and study area to complement an existing 24x7 computer laboratory elsewhere on campus. This setup also provides an opportunity to increase available hours of IT support.

The appearance of the Library building also needed updating. The two wings of the building enclose a coffee shop which was opened in 1994, set in a landscaped garden. By removing walls and increasing the amount of glass, the renovation opens up the lower level of the Learning Common to the coffee shop. The renovation provides increased hanging space in high traffic areas for the University's Art Collection. There is new paintwork, new carpets, new interesting furniture, more color, more group-oriented spaces. The renovation has also provided an opportunity to re-shelve almost the entire printed collection of books and journals. This provides better sequencing and a coherent run of journals, previously split among five floors.

But the primary focus of the Learning Common is to enhance our students' experience of university through providing extensive and accessible support for learning. A group of staff involved in the Learning Common meets weekly to plan new collaborative services. A funding submission to develop a program supporting refugee students and other equity groups has been prepared and submitted to a higher education funding body, and other initiatives are planned. The Learning Common has enhanced collaboration between staff, as it has provided us with a new common focus.

The Learning Common concept has not been supported by everyone. For some of our users, the Library is still a place for printed collections and quiet individual study. We hope to meet these needs while we also engage a new generation of students and staff.

Online Librarian

Murdoch began investigating virtual reference in 2002. e-mail reference had been available since 1995 and some librarians were keen to extend this to a synchronous service. As the Library had been an early adopter of electronic resources, readily available online help in accessing these was a natural progression.

At this time, Macquarie University Library was looking for a partner to develop virtual reference. This suited Murdoch. Macquarie is located on the east coast of Australia with a two hour time difference to Murdoch on the west coast. This meant that we could offer the service for a reasonable spread of hours. The two institutions are members of the Innovative Research Universities Australia (IRUA) group and have teaching and research strengths in common. This is helpful for librarians answering questions from the other institution's patrons.

Librarians in the two institutions agreed on a set of basic premises for the new service, which was to be called Online Librarian. The service would use commonly available software familiar to patrons. Microsoft NetMeeting was selected. At the time, it was freely downloadable, and offered both VoIP and chat, shared applications, and transfer of files. Although lacking administrative functions, such as the capacity to queue calls or provide statistics, NetMeeting satisfied the principle of using widely available software.

As detailed by Janet Fletcher et. al. (2004), the service was launched in February 2003. Interestingly, chat calls far outnumbered voice calls. Our patrons definitely preferred to chat. This method of communication was simple and flexible, and did not involve headsets or microphones. So the service that librarians had marketed as "real time real talk" was not being used for real talk!

Feedback from patrons showed that most did not use NetMeeting as their chat client, but preferred alternative products such as those offered by MSN, AOL, Yahoo!, etc. Thus, Online Librarian was being provided to only a small subset of potential patrons, with software that was not being used for its VoIP capacity. Use of NetMeeting appeared to deter adoption.

In October 2004, the service was swapped to a chat-only client, using the popular MSN Messenger, with a Hotmail address. In the first month, use quadrupled and continued to expand. 'Online Librarian' began to appear in our students' contact lists. Patterns began to appear in the librarian/student communication. A student would contact Online Librarian a few times during a session. A question would be answered and often there was no confirmation that the student was satisfied, but then the student would start chatting again with another question. This was just how Murdoch and Macquarie librarians wanted the service to be used, as a presence in the students' space. One staff member commented, "It's like having a librarian in your living room".

Before implementing chat, staff were offered training in MSN. This had the effect of popularizing the software among staff. Librarians selected user icons and swapped 'smileys'. They liked the immediacy of being able to see if a colleague was available and appreciated the benefits of synchronous exchanges. Librarians unfamiliar with chat commented that sometimes they did not understand the students' chat abbreviations. As a result, staff began swapping terminology.

As use of Online Librarian with MSN Messenger continued to increase, librarians ran up against the software's limitations. The MSN service could only be provided by a single operator. Sometimes the Online Librarian was juggling three separate chat sessions. In addition, the maximum number of users on the MSN Messenger "allow list" reached its limit and no further callers could be added. Potential new users were frustrated and use declined.

Fortunately, in 2006 Online Librarian became a demonstrator project for the MAMS (Metadata Access Management System) Testbed Federation (http://www.federation.org.au/FedManager/jsp/index.jsp). MAMS was funded by the Australian government to introduce Shibboleth to Australian research institutions. Shibboleth is open source single signon middleware. The collaborative Online Librarian was suited to this initiative, as its staff were experienced in providing chat help, but the current implementation of the service was not scalable. Shibboleth could permit identification of the institution to which a caller belonged and enable the call to be assigned to the correct institution. Multiple operators could staff the service, and if one was busy, the call would be allocated to the next free operator.

In June 2006, Murdoch and Macquarie successfully obtained a MAMS Mini-grant. A de-

veloper was employed to work with library and MAMS staff to design functionality for the new Online Librarian, while also implementing Shibboleth authentication . Previously, all calls were accepted and no authentication was required. The Psi Jabber client was selected, as this chat client is interoperable with other third party chat clients – MSN, Yahoo!, ICQ, etc. Patrons can opt to use their preferred client or chat in a Java chat box which pops up after authentication.

The project developer has enhanced the functionality of Online Librarian in a number of ways. Following authentication through Shibboleth, there is smart assignment of calls to the librarians at the student's home university. There are commands that enable calls to be transferred between frontline and secondline operators. For example, a call can be answered by a reference librarian (frontline) who transfers the call to the specialist science and engineering librarian (secondline). Most importantly, the service can now be staffed by multiple operators across both libraries. As a result, the service is now offered for eighty-seven hours per week. Librarians are encouraged to register as operators when not engaged in face to face activities. This has the effect of creating a large pool of operators and a shared workload. Initial feedback from users has been positive, and there is now enthusiasm amongst staff about the benefits of being able to provide real time support.

At the time of this writing, we are about to implement a more robust version of Online Librarian on an upgraded server. We will be evaluating the new functionality of the service and extending its use, targeting transnational and other off-campus students. It is hoped to expand the group of operators to include staff working in our other campus libraries.

Discovering Your Second Life

Murdoch University Library is the first Australian library to experiment with space in the 3D online virtual world, Second Life. We aim to learn about the interface and the conceptual decisions needed to provide library services in a Multi User Virtual Environment. Many of our clients are familiar with this kind of interface from gaming, even more so their younger brothers and sisters who will be our students within the next few years.

In March 2007, the library leased a plot of land on Cybrary City II. This is part of the forty island Information Archipelago. The island is owned by the Alliance Library System in Illinois. Alliance administers nine of the islands in the archipelago and co-ordinates many of the activities of over 500 librarians from many nations. All of our neighbors on Cybrary City II are library services. There are often other librarians present on the island to share information about how to build in Second Life, and to talk with about our real life libraries.

Second Life requires a broadband connection and a rather powerful PC system. Many of our students cannot afford this, so the Second Life land is not an attempt to "go where the users are". Rather, this provides our staff with hands-on experimentation using a social, three dimensional interactive and immersive environment.

The Horizon Report 2007 identifies virtual worlds as one of six major trends in emerging technology that will have an impact on higher education (New Media Consortium 2007). The Library is providing exposure and basic training in this information resource so people in our University community can make up their own minds about its value to education. The library plot of land provides a location and destination for any of the Murdoch University community who want to experiment with Second Life.

The library is running a series of seminars and workshops about Second Life. Murdoch reference librarian Kathryn Greenhill - who co-ordinates the Australian Libraries Building on Cybrary City in her spare time - gave a talk and demonstration about librarians in Second Life in February 2007. A large number staff from across the University attended. Starting in May 2007, the library ran a series of Second Life Seminars in conjunction with the Teaching and Learning Centre. The first session was a one-hour talk about Action Learning in Second Life by a Ph.D. student at the University of Southern Queensland, Lindy McKeown.

This talk was followed by two hands-on workshops in a library computing laboratory designed and facilitated by Greenhill. She showed participants how to create their avatars and guided them through Orientation Island. The second session introduced participants to the Murdoch Library plot, gave them a "Treasure Hunt" of activities to do there, and took them on a group tour of an educational site in Second Life.

Sessions were limited to ten people at a time, but each session was offered four times. Invitations to the workshop were sent out in a university-wide mail message. By the end of the first day, half the sessions were full and all were booked out within a week.

Some members of the university community expressed concerns about using university facilities to access Second Life, as the site contains some commercial ventures and the University does not have control over what students and staff do in there. In response, the librarian conducting the workshop ensured that the following information was part of the workshop and included in the wiki that was used as a handout (http://murdochsecondlife.pbwiki.com/).

What Are We Not Doing?

- Like the internet in general, educational sites in Second Life sit alongside porn, gambling and people out to make a fast buck. We're not hanging out there. It's not work. Don't do it here.
- We're not advising you to spend work time in Second Life doing non-work things. It's not work. Don't do it here.
- We're not advising you to spend work time in Second Life doing work things to the exclusion of other work.

What is Work Related Activity in Second Life?

Second Life is a chance to learn a new literacy and try out new ways of using technology. These things are work related:

+ learning how to get around Second Life - walk, fly, teleport, walk
+ learning to do things with objects - take, give, buy, sell, create, touch, move, edit
+ interacting with other people - IMing, chatting, viewing profiles, searching, joining groups
+ doing things with your avatar - changing appearance, editing, animating
+ exploring Second Life - attending events, exploring locations

The first workshop was held on 25 May 2007. This workshop was the first time Greenhill had shown a large group of people how to use Second Life. Participants were allowed to work through registration and Orientation Island at their own pace, following instructions on the online handout. This resulted in a disastrously chaotic session, where many participants dropped behind, were confused, and needed individual support to continue. To avoid this happening in future sessions, the instructor changed the format so that all participants completed each step together.

Linden Labs, which owns Second Life, issues frequent mandatory upgrades to the client software. This meant that the librarian running the workshop had to book an IT officer with admin-

Figure 1: Avatar Emerald Dumont using the Steps to Research on the Murdoch University Library plot of land in Second Life

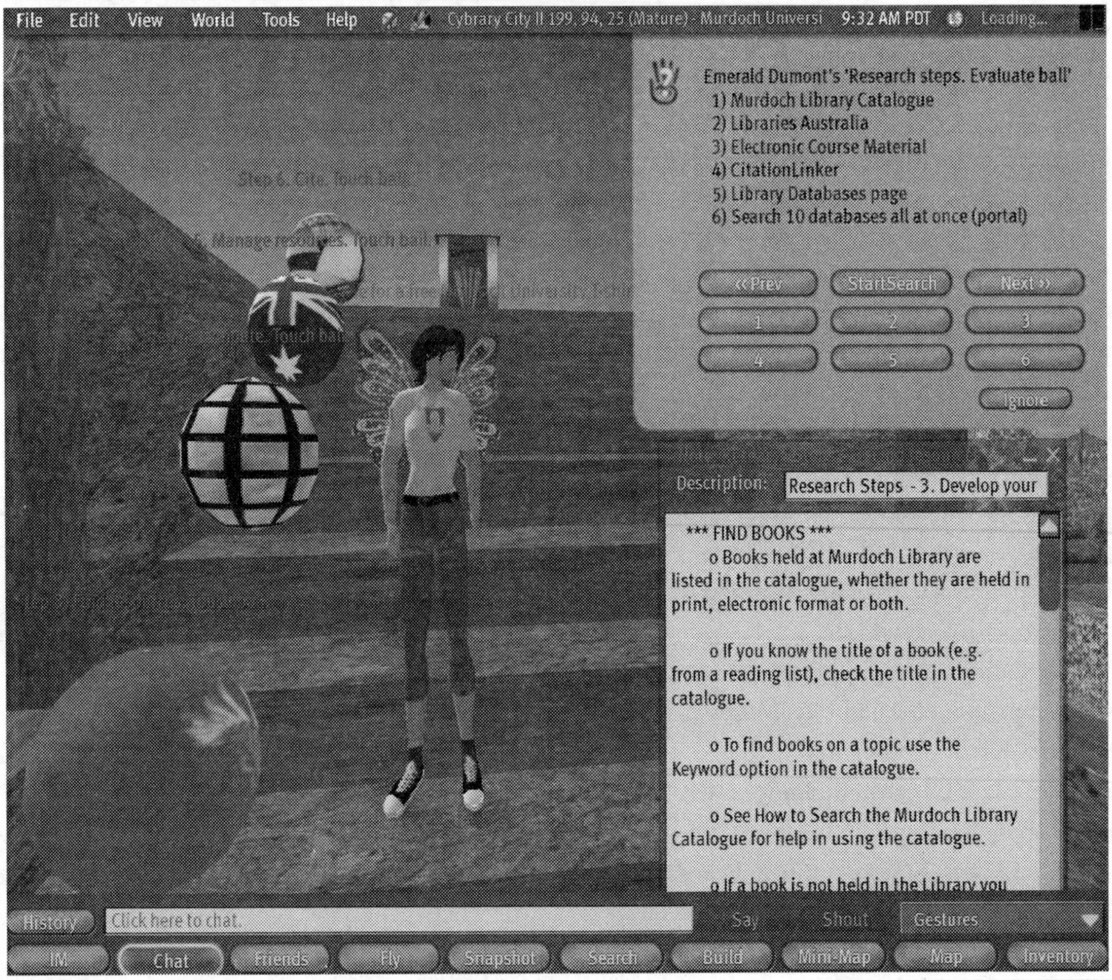

istrative rights to the PCs the hour before each session to perform a manual upgrade in case IT Services was not able to package up and push out a new upgrade in time for each workshop.

In an experiment with the Second Life interface, Greenhill is creating a "Steps to Research" installation. This is based on our library's "Beginning your Research" Web page (Murdoch University Library) . This installation is a staircase with spinning, hovering balls on every second step. Each ball has text floating above it that explains what it is. The balls are: 1. Analyze your topic; 2. Find Background; 3. Develop your research; 4. Evaluate; 5. Manage; 6. Cite. When an avatar touches the ball, s/he receives a notecard detailing the particular research step. At this stage, another small window also pops up within the Second Life interface. It contains a set of buttons to click to force the external Web browser to display useful online library resources. At the top of the steps is an old fashioned wooden radiola - a vintage radio from the early twentieth century - which presents the avatar with a Murdoch University t-shirt.

Plans for the site will depend on how the University community wants to use it. The library does not have the sufficient staffing to fully develop the site in-house. Staff from the Guild of Undergraduates, the Teaching and Learning Centre, the School of Chemical and Mathematical Sciences, and the School of Psychology have all expressed interest in contributing to the development of the site.

The Second Life address of the Murdoch plot of land is: Cybrary CityII 194, 115, 22.

MULTA – Murdoch University Library Thinking Aloud

Staff at the University Library had become interested in the application of new technologies such as blogs and RSS feeds. Kathryn Greenhill began to research this in April of 2006. In doing so, she had assumed that she would take a few hours, then produce a small report with a few suggestions.

When Greenhill began, she encountered for the first time the term "Library 2.0". She learned about sites like del.icio.us, Flickr, and Connotea, and came across the "OPAC sucks" movement. She discovered that blogging was as much about the comments as the posts. And wikis? What were those? By the time she was reading *The Cluetrain Manifesto* (Levine 1999), she realized that other library staff needed to know about these new tools and the associated new attitudes, more than they needed a few suggestions from her in a report. Within a few weeks, library staff was engaged in MULTA (http://multa.murdoch.edu.au/).

MULTA stands for Murdoch University Library Thinking Aloud. This was a collaborative learning project open to all library staff. Most of the activities took place on a site using a TikiWiki Content Management System hosted within the University. The project ran from June through August 2006.

The project aims were as follows:

MULTA is a two month collaborative project among Murdoch Library staff.

We aim to:

1. *Find out about "Library 2.0" technologies*
2. *Gain "hands on" exposure to five classes of technology*
   a. *RSS feeds*
   b. *Wikis*
   c. *Blogs*
   d. *Forums*
   e. *Social tagging*
3. *Create library wide discussion of these technologies, formally on the Webspaces and, hopefully, informally.*
4. *Investigate the technical setup required for these technologies and gain staff skills to set them up.*
5. *Create a set of recommendations about the future use of these technologies.*

Online Library 2.0 learning initiatives have been implemented elsewhere. The American Library Association's *Library 2.0 Bootcamp* (http://library2.0.alablog.org/) was running while the

MULTA site was being constructed. The strategy of using social software to learn about social software was taken from this initiative.

The Public Library of Charlotte and Mecklenberg County's *Learning2.0* course (http://plc-mcl2-things.blogspot.com/) started the week after MULTA finished. Participants completed a list of "23 things" using readily available social software sites. This course has since been used by several library systems worldwide.

Five Weeks to a Social Library, described as the "first free, grassroots, completely online course devoted to teaching librarians about social software and how to use it in their libraries", ran from February to March 2007 (http://www.sociallibraries.com/course/). Like MULTA, this course used a Content Management System for participant blogs and other functions such as chat and course outlines. A screencast about MULTA (Greenhill 2007) was part of the syllabus for the "Five Weeks" course as material for Week 5, Selling Social Software@Your Library.

Although MULTA was open to all library staff, every library section was asked to send at least one representative. All librarians were encouraged by their supervisors to attend the first meeting where the course content was outlined. Take-up varied from week to week, but about half of our staff participated at some point during the project. Staff who did not participate saw what their colleagues were doing and heard them talking about their activities. The vocabulary of Library 2.0 began permeating the library.

Participants attended a start-up meeting which outlined the project, a midway meeting which asked for feedback, and a final meeting in which participants discussed what they had learned and future uses of emerging technologies in our library. Every Friday there was a hands-on session in a computer lab. This started as an open house for any staff who came with reflections and questions. As a result of feedback at the midway meeting, these sessions developed into a more formal step-through of specific tools.

Every week, participants were given a set of three readings and two or three tasks to complete. There were two "catch up" weeks with no set readings or tasks. Each set of tasks related to the week's new Web tool. For example, during Week Six, which was Wiki week, the readings were titled *Wikis, Local Librarians 2.0* and *Radical Trust*. The tasks included viewing a screencast about how to edit a wiki, playing with the wiki page associated with their login, and adding a suggestion to the collaborative *Recommendations* wiki.

Participants read about a different aspect of the same three topics each week. The topics were New Web Tools, Library 2.0, and Memes. Below is a list of readings. Readings with the same number were read in the same week. The Ranganathan reading was extra.

Topic One. New Web Tools. 1. Content Management Systems; 2. Forums; 3. RSS Feeds; 4. Blogs; 5. Wikis; 6. Social tagging

Topic Two. Library 2.0 1. Web 2.0; 2. Library 2.0 PART 1; 3. Library 2.0 PART 2; 4. User 2.0; 5. Local Librarians 2.0; 6. Where 2.0

Topic 3. Memes 1. Meme; 2. Internet Quizzes; 3. The Long Tail; 4. The Cluetrain Manifesto; 5. Radical Trust; 6. Curvy Models; 7. Ranganathan's Five Laws of Library Science

After the initial 100 hours of setup, the MULTA site evolved based on the content created by the participants. By the end of the project, several staff had begun blogging. By week three, one staff member had created a wiki for staff to collaborate on a program timetable for practicum students. Another two staff members created a page defining blog and wiki terms - memorably coining the term "CatalogueAflogOblogOdogOphillia" (This was defined as "Being excited by cataloguing about your dog in a blog and going on about it"). People uploaded images and files. There were a couple of experiments at putting staff minutes and reports on a blog or wiki, and then asking for comments. Staff did not necessarily follow the weekly timetable and often did only the tasks that interested them.

The project achieved all of its aims. Staff who were involved did learn about Library 2.0 and tried out some new Web tools. The setup of the MULTA site developed in-house skills in configuring social software sites. The Recommendations wiki produced at the end of the project had over twenty-five suggestions for future usage of the new technologies. (Murdoch University Library 2006) There were several factors that contributed to this success.

- *Others joined in.* Library staff welcomed the participation of other campuses and sections of our university, notably our Teaching and Learning Centre. All library participants were enriched by the knowledge of participants from outside the library.
- *Staff had catch up breaks.* Six weeks of material was programmed over nine weeks, allowing staff to take breaks and still finish at the same time as the others.
- *The project was pitched at early adopters.* There was quite a jump in skills for those who completed all the tasks. These people served as models for the rest of staff.
- *The project created a community of learners.* The librarian who designed and facilitated the course monitored the site and provided suggestions to participants via e-mail, but had few contact hours on campus. As a result, a community of peer to peer learners arose.
- *Successes were celebrated.* All staff, not just participants, were e-mailed a summary of "what happened in the last week", outlining and publicly celebrating the achievements of participants during the last week.

Greenhill has concluded that, in retrospect, she would have would have done at least two things differently when facilitating the MULTA project. First, she would have included an online progress chart that recorded when each participant completed an exercise. This strategy was described in the Webinar, "Hopping into Library 2.0: Experiencing Lifelong Learning" (2007), which covered the Yarra Plenty Regional Library's experience with the "23 Things" program. This feedback would have been a useful way of encouraging staff to complete all tasks. Second, she would not have presumed that everyone who attended a Friday workshop had completed that week's reading. She would have spent the first 10 - 15 minutes reviewing the required readings and tasks for the week.

As a result of MULTA, the library has implemented an in-house blog for reference staff, using self-hosted Wordpress. The library has formed an RSS Working Party that examines how best to educate our library users about RSS, how to output catalogue information like a new books list via RSS and how to pull RSS feeds into pages within our library catalogue. The hands-on workshop component of MULTA is now run as part of the Emerging Technology Group.

Emerging Technology Group

After the MULTA project ended, library staff took a break from actively training and formally discussing Library 2.0. This gave the "first wave" of understanding time to percolate through the library. The construction of the Learning Common and the resultant renovation of most of the library took up much staff time and energy.

In March 2007, the experience with MULTA led to the formation of a Library Emerging Technology (LET) Group. Kathryn Greenhill co-ordinates this group. Initially LET meetings ran for an hour a week. The first half hour was a hands-on session in a PC lab open to all staff who wanted to learn about a new Web 2.0 tool. The second half hour was reserved for project work by a core "getting things done" group.

These staff members volunteered to take responsibility for completing experimental projects. Half an hour for hands-on learning, however, was too rushed, so the format was changed to project work one Friday, and hands-on session the next Friday.

Before setting up LET, Greenhill met with her supervisor and the Director of the University Library to decide the best way to implement it. These three decided that it was important that the LET group focus on new attitudes of Library 2.0 as well as new tools. They also wanted to ensure that learning about new technologies was seen as everybody's business and not limited to those who participated in LET. Finally, they decided the core outcomes they wanted from the group - particularly that it complete identifiable projects and not just talk about ideas - and then sat back and let the group decide how to go about it.

Before launching LET, the three librarians discussed the group's membership. They considered whether to "tap people on the shoulder" to join the group so that it had a mix of people with skills from different work areas and people who needed to know about new technologies for their jobs. This seemed counter to the attitudes of transparency the group was exploring, so membership was opened to everyone. An undergraduate who is very technologically competent joined the group after hearing about it from the Director of Library Services. This student gives the group feedback on how undergraduates regard our library.

These are the Terms of Reference of the LET Group:

Purpose:

• To discover, incubate and communicate new technological tools so we can provide better service to our clients.

• To discover, understand and communicate new attitudes and expectations which come with the use of new technological tools.

Method

This is done by:

1. Experimenting with using new Web tools to run the business of the group.

2. Welcoming input and attendance by any member of library staff to any meeting/event.

3. Maintaining current awareness of useful new technologies.

4. Assessing the potential of very new Web tools, which may be unfinished or in beta, by hands on experimentation where feasible.

5. Accepting that some technologies assessed will be rejected after experimentation.

6. Experimenting with library service delivery in pilot projects using appropriate new technologies (e.g., podcasting).

7. Experimenting with library service delivery in pilot projects which accommodate new expectations brought about by new Web tools (e.g., allowing comments on an external blog).

8. Sharing information about useful new technologies with other library staff informally and by seminars and hands on workshops.

9. Identifying projects which could be better developed to full production by another area of the library, rather than remain the experimental responsibility of the group.

The first project for the "getting things done" team was to create local content for the large screens installed in three locations in the library as part of the Learning Common renovation. Staff were asked to submit a series of three photographs of a member of our library community discovering one of our resources - the person, the object, then both together. The first image was captioned with the person's name, the next with "discovers@our library", the third with a user centered description of the resource and how to find it. (e.g. *Jan Doe, Philosophy Student. Discovers@Our Library. Printing and laminating and photocopying. Murdoch Print, North Wing Level 3*). The focus is on the library's "hidden gems" or services relocated due to the renovations. Some of the photographs will be uploaded to the library's Flickr account and added to the "365 Days at Your Library" group (Porter 2007).

This project gives staff experience with creating user centered language, developing online content, using a wiki to keep track of the images, and playing creatively. The university has recently run a re-branding campaign with the slogan "Discoverers Welcome", so the project co-brands the library with this campaign. Although LET members are enthusiastic about the project, we are having trouble finding time to fit it in with our other "regular" work.

Tools covered so far in the hands-on sessions have been "YouTube and libraries", Gmail, PBwiki, Google Reader, introduction to Firefox, and podcasting. Topics for future workshops include bundling RSS feeds using OPML and tagging using del.icio.us/Connotea/CiteULike.

Staff take-up varies from session to session ranging from four staff to ten. The core "getting things done" group attend, but most sessions include someone who has not attended before. All staff are e-mailed weekly about what is happening at LET in order to inform even those who do not attend. Generally para-professional staff (those without professional library qualifications) do not attend, although they are invited to each session and library management would like them to be involved. Management anticipates that this group will remain in existence for the foreseeable future. Retaining student participation will be an important contribution to the group's success, helping ensure that we do not inadvertently ignore our students' interests.

Future Plans

Learning Common

The Learning Common Management group will evaluate how students and staff use the Learning

Figure 2: A "Discovering at our library" image sequence

Common and its facilities. Given the emphasis on first year students, a major component of the evaluation will be the extent to which students new to the university use the space and services, and evaluating the impact the Learning Common has on their university experience. Use by others, including academic staff, will also be measured.

Planning for a refurbishment of the Veterinary Sciences branch library will also take account of the service approach provided by the Learning Common. The Management group will also continue the development of the Learning Common Web site.

Online Librarian

Evaluation of the improved Online Librarian service will be conducted during the latter part of 2007. Increased client feedback will be sought. Librarians will invite clients to submit the feedback form which is pushed to them when they close the chat session. The Online Librarian software application may be modified in response to user feedback, and once library staff have used it for a period and discovered any glitches. It would be useful to develop a widget to make the Online Librarian chat box accessible from applications that our students use, such as iGoogle.

Second Life

In response to feedback by workshop participants, the library hosted and chaired a meeting of people interested in further exploring teaching and learning within Second Life. Several ideas were floated, leading to a second meeting calling for potential pilot projects for teaching within Second Life in the second half of 2007. As a result, six third year Information and Computing Studies students will complete a twelve week for-credit project, establishing tools, scripts, objects, and environments for at least four different teaching projects within Second Life. These projects will include distance teaching to postgraduate forensic science students, creating tools for virtual theatrical set design, and simulated

job interviews for a transition to the workforce unit. The library is the client for this project.

MULTA

MULTA was deliberately aimed at early adopters. To serve the later adopters, we plan to run a Learning 2.0 / 23 Things program for three months before the end of 2007. We aim to adapt the program to include mentors for learning groups. The mentors will be drawn from those who completed MULTA in 2006. We will also include two optional weekly sessions of hands on PC lab instruction, a variation on the original program which took place in a workplace of 550 people.

Emerging Technologies Group

While the 23 Things program is being planned and while it is running, the Emerging Technologies Group is meeting in an ad hoc way to tackle more technically demanding Library 2.0 tools. The "Getting Things Done" group is halfway through building a LibX (http://libx.org/) extension for the Firefox Toolbar. These staff are now used to reserving a couple of hours a week to experiment with new technologies, so they find it easier to make space for small projects that arise as new Web tools develop. This is very different from the way we worked before the formation of the Emerging Technology Group.

Conclusion

At the time of writing, June 2007, the Learning Common is almost complete as a building renovation, while in its early stages as a collaborative and inclusive learning space. The two remodeled floors feel bright, spacious, comfortable, and welcoming as a community meeting place. The new spaces are already heavily used by students.

The collaborative Online Librarian service continues to attract new users. Evaluation of the service and its new functionality will proceed over the next six months. Training additional staff in use of the service is another imperative.

Any spare staff time and energy has been consumed in the last half year by the impact of major renovations. As things settle down, and after some breathing space, management expects staff will have more time to put more effort into our Emerging Technology Projects.

Within Murdoch University Library, the approach to emerging technologies is a gamble. No emerging technology programs or sessions are compulsory. Rather, the librarian facilitating the projects aims to provide engaging sessions with the goal of building skills relevant to staff. Sessions have focused on easily accessible examples of tools that require new flexible, conversational attitudes, rather than those requiring great technical competence or coding skills. Compulsory attendance would give more staff exposure to the material covered. Instead, the idea is to rely on a few enthusiastic early adopters increasing their skills and taking what they know back to their colleagues. This is a slower process, but library management hopes it has a longer-term, deeper impact in raising the skills and awareness of our staff to handle even more Library 2.0 changes that the future will bring to academic libraries.

References

Fletcher, Janet, Philippa Hair, and Jean McKay. 2004. Online librarian – Real time / real talk: an innovative collaboration between two university libraries. http://www.vala.org.au/vala2004/2004pdfs/20FlHaMc.PDF.

Greenhill, Kathryn. 2007. A puppy with a new ball: engaging staff in social networking tools during the MULTA project. http://s5.video.blip.tv/0580000182423/Sociallibrary-APuppyWithANewBallEngagingLibraryStaffInSocialNetwork346.swf.

SirsiDynix Institute. 2007. Hopping into library 2.0: Experiencing lifelong learning. http://www.sirsidynixinstitute.com/seminar_page.php?sid=75.

Levine, Rick, Christopher Locke, Doc Searles and David Weinberger. 1999. *The Cluetrain manifesto: the end of business as usual*. http://www.cluetrain.com/book.html.

Murdoch University Library. Beginning your research. http://wwwlib.murdoch.edu.au/help/begin.html.

Murdoch University Library. 2006. MULTA: Recommendations wiki. http://multa.murdoch.edu.au/tiki-index.php?page=Recommendations+wiki.

New Media Consortium and EduCause Learning Initiative. 2007. *The Horizon Report 2007 Edition*. http://www.nmc.org/pdf/2007_Horizon_Report.pdf.

Porter, Michael. 2007. 365 Library Days Project: The beginning. *Libraryman*, April 8. http://www.libraryman.com/blog/2007/04/08/365-library-days-project-the-beginning/.

Yale: Taking the Library to Users in the Online University Environment

Kalee Sprague and Roy Lechich

Abstract

The Yale University Library is engaged in an initiative to incorporate Library resources and services into the diverse environments where readers and researchers conduct their daily intellectual lives—course management systems, non-library portals, personal information management tools, etc. The authors will discuss this initiative focusing on the library's efforts to embed library services and resources in Web browsers, the Yale University portal, and the university's course management system. Specific projects include: adding the library catalog to Open WorldCat, creating a browser search plugin, the production of library XML feeds for use in uPortal and Sakai, and the library's exploration of ways to provide federated search tools in the Sakai environment. The authors will highlight their practical experiences identifying, developing, and implementing these projects.

Introduction

The last several years have been an exciting time in the Yale University Library. At all levels of the organization, we have been rethinking our approach to traditional online information services. In addition to constructing new services such as federated search tools and digital repositories, we have been investigating ways to integrate our new and existing services in non-library environments including portals, course management systems, PDAs, and cell phones. In essence, we are exploring the Library 2.0 concept of "taking the library to users". We no longer want simply to bring up new services, but also to present them in the online environments where our users conduct their daily lives. This evolution in the Library's approach to online services is an ongoing process, reflected both in Yale's institutional planning efforts and in the concrete projects currently underway. In this chapter we will first discuss details of relevant institutional planning and development at the university, library, and grassroots level. We will then highlight five Library 2.0 projects that integrate library services in the browser, portal, and course management environments at Yale.

Background and Planning

In the fall of 2001, the Yale University Library started work on a long-term Strategic Plan that focused, among other things, on our online library services. The Library, in particular, was interested in integrating its online services. Services such as the library catalog, licensed journal databases, and digital image databases had been implemented independently over time, and as a result were effectively isolated from each other, with separate content and interfaces. In a rapidly maturing online world, however, users were starting to expect crossover services that provided easy access to multiple types of content at once. New developments in federated search, portal, and other Web 2.0 technologies offered the potential to provide our users with this kind of integrated access.

During the development of the Strategic Plan, the Library recognized these emerging user expectations and the opportunities afforded by new technologies. The Plan included "Integrated Ac-

Kalee Sprague, e-mail: kalee.sprague@yale.edu; and Roy Lechich, e-mail: roy.lechich@yale.edu, both at Yale University Library.

cess" as a major goal, with the intention of providing access to and seamless integration of the Library's diverse information services. Important aspects of this goal included working in partnership with users to develop new teaching and research services, and establishing an integrated library organizational structure to support the integration of services.

In December 2003, the Yale Library systems office held a multi-day retreat to further develop our plan for "Integrated Access". Associate University Librarian Meg Bellinger invited Lorcan Dempsey, Vice President of Research at OCLC, to present his white paper, "The recombinant library: portals and people", as a key talking point (Dempsey 2003). A crucial conclusion reached in the retreat was that, in an increasingly diverse online environment, the library could no longer function as the sole portal of choice for researchers. The Yale Library needed to push its services out to the richer online environment of the University – we referred to this concept as the "in-your-face-library".

The retreat generated two concrete outcomes. The Integrated Access Council (IAC) was formed to provide a formal structural framework to support the work of Integrated Access. At the same time, a group of three systems office staff (the authors and Karen Kupiec) began experimenting on a grassroots level with Web 2.0 technologies and exploring how they might apply to the Yale environment. After some initial playing and experimentation, specific project ideas began to gel. At that point the grassroots group wanted to broaden its vision by including a wider range of viewpoints and a strong focus on emerging user behaviors. Accordingly, the group proposed that IAC create a formal committee that would include key usability and public services librarians.

In January 2005, IAC approved the proposal and charged the Portal Opportunities Group (POG) to "identify specific opportunities to embed library resources and services in the diverse environments where readers and researchers conduct

their daily intellectual lives – course management systems, non-library portals, personal information management tools, etc". POG was asked to conduct an environmental scan of activities at peer institutions and at Yale, then think creatively about specific projects targeting these diverse environments. The group was asked to think particularly about the integration opportunities presented by the university-level Teaching and Learning Portal (T&LP) project, weaving this in with the Library's Integrated Access plans and the work of the grassroots systems group. A cornerstone of the T&LP effort was to implement a new course management system using the open source Sakai software (http://www.sakaiproject.org/) whose open architecture presented the library with an opportunity to establish a strong presence. Also presenting a key "in-your-face-library" opportunity was the implementation of tailored student, faculty, and staff views in the new uPortal based university portal.

Operating at this critical juncture enabled the Portal Opportunities Group to write a comprehensive report identifying over thirty projects for possible implementation (http://www.library.yale.edu/~lso/pog/Portal%20Opportunities%20Group%20Report.pdf). After presenting its report to the Library, the group began implementing selected projects.

The Initiatives

Following is a discussion of some of the initiatives that are "taking the library to users" in the online university environment at Yale.

Two Long Tail Projects

Our first two projects address Chris Anderson's concept of the Long Tail (Anderson 2004). Both serve potential niche users, who may not be regular users of the online library catalog, but who might well be drawn by the presence of the library catalog in Google or in a browser search plugin. These were good first projects in that they were "low-hanging-fruit" – effective and easy to implement.

Open WorldCat

Our first small "in-your-face-library" project in Spring 2005 was making our library holdings available to Google, Yahoo!, and other search engines through OCLC's new Open WorldCat program (http://www.oclc.org/worldcat/open/). When users search for keywords in Google or Yahoo! that are contained in the title of a book, pamphlet, score, etc, the search engine results screen will contain a result prefaced by the phrase "Find in a Library" that links to the title in the WorldCat interface and displays appropriate library holdings. Alternatively, users can link directly to Open WorldCat results by prefacing their search with the phrase "Find in a Library".

The first time a user accesses the Open WorldCat interface, he or she is prompted to enter a local zip code. The Open WorldCat interface will then list libraries that own the title in order by geographic proximity. In addition to making our holdings available in Open WorldCat, we also activated the "Web links" feature so that users could link directly to the title in our library catalog from the Open WorldCat screen. Participating in Open WorldCat was an easy first step in our quest to bring the library to users, and we have seen a slow but steady increase in monthly usage. In May 2006 there were 325 clicks in Open WorldCat through to the Yale library catalog; one year later there were 5,027 – an increase of nearly 1500%.

Library Catalog Firefox Search Plugin

The "Yale Library Catalog" search plugin was easy to create, thanks to open software and open standards for creating search plugins. Mozilla's Firefox and Microsoft's Internet Explorer include a built-in search box in the upper right hand corner, with a drop down selection list of search engines. By creat-

Figure 1. Google "Find in a Library" results

Figure 2. Open WorldCat display

ing a new search plugin, this list can be extended to include, for example, a library OPAC (Online Public Access Catalog).

Creating and implementing a search plugin is primarily a matter of creating a small text file (SGML or XML) as a search plugin description file, and then placing this file in the appropriate plugins directory (e.g. in Firefox for Windows this would generally be "C:\Program Files\Mozilla Firefox\searchplugins") along with an icon to represent the plugin.

The "Yale Library Catalog" search plugin was created in early 2006 by Jeffrey Barnett, senior researcher in the Library systems office, using a Sherlock description file. Sherlock was originally a file and Web searching tool developed by Apple for its Mac

Figure 3. Yale Library Catalog search plugin

operating system. Mozilla adapted the Sherlock description format for use in its browser suite, and created a project called "Mycroft" (named for Sherlock Holmes' older brother) to hold and host Sherlock search plugins (http://www.mozdev.org/).

The Sherlock description file is straightforward SGML, and contains information such as the URL and parameters for the search. Mycroft also serves a hosting function – by registering a search plugin on its site, the plugin can automatically find any upgrades placed there (http://mycroft. mozdev.org/download.html).

Along with the search plugin, we added an extension enhancing the functionality of the context menu in Firefox. ("Search plugins" allow the browser to access search engines, while "extensions" extend the functionality of the browser itself.) The context menu appears when a user right-clicks in the browser window. One of the options available from the context menu is the ability to search for a word or phrase that the user has selected in a Web page. The default Firefox behavior is to use the currently selected search engine for the search. The "Context Search" extension (http://www.cusser.net/extensions/contextsearch /) adds a secondary dropdown menu allowing the user to choose from the available list of search engines, including our library catalog.

Around October 2006, Mozilla released version 2 of its Firefox browser, and Microsoft released version 7 of its Internet Explorer (IE) browser. Both browsers now support (and Firefox prefers) the newer OpenSearch search description format, which uses XML. OpenSearch is a set of technologies from A9, an Amazon company (http://www.a9.com/), which includes not only the description format but also functionality to display OpenSearch results using OpenSearch RSS and Aggregators. The basic idea is the same: by creating a

Figure 4. Context Search showing Yale search plugin

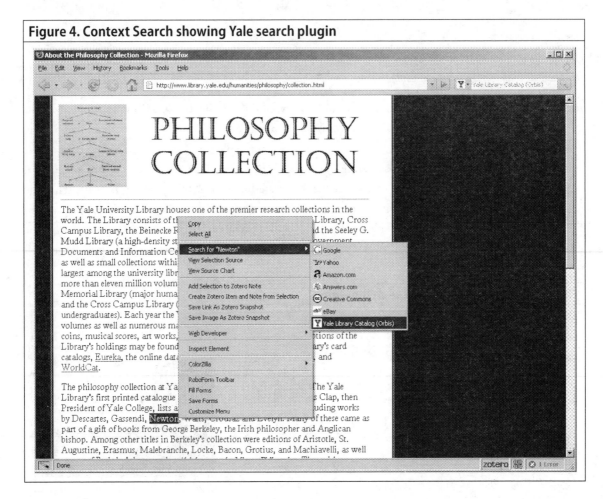

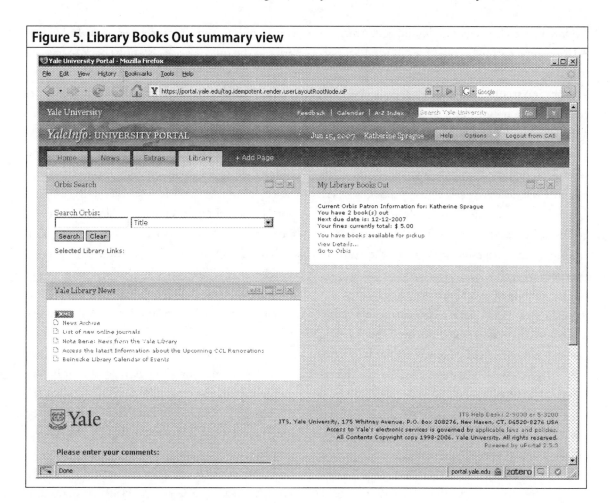

Figure 5. Library Books Out summary view

simple search description file, one can now add to the list of available search engines in both Firefox and IE. The Mozilla development site also offers a new context query extension called "ConQuery" with more functionality than the Context Search extension (http://conquery.mozdev.org/).

The "Yale Library Catalog" search plugin is available for download to the Yale community from the university's central online software library. We are planning to upgrade the search plugin to OpenSearch by Fall 2007, allowing users of both Firefox and IE to use the plugin, and hope to upgrade our context search extension to use Mozilla's new "ConQuery" plugin.

Dynamic Generation of XML Content
Library Books Out
The "Library Books Out" portal channel is our first example of taking the library to users using XML

content dynamically generated from our library catalog. "Library Books Out" is an XML portal channel that displays selected patron information from our Voyager® Integrated Library Management System in the Yale University portal, YaleInfo. As the name suggests, the channel primarily lists information about the titles a user has checked out.

The original idea for "Library Books Out" was generated in the grassroots group of three systems office staff who were exploring Web 2.0 technologies. Fortuitously, a group of central university Information Technology Services (ITS) staff (including Susan Bramhall and Andrew Petro of the Technology & Planning Group) was implementing the university portal at that same time, and were eager to enlist potential content providers. As a result, they were happy to collaborate with us to integrate library information in the portal. The project provided an ideal opportunity to both explore new technologies and build good working relationships with our colleagues in the ITS portal group.

The grassroots nature of this early work afforded us the opportunity to concentrate on core functionality, free from the usual considerations of a more formal development process. The benefit of this streamlined process was speed; once the channel was ready, we put it into production. We continued in this expedient mode after the channel went live, asking for feedback from users and implementing suggested changes in the spirit of "perpetual beta".

"Library Books Out" offers two separately designed views: 1) a summary view listing total number of items checked out, fines due, and warning messages about circulation activity, and 2) a full view that lists details of items checked out and requested by the user.

The warning messages in the summary view are particularly useful, alerting a user when they have books that are about to come due (or are already overdue), and when items they have requested are ready to be picked up. Both views have links back to the library catalog, so that users can renew ma-

terials online and/or cancel requests. Individual titles in the full view are also links back to the full title information in the library catalog.

The "Library Books Out" portal channel is designed specifically for use with Yale's implementation of uPortal. uPortal is an open source JA-SIG (http://www.ja-sig.org/) portal project, and is designed to let users leverage reusable portlets called "channel types" to accommodate common portal channel tasks. One channel type emulates a browser window; another accepts as input both an XML feed and an XSL style sheet for rendering the channel. "Library Books Out" is comprised of two components: 1) an XML Proxy portal channel developed by our ITS group that calls 2) a library Web application to authenticate the user and return an XML feed of patron information. When a user logs in, the portal sends a request for library patron information that includes the user's NetID, the university's unique online identifier. First the program uses Yale's locally developed, open source Central Authentication Service (CAS) to authenticate the NetID (http://www.ja-sig.org/products/cas/). Then a Java Server Page (JSP) program runs a SQL query in response to gather the relevant

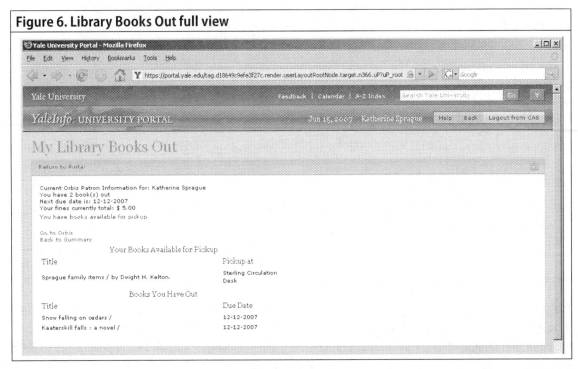

Figure 6. Library Books Out full view

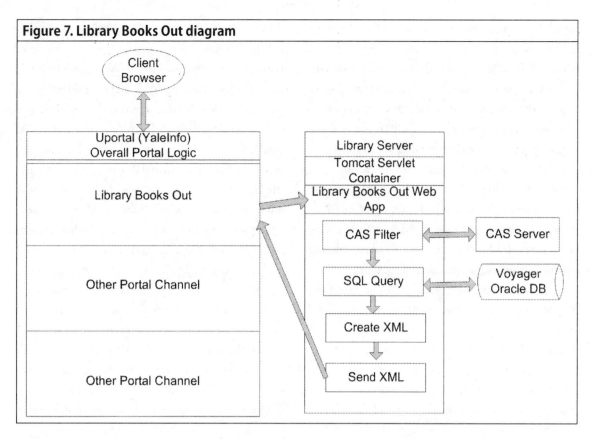

Figure 7. Library Books Out diagram

data from our Voyager Oracle database. The result set is used to generate an XML document, which is then returned and rendered using an Extensible Stylesheet Language Transformation (XSLT) style sheet (a type of style sheet that transforms XML into other formats) that contains uPortal specific logic for switching between the summary and full views. The XML is delivered to the portal, where the Library-designed XSLT style sheet is applied, and the appropriate summary or full view of the "Library Books Out" channel is rendered.

The "Library Books Out" portal channel was an exciting development for the Yale Library because it was our first example of using XML to dynamically integrate library catalog content with the university portal. We are currently looking into new methods for converting "Library Books Out" into a cell phone and PDA-enabled notification service.

Course Reserves Feed

The Course Reserves feed was our next project to use dynamically generated content to "take the library to users". Course Reserves is an XML feed of course reserve list information from our library catalog. We first got the idea for the Course Reserves feed while brainstorming for ideas to follow up on our work with the "Library Books Out" channel. Course reserve information offered an intriguing opportunity to create a mashup of library and central class information, along with an opportunity to explore a new type of portal technology. This project was also significant because it was the first project to develop under the auspices of the Library's new integrated access structure – with formal input from the Integrated Access Council, the Portal Opportunities Group, and our central ITS group. Our grassroots experiments now had a larger, more mature organizational framework in which to develop.

At the outset, the Library's Course Reserves feed had the interest of two likely consumers: the ITS portal group, for a "Course Readings" portal channel, and the ITS course support group, as a source of content for Classes, Yale's locally-developed course management system. After the three groups met to discuss specifications for the Course Reserves feed, it was clear the first and most critical issue to resolve was the fact that many Course IDs in the library catalog did not match those in the university's systems. The Library was using legacy department codes that did not match the official university department codes. In consultation with the Library's Access Services department, the systems office embarked on a labor-intensive project to change the Library's department codes, with new workflows to ensure future compliance with the university. The Library's support for this project confirmed the growing recognition of the importance of the "taking the library to users" service model.

After establishing the initial criteria and creating a match point for the feed, we moved on to develop the feed itself. In contrast to the "Library Books Out" channel, development of the Course Reserves feed did not involve end-user interface considerations. Course Reserves is, in essence,

a Web service in that it is designed to generate XML in response to another application's Web request. (Strictly speaking, a Web service should have a self-describing Web Services Description Language (WSDL) document and be published in a Web services registry (http://www.w3.org/TR/wsdl)). The feed is produced using JSP and Java technologies. Once invoked, the application uses the URL's query string to build and execute a SQL query against our catalog database for the requested department and course code(s). It then returns an XML feed of course reserve list information.

The feed includes information about the Title, Author, Call Number, and Location associated with each course reserve. In addition, three types of URLs are provided with each title in the feed. For books and other materials that are primarily listed in the library catalog, the feed provides a title link back to the full catalog record. Links to Table of Contents and other independent content related to a book are provided as independent URLs associated with each title. Electronic reserve (e-re-

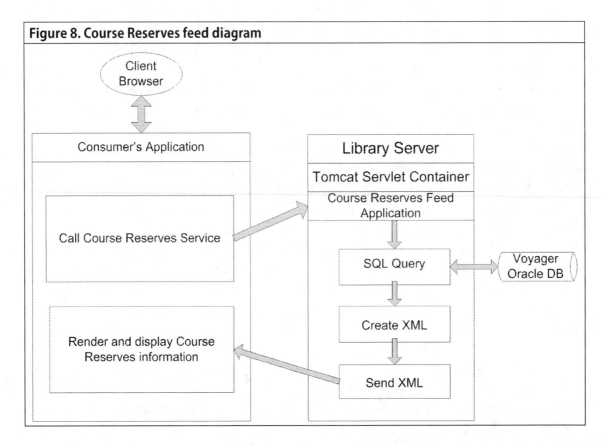

Figure 8. Course Reserves feed diagram

serve) materials have a special link associated with them labeled "Click to access article" that points to an OpenURL for the full text of the associated article or book chapter.

The Yale University portal was the first environment to consume the Library's Course Reserves feed. The ITS portal group developed a special type of hybrid portal channel that uses information from two different sources: the course management system and the Library's Course Reserves feed. For each course a student is registered for, this hybrid "Course Readings" channel displays a mashup of 1) the syllabus and class information associated with each course, and 2) any associated course reserves.

The second environment to consume the feed was the university's implementation of the Sakai course management system, called classes*v2. We first got the idea of embedding the Course Re-

serves feed in Sakai after seeing a conference demonstration of a similar project implemented by the University of Michigan. Both ITS and Library staff attended the conference, and came away excited by the idea of creating a custom Sakai tool to consume the Library's Course Reserves feed. Consequently, Michael Appleby in our ITS Academic Media & Technology group designed a tool to derive the department and course code associated with a Sakai course Web site, execute a call to the feed, and then apply an XSLT transform to display the results.

Because a course site is ultimately owned by the faculty member teaching the course, the tool was designed to be optional, available through the "Edit Tools" list under "Site Info". Either the faculty member or their designated site maintainer must go in and turn on the tool. Since the Course Reserves feed can contain links to e-reserves (ei-

Figure 9. Course Reserves XML output

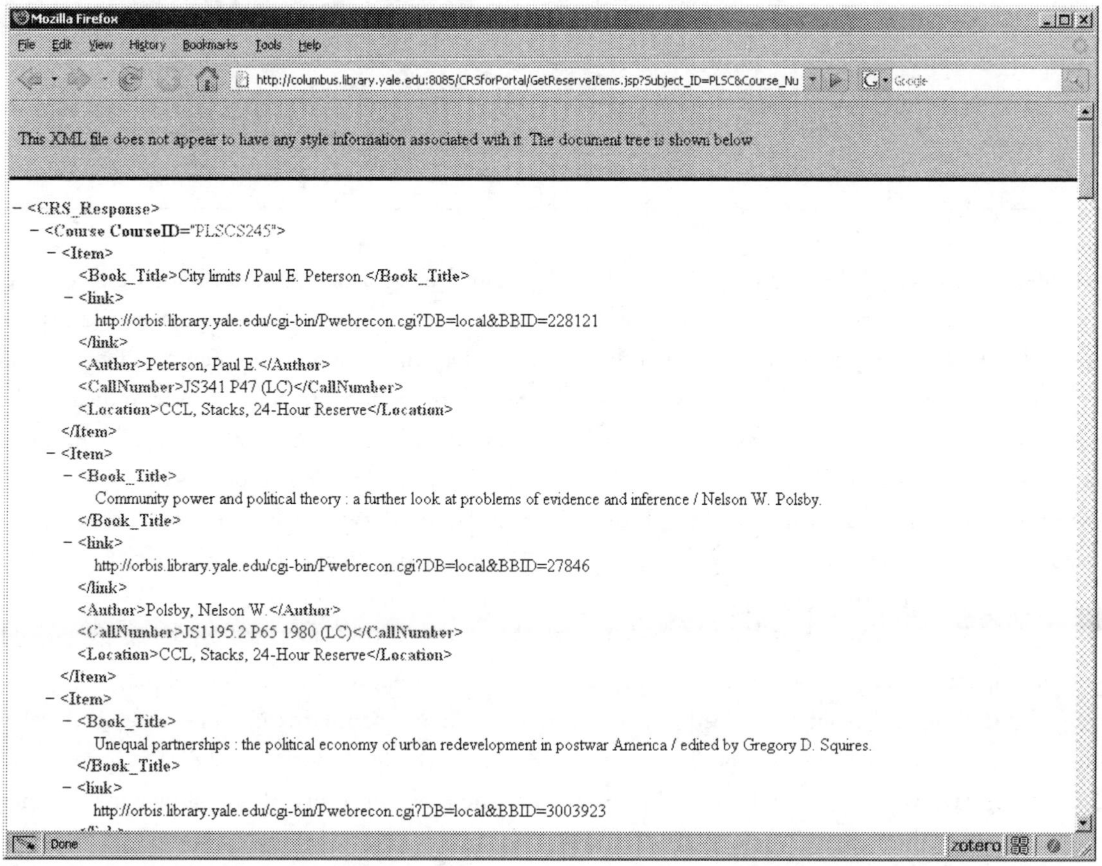

Figure 10. Course Readings in uPortal

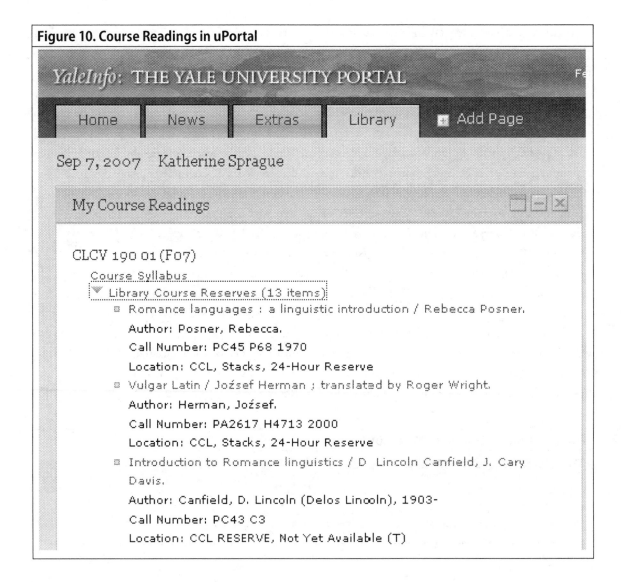

ther locally scanned PDFs or links to licensed library resources) that are restricted based on the user's IP address, the tool warns users who have an off-campus IP address that they must connect using the university's VPN or proxy server. (Yale provides a Virtual Private Network (VPN) to allow off-campus users to navigate online through the university environment as though they were on campus. Similarly, the library provides an http proxy server for accessing restricted materials.)

One important part of Library 2.0 is the process of gathering and reacting to feedback from users so that users become part of the process. Course Reserves was the first Library 2.0 project to benefit from the Library's new usability pro-

gram. During a two-semester library e-reserves pilot, a user survey was conducted on course reserves in Sakai that included comments and suggestions related to the feed. In general, users indicated that they liked having course reserves information in Sakai. However, open-ended feedback in the survey garnered two suggestions for improvement. Several respondents indicated that the order of course readings was confusing, and requested that they be organized chronologically based on weekly readings, instead of by author name. In response, we are looking into this as the next step in development of the feed (not as easy as it may seem, due to the table structure of our library management system).

Figure 11. Course Reserves in Sakai

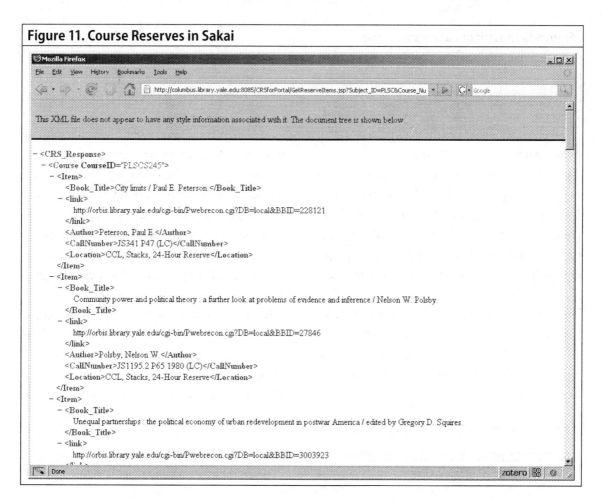

Users also requested the ability to access articles from home without having to sign in via the proxy server or VPN. Since users must initially log in to access Sakai, it is frustrating for them to be challenged again when trying to access a restricted resource like a journal article. We are working on a solution to solve this non-trivial problem.

The Course Reserves feed was significant, both as a Library 2.0 project that grew under the auspices of the Library's new organizational structure, and as a first step in pushing library information out to the online university environment in a freely accessible way. We expect the Course Reserves feed to officially go live in our course management system in August 2007, and anticipate a continuing cycle of user feedback and development.

Future Plans
Library Search Tools in Sakai and uPortal

Our next area of focus for "taking the library to users" is the integration of library search tools in Sakai and uPortal. Studies, such as the impressive Context Resource Evaluation Environment (CREE) project in the UK, have shown that users welcome the presence of subject-based library search tools in the online learning environment (Awre 2005). We have plans for integrating a number of search tools in this environment, including the addition of subject-specific search boxes in Sakai course sites, and adding links to appropriate databases and services such as Google Scholar. Also in the planning stages is an exciting new proposal to use the Open Archives Initiative framework (OAI) to create a federated search within our university portal that will provide access to our local Yale image databases and special collections. Finally, we are participating in the grant-funded Sakaibrary project to embed a federated citation search tool in Sakai.

Figure 12. Restricted access warning

Yale University Library

Electronic resources are licensed for the noncommercial, educational, or research use of the Yale community and those who are physically present at Yale library facilities. You are attempting to access a licensed resource from off-campus. Please follow the instructions to configure your computer for Off-Campus Access.

Sakaibrary

The Sakaibrary project is a Mellon-funded initiative, co-managed by Indiana University and the University of Michigan, to integrate licensed library resources with Sakai (http://www.dlib.indiana.edu/projects/sakai/). The key goal of the project is to offer users the ability to conduct federated searches against licensed library databases from within Sakai, then save the results back to a Citation List or other format in a Sakai course site.

The "Citations Helper" tool connects to existing library federated search tools such as Sirsi One Search and MetaLib using the Open Knowledge Initiative (OKI) Open Service Interface Definition (http://www.okiproject.org/). Although a connector can be written for any federated search tool, the grant limited the initial scope of the project to the two popular tools used at Indiana and Michigan. In addition to searching against library databases, the user is also offered the option of searching against Google Scholar.

As a project partner on the grant, Yale has helped establish project requirements and conduct preliminary testing of the tool. "Citations Helper" is now available in beta form in Sakai 2.4, released May 2007. Instructions for implementing the tool are

Figure 13. Citations Helper selection screen

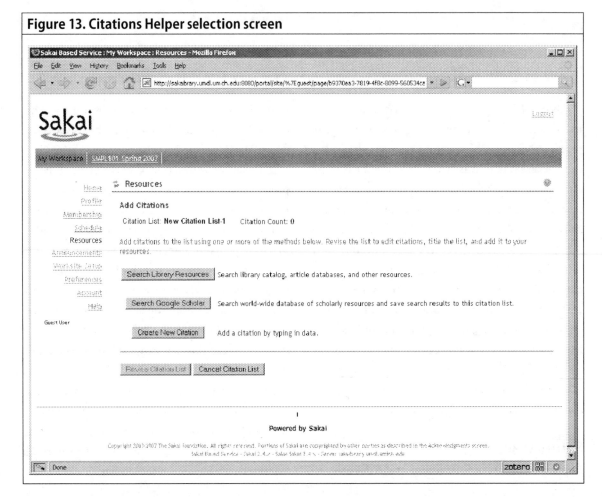

restricted to project partners, who have been asked to conduct beta testing and, if possible, pilot studies of the tool with a small number of classes. Yale is planning to participate in beta testing, but may not participate in pilot studies until Spring 2008. The goal of Yale's beta testing will be to gauge the usability and desirability of the tool. We are excited by the tool not only because it will help us support classroom teaching and research in general, but also because we hope to empower faculty and staff to create their own reading lists and bibliographies on the fly.

Future Plans

If you would like to follow the Sakaibrary project, as well as the other projects we have described here, we invite you to visit the post-publication wiki that supplements this book. We also welcome input as we track progress on these projects, and post updates on related new ideas and plans:

* Experiences converting our Firefox search plugin to OpenSearch and ConQuery

* Cell phone and PDA-enabling our Library Books Out channel

* Re-design of the library presence in the Yale Portal

* Creation of a "New Books" RSS feed for portal

* Continuing development of Course Reserves feed in Sakai

* Sakaibrary beta testing

* Development of an OAI cross-collection search

* Possible Facebook presence

Conclusion

Our various projects to take the library to users in the online university environment have been enlightening. The "silo" model of past online library

---

Figure 14. Citations Helper results screen

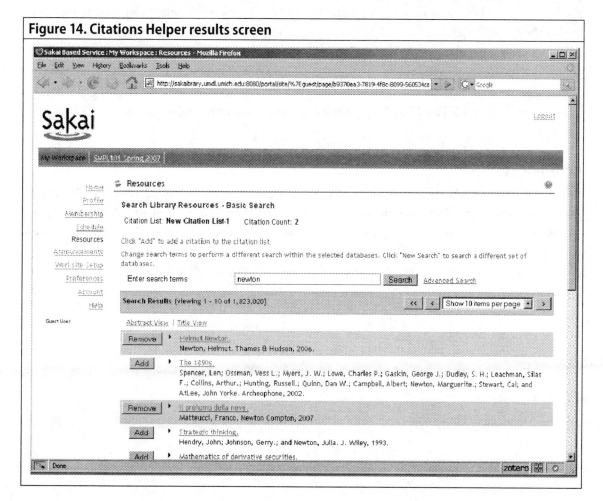

services no longer serves the needs of users who increasingly work and play in the broader online environment, and who expect quick and easy access to resources from their favorite interfaces. These Library 2.0 projects to "take the library to users" have been effective in moving the Yale Library's online services towards more integrated access.

Two things have been key to the success of these projects: the freedom to experiment at an informal grassroots level, and the formation of an organizational structure to support integrated access initiatives. Work at the grassroots level, by informal groups of individual staff, can be a low cost, yet effective means to incubate new ideas. A strong organizational framework, however, is needed to support institution-wide planning and to allocate the resources necessary to implement projects of significant scale. This framework, then, can support both centrally planned initiatives as well as projects, such as the Course Reserves feed, generated at the grassroots level.

As we have worked to push library services out to the broader university, we have seen the advantages of other aspects of Library 2.0, like "the long tail," "perpetual beta," and the growing importance of user assessment. Easy-to-implement services, such as search plugins, address the long tail requirements of niche users and enable the quick creation of a broad range of tools. The perpetual beta model allows for a fast and flexible development approach that avoids the necessity of an extensive specification and approval process that can weigh a project down and delay its roll-out seemingly indefinitely. This ongoing beta and constant re-evaluation, including user assessment, create the agility to respond to rapid changes in technology and user needs. Finally, we have found it is vital to both include users in the development process and provide them with tools that support independent research activities.

As always, users' expectations are constantly growing, keeping pace with the rapidly expanding pool of available information. The library's ongoing challenge is to meet this need. Happily, a lot of good work is currently being done in the library community to keep libraries at the center of online research. Library 2.0 initiatives, like the ones we have described at the Yale Library, are improving service for our users while ensuring the library's active role in the evolving online world.

References

Anderson, Chris. 2004. The long tail. *Wired* 12 (October). http://www.wired.com/wired/archive/12.10/tail.html.

Awre, Chris, Gabrial Hanganu, Caroline Ingram, Tony Brett, and Ian Dolphin. 2005. The CREE Project: investigating user requirements for searching within institutional environments. *D-Lib Magazine* 11 (October). http://www.dlib.org/dlib/october05/awre/10awre.html.

Dempsey, Lorcan. 2003. The recombinant library: portals and people. *Journal of Library Administration* 39 (4): 103-136. http://www.oclc.org/research/staff/dempsey/recombinant_library/.

Delivering Targeted Library Resources into a Blackboard Framework

Richard Cox

Abstract

This chapter describes the planning, development, and implementation of an application that pushes library content into the Blackboard course management system. Developed by the Electronic Resources and Information Technology Department (ERIT) at the University Libraries, University of North Carolina at Greensboro (UNCG), this tool is built around a number of technologies and methodologies including SOAP Web services, ASP.NET, Java, AJAX, and Adobe Flex. Through this application, the library provides up-to-date, customized links to databases and e-journals at the course level, thereby establishing a presence at a point of need. This application may be the first to integrate library content dynamically into Blackboard at this level and scale.

Introduction

Despite the breadth of quality resources made available online by academic libraries, many researchers spend relatively little time on library Web sites. Users look for simple interfaces that return relevant results immediately. They often do not want to learn multiple or complex library or learning systems, nor do they want to deal with several sign-ons across campus.

Like many development projects, the Blackboard initiative at the UNCG University Libraries was born out of the need to solve a specific problem. In 2003, as a member of ERIT, I first began looking at our Reference Department's Subject and Course Guides. This collection is a sprawling set of static Web pages that now totals a whopping 15.4 MB and encompasses 1,469 files and 166 folders. The Web pages contain the types of resources one would expect to support classroom instruction within UNCG's subject areas– relevant journals, databases, contact information, and so on. When one combines the generic data formats and categories, the repetitive look and feel, and the inherent challenges involved in maintaining over 1,000 high-traffic Web pages, it was apparent to me that the Subject Guides needed to be generated through a database application. This move would reduce the maintenance load to a much more manageable number - probably less than ten pages - and add a high level of searchability and portability to the information.

An ad hoc working group was created to revamp the Subject and Course Guide areas of the University Libraries' Web site. The group combined the technical skills of ERIT with the subject expertise of the Reference Department. ERIT put together a SQL Server 2000 database that contained a great deal of information related to our vendor database subscriptions, including breakdowns by subject area and subject-based RSS Feeds. This "metabase" has been informally dubbed VDBS (Vendor Database Services) and to this day powers the University Libraries' online database listings by both title and subject (http://library.uncg.edu/dbs/). Unfortunately, when the Reference Department reviewed the progress of the project, disagreements led to its demise. Some librarians in the department wanted the more standardized,

Richard Cox, University Libraries of the University of North Carolina at Greensboro, e-mail: richard_cox@uncg.edu

easily maintained design, while others wanted complete control over every element on their pages despite any maintenance overhead. ERIT did not want to develop a product for a client that could not agree on what it wanted. It was not feasible to build a database application to recreate the pages as they currently existed while at the same time including infinite customization options.

As a lead developer and project manager for ERIT, I found it difficult to allow such a worthwhile project to fade away. Moreover, as an applications programmer, I believe in the interrelatedness of projects, and that no application should stand alone. While pondering the issues relating to our subject pages and the orphaned VDBS application, it became apparent to me that the central point of contention was the user interface. If this issue could be eliminated, progress might be made. A personal interest in Web services and their potential uses led to what would become the Library Resources project: the delivery of robust, targeted library resources into Blackboard at the course level.

The strategy behind the Library Resources project reflects principles of Library 2.0. We are building a component-based application that pulls together resources from multiple locations and in different formats. As a lightweight approach to applications development, Library Resources is open to ongoing modification. As a result of its XML-based format, its content can be repurposed for more than one type of device. This is an approach that embodies the Library 2.0 concepts of perpetual beta and the long tail. The Library Resources project is most closely tied to Library 2.0 in its user-centricity and tight integration with UNCG's e-learning environment, Blackboard. By delivery library content to Blackboard, we are able to meet users' needs when, where, and how they need it and in a way that not only leaves behind the library's walls, but the library's Web space as well.

This methodology is attentive to needs pointed out within the OCLC 2003 Environmental Scan, which notes that users are looking for disaggregation, self-service, seamlessness, and satisfaction (http://www.oclc.org/reports/escan/). The Library Resources project, with a native user interface within Blackboard (or, really, any Course Management System), provides a single login system, relevant resources where the users already are, and content customized to the needs of users at the time and place of need. As a result, each of the needs identified by OCLC is addressed through the use of Library 2.0 concepts.

The Library Resources project is a Web 2.0 application on both front and back end. The two browser clients, detailed below, are based upon two Rich Internet Application (RIA) techniques. One is an Adobe Flex-based solution, while the other is based upon Ajax and JSON utilizing CSS and XHTML for markup. On the back end of the application, the University Libraries is delivering data via the open-source JSON.NET and, most importantly, XML-based Web services Application Programming Interfaces (APIs).

What Are Web Services?

The World Wide Web Consortium (W3C) defines Web Services as providing

> A standard means of interoperating between
> different software applications, running on
> a variety of platforms and/or frameworks.
> Web services are characterized by their
> great interoperability and extensibility,
> as well as their machine-processable
> descriptions thanks to the use of XML
> (World Wide Web Consortium 2007).

To put it another way, Web Services are a platform independent method by which differing systems may seamlessly communicate with and transfer data between one another. The normal mode of communication is via the SOAP (Service Oriented Architecture Protocol) XML standard (http://www.w3.org/2000/xp/Group/), using WSDL

(Web Services Description Language) (http://www.w3.org/2002/ws/desc/). SOAP and WSDL are both XML-based languages. SOAP is the primary protocol over which Web service requests and responses are transmitted between the client and server, while WSDL is a description of all of the actions the Web service is capable of performing, as well as how the clients and servers should interact. WSDL is generally used for automatically generating code (based upon the WSDL definitions) and for Web service configuration.

Amazon.com provides a well-known example of a Web service. The site contains a section entitled "Where's My Stuff?," where customers can track their recent United States Postal Service (USPS) or United Parcel Service (UPS) orders. After logging in to Amazon.com, they can select a link for the appropriate shipment, and voilá—their tracking information appears *on the Amazon.com* Web site. This occurs without redirecting customers to the USPS or UPS sites. How is this accomplished? Web Services. When customers select the "track" button, the Amazon.com Web server connects to the appropriate Web service, sending along the tracking number and using a format specified within the USPS or UPS WSDL. The Web service then searches the provider's own databases and returns a response, also conforming to the WSDL definition. The Amazon.com Web application for-

mats the returned data and presents the results to the user. Thus timely tracking information is made available to Amazon.com customers directly from USPS (United States Postal Service 2005) or UPS (United Parcel Service) without leaving the Amazon.com storefront. This portability across different systems and servers from a central data source makes Web Services an ideal model for delivering resources within Blackboard or other applications outside the library network and Web space.

The Initiative

The Library Resources project at UNCG is an application that pushes library content into the campus Blackboard course management system, thereby serving users at a point of need. This project was built by ERIT under the direction of the author, who was also the primary application developer.

The Back End and Administration

The back end and administration for the Library Resources project consists of several distinct content components brought together into a single administrative interface. Microsoft's Active Directory was utilized in order to provide both security and librarian-related information within the project, while also benefiting from data originating within three other, stand-alone ERIT or UNCG applications: Banner,

Figure 1: Amazon.com Track Your Order Web Service

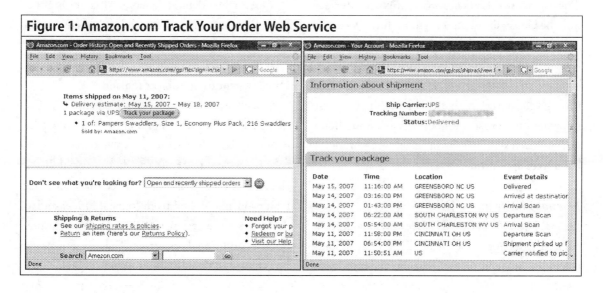

Journal Finder, and VDBS. Pieces of each program are pulled together into a new administrative interface called the Library Resources Content Administration Tool which lies behind and drives the Library Resources project. It cannot be stressed enough how much more complex an undertaking this project would have been if not for the ability to leverage preexisting tools and applications in constructing the Library Resources Content Administration Tool.

Windows Server 2003 Active Directory
Microsoft's Active Directory is a Windows Server-based implementation of the LDAP (Lightweight Directory Access Protocol) standard. Among its many uses, Active Directory organizes network objects such as users and computers into a centralized data store, and provides centralized authentication services for the Windows environment. The user storage and authentication pieces of Active Directory are used to pull librarian subject and departmental liaison information into the Library Resources database, and its authentication procedures monitor access to and rights within the administration tool. We use this information to build a link from a Blackboard course to the e-mail (and potentially Instant Messaging) account of the relevant subject expert in the Reference Department.

Banner Student Information System
The University Libraries maintains an interface into the University's Banner system (http://banner.uncg.edu/). Banner is a comprehensive computer information system that contains information on courses, students, faculty, staff, and alumni. It is through this interface that ERIT pulls new course information (course, number, section, and abbreviation) each semester for inclusion in the Library Resources application.

Journal Finder and VDBS
Journal Finder is an OpenURL resolver and knowledge base developed locally by ERIT (http://journalfinder.uncg.edu/uncg/). Journal Finder includes a subject area-browsable interface based upon the areas of study at UNCG. Journal listings by subject within Journal Finder are accessed by the Library Resources administrative tool.

VDBS, as mentioned above, is a SQL Server 2000 database that contains vendor database subscriptions, including the capacity to sort by subject area. As with Journal Finder, database information is acquired by the Library Resources administrative tool from VDBS broken down by subject. Using our extant Journal Finder and VDBS databases, we can push into Blackboard links to the most relevant e-journals and databases for each individual class.

Library Resources Content Administration Tool
Of course, someone needs to decide which library resources are most critical for a given class or area of study. The assignment of particular resources to specific classes is accomplished through the Library Resources Content Administration Tool. Access to and permissions within this tool are overseen by Active Directory. The administration tool then completes several tasks automatically, storing the results within a new SQL Server database:

+ Associate librarians, also provided from Active Directory, with their liaison subject/course responsibility area, creating the Library Liaisons listings

+ Attaches default liaisons to courses pulled from Banner within their subject/course responsibility area

+ Generates contact information from Active Directory for each Subject Liaison

Once logged into the system, a subject liaison may change liaison assignments on a course-by-course basis and maneuver between semesters. The core functionality of the tool lies in the ability of the liaison to associate specific courses with electronic journals culled from Journal Finder and/or databases pulled from VDBS, as well as a limited range of additional resources. These resources can be assigned in three distinct ways:

1. An entire subject area (all English courses)

2. An entire course level (all English composition [101] courses)

3. A specific section of a course (English 101, section 01).

As new resource associations are created within the administrative tool, they are dynamically picked up by the Library Resources Web Service and populated into Blackboard. As a result, we are customizing content for each class or entire groups of classes, all in real-time in order to meet the immediate needs of both instructors and students.

Taking It to the Masses: Powering the Web Service

The UNCG University Libraries works within a Microsoft development environment, but a similar architecture could be built based upon any number of frameworks or languages, including J2EE (Java), PHP, Perl, Python, or a number of other options. The Library Resources Web Service is built in ASP. NET 2.0, and looks for three distinct parameters in any SOAP request: academic departmental abbreviation, course number, and section number. Once the .NET application has checked the validity of the request, it will query the SQL Server 2000 database fronted by the Content Administration Tool and return the relevant records (journals, databases, and liaison contact information) to the client via a SOAP response.

Blackboard and Adobe Flex

In coordination with UNCG's Blackboard Application Administrator, who manages all programs built to interface with Blackboard in addition to the course management system itself, we were able to create a Web services client as a Blackboard Building Block. A Building Block is an application built to work within the Blackboard framework and extend its functionality via openly available APIs. We attempted to do this by having Java, Blackboard's programming language of choice, speak directly to ASP.NET over the campus network. Due to network configuration issues, this proved unwieldy. As a result, we had to turn to a Web browser/client-based approach. We chose Adobe Flex because it is the client-side

Figure 2: Content Administration Tool, sample course listing

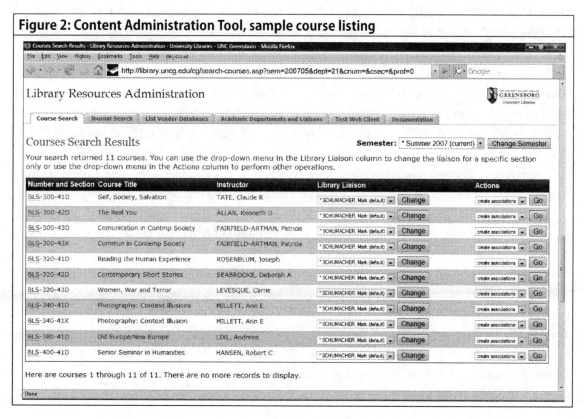

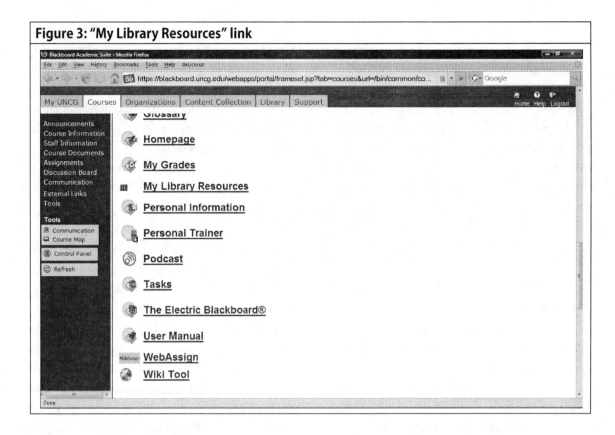

Figure 3: "My Library Resources" link

development platform the Blackboard Application Administrator is most familiar with. Adobe Flex is a Flash-based application framework used to create rich client-based, cross-platform Web applications (http://www.adobe.com/products/flex/).

The Library Resources/Adobe Flex Building Block is passed to the standard three course parameters by Java. Flex then initiates a SOAP request to the University Libraries Web service, which returns a list of e-journals, vendor databases, and contact liaison information. Flex then takes the returned XML data and formats it for the user as Adobe Flash.

The User Experience

When students log into UNCG's Blackboard environment, they see a list of courses in which they are enrolled. After selecting one, they go into that course and see a button labeled "Tools," which in turn leads to a "My Library Resources" option. Selecting this link opens a new page within the primary frame. This contains the results of the Web services data request, laid out in a familiar table format.

Once students have selected a journal or database from the "My Library Resources" table within Blackboard, they are redirected through a library Web server which transparently verifies that their request is coming from within Blackboard, and therefore pre-authenticated as affiliated with the University. As a result, students do not need to be diverted through the University Libraries' authentication mechanism before being passed on to their chosen resource. This is an important step in the process, as it eliminates the necessity for multiple sign-ons. This can be very frustrating to users.

The Good and the Bad
Technology
The client portion of the service application relies heavily upon Flash Player version 9. This is a small, widely installed browser plugin with which many students are familiar. As of March 2007, the version 9 player had was installed across 84% of Internet-enabled devices in the United States and Canada (Adobe Systems Incorporated 2007a). In

addition, Flash 9 is the installed player across the UNCG campus computer labs. For an overwhelming majority of users, therefore, access to library resources within Blackboard is a seamless process. The UNCG Division of Continual Learning utilizes a great deal of interactive Flash applications in its online courses, and as a result should be able to readily utilize the available code base in the same Flex tool as employed in Blackboard.

There were a number of technological challenges faced in implementing this application. As we debugged and overcame one hurdle, another tricky area was uncovered. The Blackboard Application Administrator and I believed that we were having difficulty getting ASP.NET and Java to talk to one another because we were not very familiar with each other's programming language of choice. This turned out not to be the case, as the two platforms were having no communication issues. Rather, we discovered that the UNCG network architecture was placing limitations on port 80 communications which prevented server-to-server communication. This, our greatest hurdle, was dealt with by the

adopting a browser client-based approach. Such an approach brought its own set of concerns, and we had to circumvent cross site scripting (XSS) security vulnerabilities (CGISecurity.com 2002) through the implementation of an Adobe Flash cross domain policy file (Adobe Systems Incorporated 2007b).

Unfortunately, our solution is not as portable as we would like, as it requires knowledge of both Flash/Flex and Java in order to modify the interface for a customized implementation and to access the Web service. The high degree of required programming skills could reduce the usefulness of the tool if we wanted to utilize it in an environment outside of Blackboard, for example embedded within departmental Web pages. Another client, with less of a technological overhead, was required if we wanted to utilize our application in other environments. This will be addressed below.

Usability

From the user's perspective, the approach is streamlined. The interaction required from the students using the Flex-based approach is relatively minimal.

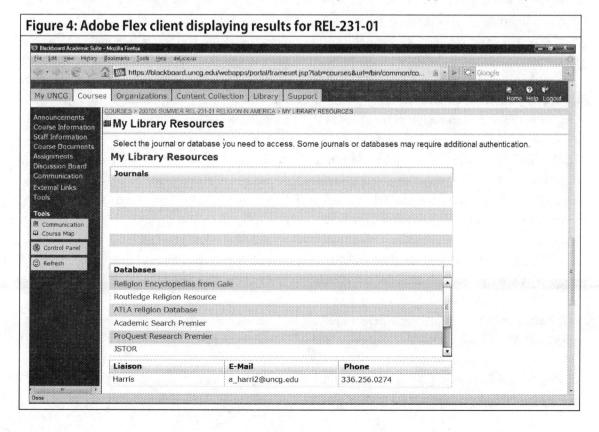

Figure 4: Adobe Flex client displaying results for REL-231-01

They select a link from a list of targeted resources, and are connected to their information without the requirements of additional authentication. Should they encounter difficulties or questions, the contact information for their subject liaison is provided on the same page as the data sources.

Because of the need for a default implementation that would place no burden on our teaching faculty, the Flex client is buried fairly deeply (three levels to be exact) within a course. Without directions - be it from teaching faculty or as a result of library instruction efforts - or a goodly amount of simply playing around with Blackboard course navigation, many students are not aware of the project's existence. In addition, there is a lack of customization options with this approach. The presentation layer is standard across all courses, and does not reflect the individualized approach that course builders in Blackboard may take in designing a distinct presentation for their class. As a next step, we need a way of implementing a Web service client on the browser that addresses these concerns as well as other issues including the limited portability and high degree of required technical expertise in developing with Flash/Flex and Java. Enter JSON and AJAX.

Bringing JSON into the Mix

JavaScript Object Notation (JSON) is, like SOAP, a data interchange format. While SOAP is an XML-based format, JSON is a subset of JavaScript. Essentially, it is a JavaScript object containing an array of data and, as a result, is lightweight, nimble, easy to read, and portable (http://www.json.org/).

ERIT has completed work on the beta version of an AJAX Web services client for our Blackboard tool using JSON as the data exchange format instead of SOAP. While not a programming language, AJAX (Asynchronous JavaScript and XML) is a programming technique that allows for small sections of a Web page to be reloaded either at a specified time by the application or through interaction with the user. This allows for greater interaction between the user and the Web site or application, as well as enhanced usability, speed, and functionality (Garrett 2005). Generally, AJAX Internet applications are created through the use of:

• XHTML and Cascading Style Sheets (CSS) for markup and styling

• JavaScript and the Document Object Model, especially the XMLHttpRequest Object, for client-side programming (http://www.w3.org/TR/XMLHttpRequest/)

• A data exchange format, generally either XML or JSON

AJAX is in many ways the backbone of Web 2.0 (thus Library 2.0), as it is the programming method many Web 2.0 applications rely upon. Examples include Flickr (http://www.flickr.com/), Gmail (http://www.gmail.com/), and Microsoft Virtual Earth (http://maps.live.com/).

AJAX offers a number of benefits. One is that clients become AJAX applications instead of Flash/Flex objects. This removes the requirements for the Flash plugin. As another benefit, an AJAX approach lowers the technology barrier by placing the pre-existing JavaScript functions and objects used to call the Web service and convert the resulting array from JSON to XHTML into remote files. The piece of simple JavaScript shown below is all that need be included on the client Web page.

```
<script type="text/javascript">
function buildResource() {
  var url = "http://library.uncg.
edu/cgpub/json.aspx";
  url += "?dept=lis";
  url += "&crs=688e";
  url += "&sec=01";
  url += "&output=json";
  url += "&callback=jsonResults";
  getJson(url);
  }
addLoadEvent(buildResource);
</script>
```

Web or Blackboard course developers need only edit the three lines shown in bold, substituting the information specific to their courses. The bulk of the programming work is accomplished through calls to remotely linked-in JavaScript files that the developer need never access. Changes to the Web services request parameters are written in plain text rather than embedded inside a Flex object. In addition, AJAX utilizes standards-based languages such as valid Document Object Model (http://www.w3.org/DOM/), CSS, and XHTML, which are similarly understood across multiple clients without the need for a plugin. As a result, the AJAX client module can be embedded anywhere within an online course that the developer or instructor chooses. Another benefit of utilizing Web standards instead of Flex is that the structure is based on meaningful HTML elements, e.g., headers, a data table, and a definition item list, making the presentation manipulable through the use of an additional, locally maintained and created CSS file. Developers can change the presentation of the displayed data to fit the needs of their course using the same tools as those used in the construction of the course itself.

It is important to note that while the above AJAX approach requires the developer to manually add a piece of code to delineate the different courses, the standard Flex implementation does not have any extra code for the developer to add. All course designation changes occur from within the Blackboard application.

How the AJAX Client Works

Blackboard course developers input the three standard course parameters into the JavaScript as shown in the example above. When students visit the site and the page begins loading, the JavaScript initiates an Http request to a proxy service residing within the University Libraries Web environment. The proxy issues a call to the Web service based upon the provided course parameters. The SOAP response is then converted into a JSON object array which is returned to the requesting Web page for processing. JavaScript

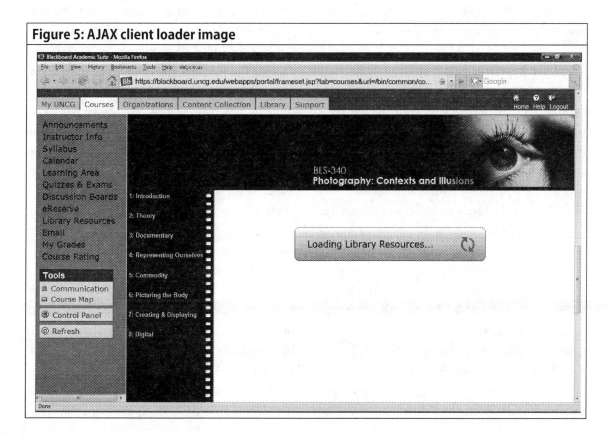

Figure 5: AJAX client loader image

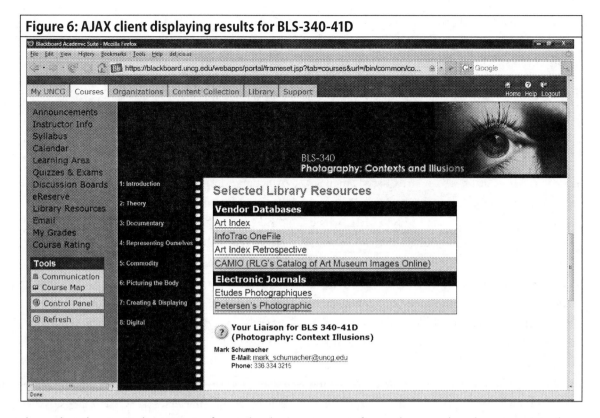

Figure 6: AJAX client displaying results for BLS-340-41D

then takes the received array, transforms the data into XHTML, and embeds it dynamically into the page. Applying a default or localized style sheet then completes the transformation for the users.

The User Experience

The user experience with the AJAX client will vary depending on the design of the online course component. Generally, users log into Blackboard and select a course from the list of those in which they are enrolled. Assuming that they have chosen a course with a uniquely designed online component, access to the Library Resources service can be achieved in any number of ways. Usually, the service is available on the home page of the course or through a link within the course navigation to a page containing the client. Such a page might also link to other library materials within Blackboard, for example electronic reserves. Nothing prevents librarians from including other materials from appearing on the same page as the Library Resources service client.

When users select the link, a page opens and a default "Loader" image will briefly appear. This image informs the user that there is activity happening, while behind the scenes JavaScript begins communication with the University Libraries Web service and formatting data for the screen.

Once the AJAX client has received the response data set and formatted it, a JavaScript function removes the loader along with any other placeholder content, and then writes the Library Resources information to the screen, laid out in table format. In several test cases, the loading occurs fast enough so that the loader image is never seen by users. This result will vary based upon a number of variables including the size of the page, amount of data being transferred, bandwidth availability, and the speed of the user's Internet connection.

Once users have selected a journal or database, the process is very much like that of the Flex client, in that they are verified as affiliated users within Blackboard, and redirected as necessary. Like the Flex Building Block, the necessity for multiple sign-ins is eliminated.

Should JavaScript be disabled or the connections to the Web service fail, the application writes a set of default links to resources hosted on the University Libraries' Web server. As a result, users are always provided with resources, though the dynamic results are tailored to their immediate needs.

Flex vs. AJAX

In comparing the different Web services client implementations, the JavaScript-based AJAX/JSON client is a much more flexible, faster solution than the Adobe Flex version. The AJAX client allows for a greater degree of customization, has a slightly smaller footprint and faster load speed, and can be implemented easily both within and outside of Blackboard (or any other Course Management System) at any point within a course hierarchy. The client can be broken into remote components hosted by the University Libraries for ease of managing functionality or adding new functions. In addition, it requires only a minimal amount of code work, limited to the editing of three variables. Developing a Flex client that would operate outside of Blackboard would require in-depth knowledge of Adobe Flex/Flash.

On the other hand, the Adobe Flex client has the benefit of being always available within Blackboard as a Building Block, whether or not there is a customized course component available. This would theoretically give a larger presence for the University Libraries, even if not in an optimal location. The Flex object has the added benefit of being the preferred format for UNCG's Distance Education unit. Coordination with this unit is a key component of extending our reach beyond the library walls to the widest possible student audience. The Flex client also precludes the requirement for the developer to maintain any code, even the three lines required for the AJAX solution.

Where We Are Today

In late 2006, ERIT began building the database that would drive the Web service push into Blackboard. The initiative launched in beta in January of 2007 with the push of the Adobe Flex client to our production Blackboard server. During the Spring 2007 semester, we pushed content into thirty courses within the UNCG Blackboard framework.

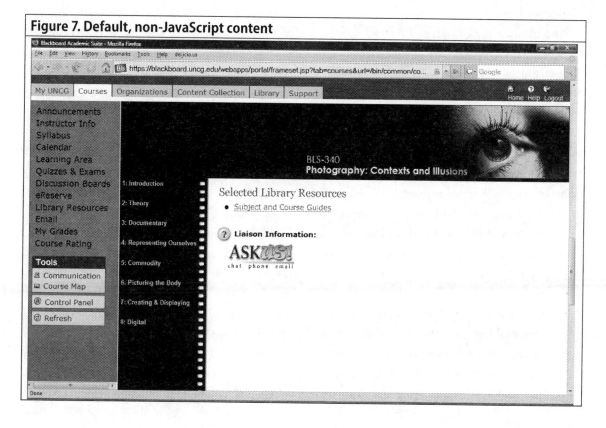

Figure 7. Default, non-JavaScript content

Based on anecdotal feedback derived from library instruction courses, the initial response has been positive. During the summer, we conducted targeted training on the use of the Content Administration Tool to our subject liaison librarians who did not participate in its beta development. We also began teaching first year students to locate and use the Library Resources service. Our first courses utilizing the AJAX/JSON client went live in beta over the first summer course session. ERIT expects a full release of the application to our subject liaisons and interested instructors in time for the Fall 2007 semester.

Future Plans

We expect to implement the default Adobe Flex/Java implementation of the tool campus-wide before the end of the Fall 2007 semester. As the Flex client goes fully live, the beta testing of the AJAX/JSON Web services client will continue until January, 2008, when it will move out of beta and be marketed to various course builders across the University as the preferred method with which to consume University Libraries Web services.

As a result of the University Libraries' successful work with UNCG's Blackboard Application Administrator in creating the Library Resources project, Web services and AJAX are being considered as the primary means through which Blackboard will accept interaction with outside units within the UNCG community. In addition, there are early discussions regarding turning over the "Library" page in Blackboard, a static tab that links to our home page, to ERIT for development and administration within the Blackboard framework. This would allow for the potential development of expanded integration of targeted resources across the platform.

From here, a number of options are being considered for building upon the initiative and using the same administration tool to drive other services. For example, additional resources could be pushed into Blackboard using the same ap-

plication. These might include on-screen contextual Instant Messaging, course-level federated searching, e-Reserve listings, and links to more extensive resources from within the library. JavaScript-based clients similar to the implementation in Blackboard could bring the Web service to departmental Web sites or be utilized to expand the reach to distance education students through other means.

The tools built for the Blackboard initiative also could be brought to bear within the library Web space, providing deeper integration with new AJAX and ASP.NET-driven course and subject guide dashboards. These might potentially feature built-in, on-page IM widgets, course and subject-related news via RSS feeds, and customizations based upon the selection of a specific course or subject.

Conclusion

Through the need to solve a basic technical concern, UNCG University Libraries has been able to leverage technologies such as SOAP and applications available on campus in a new way for academic libraries. By providing library data only, and employing user-adaptable clients, we have been able to tackle concerns about the presentation of library resources by moving them beyond the library space into the user space where they can be customized to meet the needs of their given context. Through use of the Library Resources project, the University Libraries has begun integrating deeply into the user space, presenting the right resources at the point of need.

By bringing this project to its current stage, ERIT has been able to leverage various 2.0 technologies and concepts in an academic library environment. Web services, though an older technology, have only recently gained wider acceptance outside of large enterprises, especially when used in conjunction with a flexible Rich Application Interface (RAI) such as those achieved through the use of newer programming techniques such as AJAX and Adobe Flex. Through the portability of Web services, we can drive multiple interfaces across multiple platforms and servers from one resource - all updated simultaneously from a centralized, locally maintained database. The extensibility of this programming technique is limited only to the imagination of the implementation team, the bandwidth available, the immediate needs of the user, and a little common sense.

Additionally, through this tool the UNCG University Libraries has been able to address user needs as described in the OCLC 2003 Environmental Scan. Most users do not want to be confronted with the full range of resources; they only want the ones targeted to their current needs. This is achieved by the Library Resources project by pushing the resources deeply into the user's academic space at the course level. The tool allows users ready access to course-related library information while also providing a means to contact a librarian should the need arise.

Finally, we tried to make the client tools easy to use, with a minimum of links required for accessing the Library Resources Building Block. We were able to achieve this ease of use both within the Blackboard hierarchy and within the process needed to get to the resources.

The Library Resources project addresses the primary, user-centric mission of the library. It also looks toward the future as we seek new ways to propagate our services beyond the library walls.

References

Adobe Systems Incorporated. 2007a. Adobe Flash Player version penetration. http://www.adobe.com/products/player_census/flashplayer/version_penetration.html.

_____. 2007b. TechNote: External data not accessible outside a Macromedia Flash movie's domain. http://www.adobe.com/cfusion/knowledgebase/index.cfm?id=tn_14213.

CGISecurity.com. 2002. The cross site scripting (XSS) FAQ. http://www.cgisecurity.com/articles/xss-faq.shtml.

Garrett, Jesse James. 2005. Ajax: A new approach to Web applications. http://www.adaptivepath.com/publications/essays/archives/000385.php.

United Parcel Service. Integrate tracking tools. http://www.ups.com/content/us/en/tracking/tools/.

United States Postal Service. 2005. Delivery information APIs. http://www.usps.com/webtools/delivery.htm.

World Wide Web Consortium. 2007. Web services activity statement. http://www.w3.org/2002/ws/Activity.

http://acrl.ala.org/L2Initiatives/index.php?title=Chapter_4/

Adapting an Open-Source, Scholarly Web 2.0 System for Findability in Library Collections (or: "Frankly, Vendors, We Don't Give a Damn.")

Bethany Nowviskie, Elizabeth Sadler, and Erik Hatcher

Abstract

In response to economic and institutional problems facing traditional humanities scholarship, NINES, an independent digital publishing initiative housed in our main research library at the University of Virginia (UVA), has developed the Collex system. Collex is an open-source tool that enables Web 2.0-inspired interaction with federated online collections. Through an informal collaboration with NINES, the UVA Library is adapting this scholar-driven social software system into Project Blacklight, a faceted OPAC with relevancy ranking. Blacklight is designed to address issues of findability in complex library catalogs. This chapter describes Collex and Blacklight and discusses these aligned projects in terms of the value of a technical partnership between libraries and the scholarly communities they serve, communities which are beginning to take an active interest (albeit from a different perspective) in interface design and access to digital collections.

Prelude

"Fiddle-dee-dee," she sighed, slumping over the keyboard and arching an elegant brow at her search results. "With an OPAC like this, what's a girl to do?"

"Why, Miss Scarlett!" the Tarleton twins exclaimed in unison, nearly spilling their mint juleps. "Everybody knows that library catalogs are problematic. The data's notoriously inconsistent, user requirements are complex and ever-changing, and institutional inertia is a force to be reckoned with. Besides," they said, eyeing her query, "You've got 153 results! What you're looking for is bound to be in there, somewhere."

Scarlett read the first search hit aloud: "Kissin', Twistin', Goin' Where the Boys Are. Volumes 1-5. A sound recording by Connie Francis."

"There you are!" smiled Brent.

"What could be more fitting?" Stuart asked, and skimmed through the first page of results: "*Hands-on Art Activities for the Elementary Classroom*, a book on the Battle of the Somme, *Modern Japanese Theatre*, something on planetary nebulae… oh, look! *The Wind Done Gone*. That sounds interesting."

Scarlett smoothed her hands petulantly over her green sprigged muslin. "But I'm searching for *Gone with the Wind*!"

Dr. Bethany Nowviskie, e-mail: bethany@virginia.edu; and Elizabeth Sadler, e-mail: bess@virginia.edu, both at the University of Virginia; Erik Hatcher, e-mail: erikhatcher@mac.com

Figure 1. Searching for "Gone With the Wind" in Virgo, the University of Virginia Library's Sirsi-based online catalog

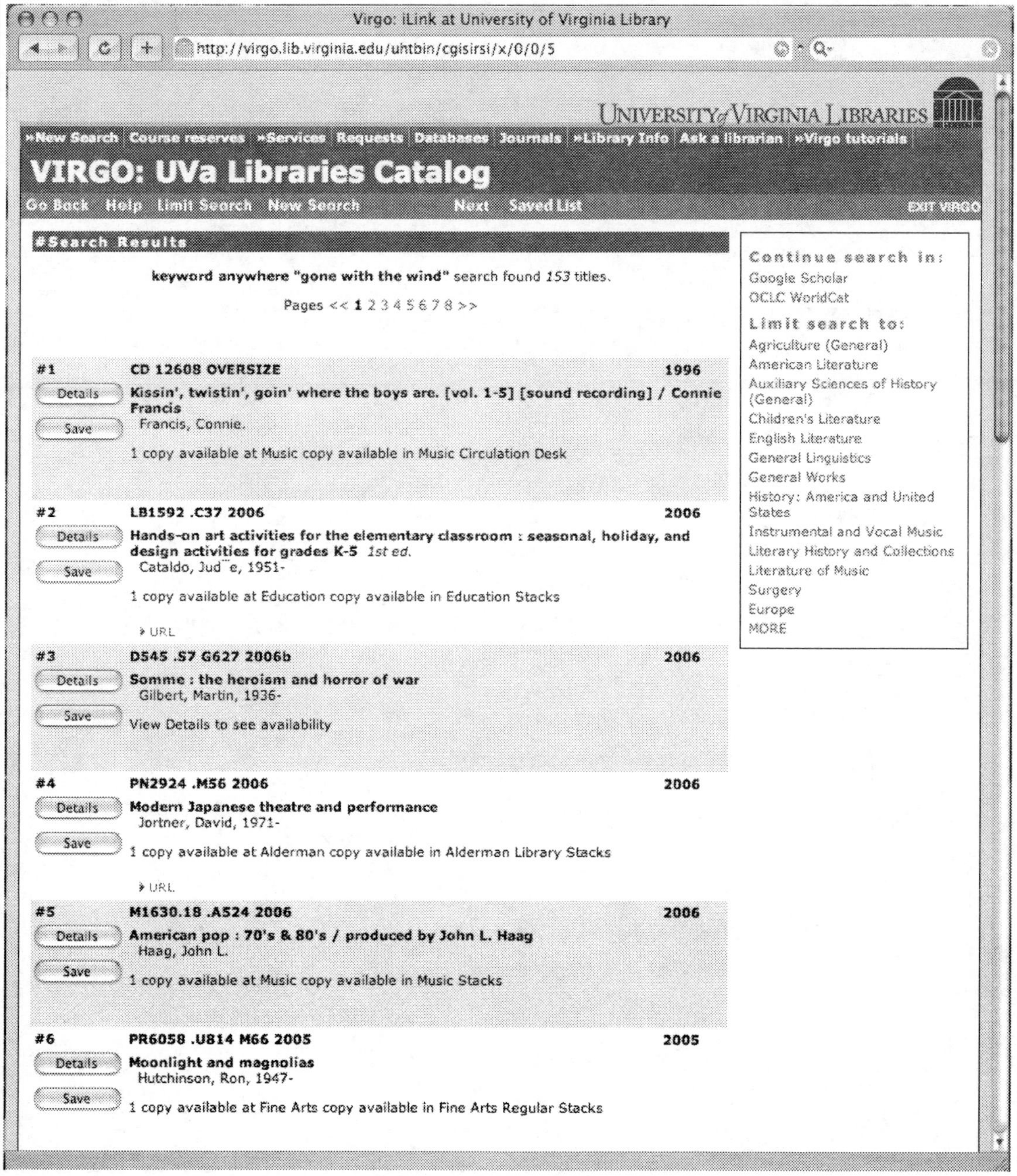

At that, a tall, dark stranger leaned forward from the shadows of Tara's whitewashed columns. A little smile played about his mustachioed lips, and his eyes, which had seen so many cataloging systems come and go, met Scarlett's knowingly. "Try Project Blacklight," he said.

Introduction

An Origin in Digital Humanities

Project Blacklight is both an open-source software system and a local, social experiment in developing next-generation online public access catalogs (OPACs). This chapter will describe both aspects of the project: the software and its evolution from a

---

Figure 2. Searching for "Gone with the Wind" in Project Blacklight. Relevance ranking ensures meaningful results, and facets enhance findability

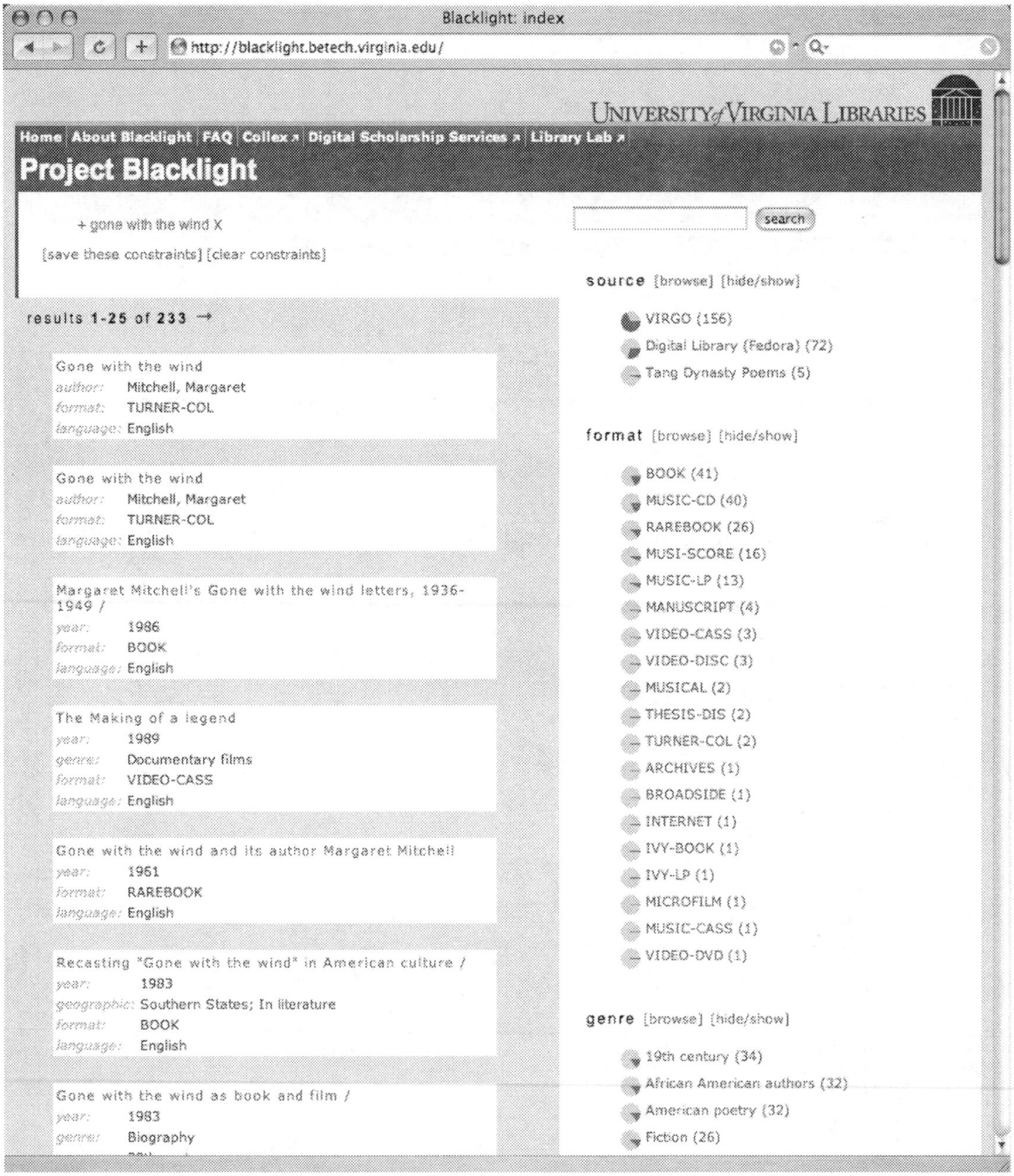

---

scholar-driven response to problems in research and publication, as well as the under-the-radar approach the Blacklight team took in conceptualizing, developing, and implementing it in the UVA Library. The tool itself, brought into being through unofficial, grass-roots collaboration among librarians and digital humanities faculty and staff at UVA, is a clean, customizable OPAC based on the faceted

browsing paradigm that has emerged over the last few years as a compelling component of Library 2.0. Blacklight joins a groundswell of effort to develop open, extensible, inexpensive alternatives to proprietary faceted browsing systems currently marketed to libraries. (Commercial vendors and proprietary systems include Endeca, AquaBrowser, and Primo. Other open source projects and solutions include

Flamenco, eXtensible Catalog, LibraryFind, eIFL's "Library in a Box" and FacBackOPAC.)

Our prototype implementation of the system is called "Blacklight" (another name for long wave ultraviolet light) because it enhances the findability of 3.8 million UVA MARC records through a robust search-and-browsing system based on Solr Flare and Ruby-on-Rails. Less punningly, we like the Blacklight name because of the shift in perspective that comes about when work such as ours sheds a different light on familiar data and problem sets. To some extent, this informal undertaking operates on a new wavelength for libraries, dem-onstrating that digital tools and analytic methods originating in scholarly projects (that is, from the community the Library has typically served) can feed back into our most fundamental cataloging and retrieval systems in illuminating ways. In other words, the success of Blacklight shows that the 2.0 versions of digital humanities and library science can (and should!) operate hand-in-hand in sharing novel approaches to issues of access and interpretation.

Blacklight is a distillation of the core faceted browsing component of Collex, a larger knowl-edge-discovery, folksonomical, and online pub-

Figure 3. The NINES instance of Collex, currently aggregating full text, thumbnail images, and metadata (including tags contributed by users) for nearly 180,000 digital objects from two dozen contributing Web sites and institutions

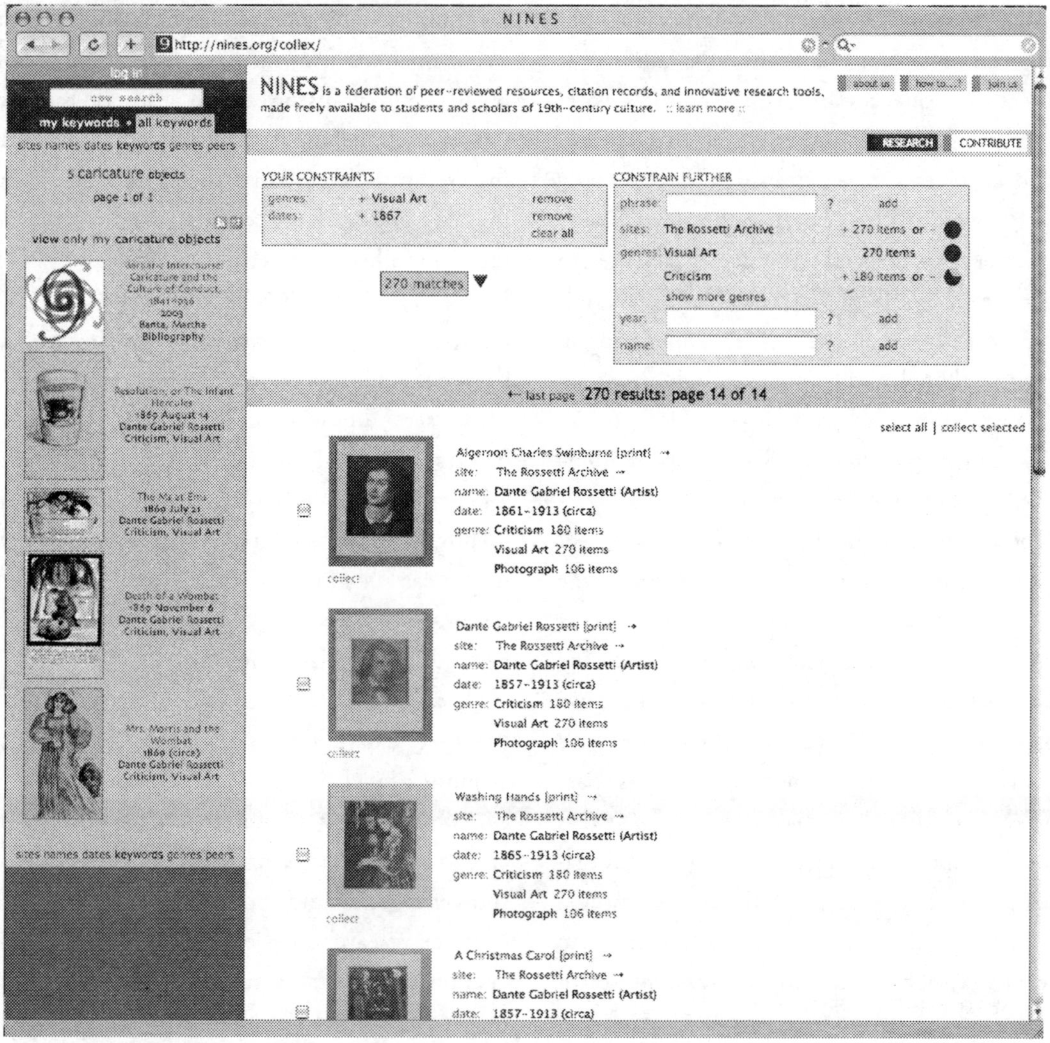

lication system developed for scholarly research communities like NINES (the *"networked infrastructure for nineteenth-century electronic scholarship"*) by designer Bethany Nowviskie and programmers Erik Hatcher and Jamie Orchard-Hays. Collex was conceived by Nowviskie in relation to what scholars term the great "publishing crisis" of the humanities (see http://www.nines. org/). This debilitating situation is known to librarians–from a vantage point slightly higher on the academic food chain–as the "serials crisis:" a cascading sequence of cut-backs and constraints that stem from an astronomical rise in the cost of journal and scientific database subscriptions. Resulting financial pressures hamper the ability of libraries to sustain humanities collections, and as libraries purchase fewer scholarly monographs, scholarly presses retreat to more marketable publishing ventures. This chain of events culminates in severe consequences for faculty and their work, and graduate students and unestablished, tenure-seeking scholars at research institutions typically bear the brunt. This is because the slow-moving "publish or perish" social structures established to evaluate and reward original research in the academy almost *depend* on that research appearing in conventional book and printed journal format, an increasingly untenable proposition.

Why is this issue relevant to work being done by librarians on next generation catalog interfaces? The crisis in publishing and tenure is one of a number of interrelated affairs transforming the face of humanities scholarship: the open-access and free-culture movements, coupled with the rapid digitization of our inherited cultural archive and a sea-change in the way younger scholars and students expect to *interact with* (and not just passively receive) digital media, seem to prime this particular moment for lasting change. Self-organizing academic co-ops like NINES have formed in response to all of these factors, in an attempt to undermine the obviously outmoded assumption of the scholarly profession that serious research and

vetted publication can only be carried out in print. As scholars turn their attention to online environments, they become increasingly conscious of and interested in matters of access, interface, findability, and remix culture.

NINES and its Collex tool (funded by the Mellon Foundation and under development since 2003) were designed to provide an electronic environment where peer-reviewed scholarship could be federated, searched, browsed, collected, and commented upon, and then "remixed" by end users into new, born-digital forms: annotated bibliographies, course syllabi and reading packets, illustrated essays and online journals, maps, and timelines. It is the hope of NINES's steering committee, its editorial boards, and its UVA-based technical team that a vital, free-culture research community will emerge around this semantic-Web, open-archives-inspired federation of nineteenth century historical and aesthetic resources. Collex itself includes a wealth of dynamic features inspired by Web 2.0 and social software, including: tagging and tag clouds; syndicated Atom feeds on folksonomy terms; a Google-suggest-like search field that updates with valid options as the user types; saved, shareable searches keyed to personal logins; dynamic information visualizations; serendipitous "more-like-this" suggestions based on textual similarities, shared metadata, and patterns of scholarly use; and a drag-and-drop "exhibit" builder for Creative Commons-licensed user-created content–all made freely available for research and pedagogy within a customizable, browser-based AJAX interface.

These social software and remix culture features–so exciting to scholars–in truth cluster around a much more crucial component: at the core of Collex is a powerful search engine and faceted browser that brings disparately-encoded resources together and allows for the construction of complex research queries in an intuitive, iterative fashion. It is, at its heart, a faceted cataloging system, designed both *by* and *for* the same academic user group that is a research library's most avid and exacting constituency. The UVA Library's project Blacklight has been distilled from this core Collex feature.

The Initiative

The Dream of a Usable OPAC

The promise of Collex as an improvement to existing OPAC systems was immediately obvious to librarians at UVA, particularly to Bess Sadler, a key proponent of our Collex/OPAC mashup. In fact, Collex was in many ways a digital instantiation of the information-seeking strategies that information behavior theorists have described for some time, and that librarians have long hoped to support in a next-generation OPAC.

Since the 1990s, a growing body of research and evidence has documented the importance of serendipity to the information-seeking behavior of scholars (Foster and Ford 2003; Williamson 1989). This research into serendipitous information gathering in libraries indicates that browsing library stacks has played a crucially important role in scholars' research lives. The advent of journal databases, electronic texts, and geographically dispersed library collections has therefore been a mixed blessing for scholars; although known items are easier to find, without the creation of tools for serendipitous browsing of digital collections, many scholars feel robbed of their most fruitful and enjoyable information gathering strategies (Sadler and Given 2007).

Equally important, especially as digitization of archival materials increases and more scholarly material is born digital, is scholars' need for tools they can use to interact with this content—without the need for intermediaries such as reference librarians. Humanists tend to be solitary researchers, and they tend "to view the search for information as being as important as the information itself" (Delgadillo and Lynch 1999, 248). Given these preferences, the tools we provide for interacting with library collections can be of supreme

importance in determining whether or not a given collection will be used.

The quest for a serendipitous browsing interface for large data collections is ongoing and interdisciplinary. Current thinking about this kind of interface design benefits from theoretical and experimental work in the areas of ecological psychology (Norman 1988; Vicente and Rasmussen 1992), humanities computing (Ruecker 2003), human-computer interaction (Morville 2005), and of course library and information studies (Birchall and Rada 1995; Delgadillo and Lynch 1999; Foster 2002; Foster and Ford 2003). We have also been influenced by other attempts to create a working OPAC that re-captures the serendipity of browsing, such as Belmont-Abbey College's 2002 Antarcti.ca-based catalog, and of course North Carolina State University's highly successful collaboration with Endeca (Beagle 2002; Waller 2002; Antelman, Lynema and Pace 2006).

Just as we began thinking of the scholar-driven Collex project as a fruitful starting point for practical implementation of an improved UVA OPAC, the concept itself had reached a boiling point in blogs, conference papers, and library task force conversations. For instance, Karen Schneider's influential 2006 series of articles, "How OPACs Suck," lists eighteen "key features common to most search engines (even the least expensive) [that are] often missing in online catalogs." These include: relevance ranking; word stemming; field and object weighting; spell checking; support for the refinement of original queries; use of popular query operators (e.g. Boolean operators, wildcards, case sensitivity, and proximity searching); flexible configuration for default search settings; the ability to construct complex queries within a single search blank; sort flexibility; support for international character sets; faceting; easily-customized search result pages; better logging; and an interface that does not require administrators to have highly specialized technical skills in order to make meaningful changes (Schneider).

The University of Virginia's Online Library Environment committee (OLE) had recently drafted a similar list of requirements for its dream OPAC. Most of these features, especially relevance ranking and faceted browsing, were beautifully implemented in Collex. Additionally, Collex was already capable of handling many different kinds of objects, such as TEI marked-up texts and media files such as digitized images. And indeed, the incorporation of non-catalog data and digital library material into an integrated system was a crucial requirement of any future UVA Library catalog. Since UVA's bibliographic catalog and digital repository were both difficult to search, it was tempting to envision Collex as an integrated solution for these problems.

Mostly through word-of-mouth in the code4lib library developers' community (http://www.code4lib.org/) and through a few high-profile blog posts and conference presentations, excitement about Collex and its possible adaptation into a next-generation OPAC spread quickly in the latter part of 2006. Hatcher presented Collex at national and international library conferences, including that of the Digital Library Foundation in Boston, a Lucene summit at the University of Windsor, and an Electronic Information for Libraries "Library in a Box" meeting in Cupramontana, Italy. The concept of Collex as an affordable, open-source, next generation library catalogue resonated with many librarians who wanted the benefits of relevance ranking and faceted browsing, but also knew they could not afford commercial solutions on offer.

Unfortunately, adapting Collex to handle MARC records and other library data was not as easy as librarians had hoped. In its initial implementation, Collex was not written with MARC and other library standards in mind, and it expected data in a format closely tied to the NINES workflow and the specialist interests of nineteenth century scholars, not those of general catalog users. In order to become an OPAC it would need to be significantly re-engineered. At the same time,

UVA Library's administration, though intrigued by the possibility of a Collex-based OPAC, was reluctant to commit funding to an untested project. The core team of Collex enthusiasts (which had expanded to include several members of the UVA Library staff, led by Sadler) was offered a chance instead: if we could prove that Collex, or a Collex derivative, could index and search our 3.8 million MARC records, then the library would consider pursuing the project in a more formal and resource-intensive way. Library staff who wished to be involved would be allowed to work on the project, as long as doing so did not interfere with their regular duties. A similar compromise was reached with the administration of the NINES project: Hatcher and Nowviskie would be granted time to develop the OPAC idea insofar as the work they produced would also benefit NINES, which was, at this time, exploring the idea of indexing citation records from special collections libraries into Collex for scholarly annotation and re-use. Armed with no funding and no explicit commitment of staff time, we happily set off to write an OPAC (see http://blacklight.betech.virginia.edu/).

The Birth of Blacklight

Metaphorically speaking, Collex is Blacklight's ancestor, but (unlike Collex) Blacklight itself consists of very few lines of custom code. We have intentionally aimed for simplicity, elegance, and maintainability in our development of the system. As described, Collex includes features well beyond Blacklight's initial scope. These include: collecting by tagging and annotating, Atom feeds for all aspects of collections, robust saved searches, hierarchical facets, serendipitous "more like this," and AJAX as-you-type suggestions. In this section we will first look at commonalities between the Blacklight and Collex projects, and then we will focus on their differences.

Collex and Blacklight share two foundational technologies: Solr and Ruby on Rails. We will begin here with a discussion of Rails, which we have chosen as a framework because we believe that software development should be user interface driven. Rails is the current darling of the Web development world because of its emphasis on convention over configuration, which minimizes the code that must be written in developing Web 2.0 applications. Ruby itself is a dynamic language with a malleable syntax, facilitating the construction of domain specific languages (DSLs) which allow content experts (not necessarily Ruby experts) to leverage a powerful dynamic environment.

Rails consists primarily of two DSLs: ActiveRecord for mapping data to and from relational databases and a Web framework for easily mapping Web interactions to server-side behavior. As an example of the elegance of Rails, the complete faceted browser and full-text search capability of Blacklight's Web tier can be expressed as follows:

```
class BrowseController <Applica-
tionController
  flare
  end
```

The central line above invokes a Solr Flare plugin (to be discussed later), which incorporates the adding and removal of facet and full-text search constraints, AJAX suggest terms, and other features. The simplicity of Rails has made it possible for NINES scholars to get knee-deep into Collex and Blacklight code, actively editing and committing changes. Rails makes Web development for scholarly and library projects much less daunting than in the past.

The Rails components of Blacklight and Collex interface with Solr, which is a widely-used, open-source, enterprise-scale search engine built on top of the highly scalable Lucene engine. Solr itself interfaces over HTTP, enabling interoperability with practically any environment. To Lucene's blindingly fast relevance-ranked full-text search, Solr adds caching, highlighting, and faceting. Not only have Collex and Blacklight benefited from Solr, but Solr itself has benefited from our development work on these projects. We have made several direct enhancements to the open-source Solr project during the development of Collex and Blacklight.

While it is straightforward to communicate with Solr from any environment, particularly

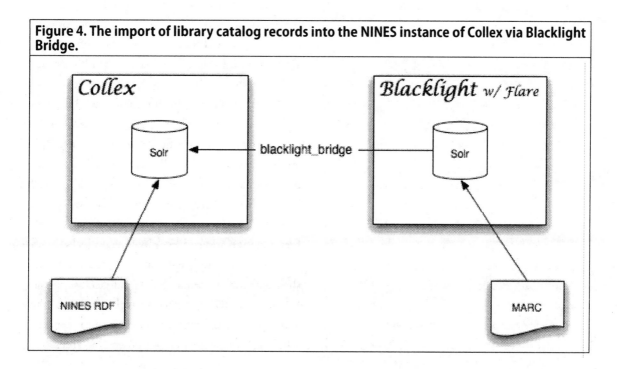

Figure 4. The import of library catalog records into the NINES instance of Collex via Blacklight Bridge.

Ruby, it is handy to abstract the details of that communication into a more legible and reusable form. As we distilled Blacklight from Collex, we developed "solr-ruby," a Ruby library, to bridge the two technologies cleanly. Adding a document to Solr, for example, is as easy as this:

```
solr = Solr::Connection.
new("http://localhost:8983/solr")
    solr.add(:callnumber =>
PS3525.I972G6, :title => "Gone
With the Wind", :author => "Mar-
garet Mitchell")
```

We released solr-ruby under an open source license and it is now available alongside Solr proper at the Apache Software Foundation. Prior to the development of solr-ruby, Collex used custom code to interact with Solr, but that system has since been refactored to use our library, thereby eliminating many lines of code.

The solr-ruby library makes it easy to map data from their original sources into Solr via the Mapper facility. A condensed example of our method for bringing MARC data into Blacklight looks like this:

```
mapping = {
 :id => :'001',
 :subject_genre_facet =>
[:'600v', :'610v', :'611v', :'650v',
:'651v', :'655a'],
 :subject_era_facet => [:'650d',
:'650y', :'651y', :'655y'],
 :subject_topic_facet =>
[:'650a', :'650b', :'650x'],
 :subject_geographic_facet =>
[:'650c', :'650z', :'651a', :'651x',
:'651z', :'655z'],
 :title_text => :'245a',
 :author_text => :'100a',
 :call_number_text => :'050a',
 :source_facet => "catalog"
 }
```

Several library catalogers of our acquaintance have immediately grasped these mappings and quickly suggested additions. A very similar structure (the "Blacklight Bridge") maps select library data from Blacklight into the NINES version of Collex, and has been maintained by the NINES editorial board.

Another layer open to reusability distillation is the user interface, particularly in the areas of faceting and searching. Again, during the development of Blacklight, we took the opportunity to generalize. We therefore developed Solr Flare, a Rails plugin providing basic state management for user-specified query constraints, actions for interacting with facets, AJAX suggest, and full-text search. The Flare plugin is used by both Blacklight and BlacklightDL, a special implementation of the tool for UVA's Fedora-based digital library. Flare is a bit too simplistic for the needs of Collex at this point, though our hope is to generalize some Solr interactions needed by Collex into Flare. Generalization is a particularly urgent task because Collex is drawing increasing attention in the scholarly community beyond NINES. A group of historians led by Gaelic scholar Michael Newton was recently awarded an NEH Digital Humanities Start-Up Grant to build the first instance of Collex outside the NINES content area. This project, entitled "Finding the Celtic: a Digital Humanities Collaboratory," will contribute refactored code and temporal and geographical visualization methods back into Collex (see http://celtic.ibiblio.org/).

How does Collex differ from Blacklight? Collex benefits from a small but dedicated team of professional staff and has been able to go well beyond Blacklight's simple faceted browsing and full-text search thanks to a couple of years of effort in design and coding. However, in its NINES instantiation, it does ask that contributors convert their data into a normalized Resource Description Framework (RDF) structure to better aggregate and represent the interests of nineteenth-century scholars. This scholarly pre-processing frees our development group from dealing with variations of data formats and allows us to focus to a greater degree on the application itself. In contrast, Blacklight ingests data directly from binary MARC files, TEI files, and HTML scraping of online electronic resources, all using mappings similar to those shown above. Its generalized mapping framework should make it easy to expand of this list of data formats.

A key feature of Collex *not* included in Blacklight is user-contributed metadata or folksonomy "keywording." The Solr search server is at the heart of this tagging. As a user tags and annotates an object, metadata is written, via ActiveRecord, to a relational database table of "interpretations." At the same time, the data is indexed into Solr. (In this context, it is important to note a general search engine best practice: that original data should be maintained outside the search engine. It is essential that developers be able to re-index data fully when changing their indexing configurations.)

Syndicated content via RSS feeds could be considered the first Web 2.0 enabling technology. We chose to support a newer and more robust protocol, Atom, and eschew often-confusing, legacy RSS "standards." Users can subscribe to feeds of collected objects with specified keywords, NINES-valid genres, contributing archives, or agents. It is also possible to subscribe to one of these threads within the collections of a particular Collex user. For example, you might wish to follow the activity of a collaborating colleague as she assigns a particular keyword of interest to NINES objects. Users can subscribe to feeds by keyword, NINES-valid genre, contributing archive, or agent, either globally or specifically for any Collex user. By tuning into select collection activities at one or more of those levels, they can also stumble upon other objects of interest. Our plan is to evolve the syndication of content such that remotely hosted archives can use the tags, exhibits, and connections in Collex in any way desired, in other words, to develop a kind of in-

formal Collex API. If a similar feature were available for Blacklight, UVA Library patrons would be able to access catalog data in many different online spaces and venues.

We have recently added hierarchical faceting to Collex as a user interface improvement. This is currently used for the NINES "archive" facet, to organize contributing resources into categories (such as library catalog records or entries for scholarly presses) and sub-categories (such as individual journal titles within a larger category of journal material). We implemented this hierarchy within a relational database, separate from the Solr index, so that categorizations can be changed at run-time without the need for reindexing.

One interesting feature of Collex, its "more like this" entries, enhances research serendipity in the NINES data set. As described above, this feature offers users a selection of objects related to any currently displayed object. Analysis is enabled by a custom Solr request handler using an open-source Lucene add-on. A similar and more generalizable MoreLikeThis feature has been proposed by open source developer Bertrand Delacretaz. When incorporated into Solr, this enhancement could be used to replace our Collex-customized version, and a similar feature is desirable in Blacklight.

Collex also includes AJAX suggest, one of Karen Schneider's suggestions for an improved OPAC. As a user types terms in Collex search boxes, matching suggestions—complete with frequency calculations within the user's given set of constraints—are displayed in a selectable dropdown menu. These suggestions lessen the need for automated spell checking and word stemming, and show other similar word forms, making misspellings in the original corpus visible and navigable. This feature is not present in the current version of Blacklight.

While we recognize the great value of those social software and Web 2.0 features already present in Collex, the scope of our work on Blacklight was deliberately limited to the core relevance ranking and faceted browsing components that would so drastically improve findability in our library's catalog. The narrowness of our scope was in part because the project to develop Blacklight from Collex had to operate as a small, under-the-radar, "skunk works."

Wikipedia defines "skunk works" as a term "used in engineering and technical fields to describe a group within an organization given a high degree of autonomy and unhampered by bureaucracy, tasked with working on advanced or secret projects" (2007). An unofficial, cooperative working arrangement along these lines turned out to be an ideal incubator for Blacklight and, nourished by the enthusiasm of Library staff and of the code4lib community at large, our work began to coalesce. The flexibility of the underlying technology (Solr, Lucene, and Ruby on Rails) meant that the software could be written and refactored quickly, and the energy of the NINES community fueled Collex development, which contributed positively to our understanding of what was possible in future versions of Blacklight. The project soon outgrew its home on our laptops and was granted space in the Library's development environment.

This environment supported the construction (by Hatcher) of Solr Flare, the Rails-based interface to Solr described above; several iterations (with the assistance of Chris Hoebeke, UVA's Integrated Library System (ILS) and OPAC administrator) of a MARC-to-Solr indexer; and two versions (designed by Nowviskie) of a simple user interface for searching and browsing on facets. After a few short weeks of trial and error, UVA's 3.8 million MARC records were ingested and the system was tested in terms of functionality for different kinds of queries and usability on different browsers and platforms. In late March, 2007, we were able to show off our new toy before a UVA Library decision-making body. The response of Library administration (like the user response we had already gathered in informal demos) was uniformly enthusiastic. We were cheered and encour-

aged, but it was too soon to celebrate. It was time to start planning.

Responsible Decision Making

In the Web 2.0 world, with every focus on fast development, perpetual beta, and agile response to user needs, it is easy to forget that large institutions cannot change directions quickly. Libraries are required to request funding for projects well in advance, and they must integrate any new products and services into existing workflows and staff allocations. Most importantly, libraries need to think strategically about the future, and ensure that they are investing their always-limited human and financial resources in a manner that will produce the greatest long-term benefit to library patrons and their host institutions. Decisions cannot be made without weighing all options and taking available resources into consideration.

Some hard questions face us in this project. Do we have proper staffing in the Library to support development of a new OPAC in addition to everything we already do? How can we build deeper expertise in these new technologies across our workforce, so we do not find ourselves overly dependent on one or two people? What about systems administration of a whole new suite of software when our IT department is already over-burdened? If it breaks, who will fix it? Will our ILS vendor come out with a similar product soon? Are there existing open source projects we should join instead of fostering our own? Should we have a local OPAC at all, or does the future lie in a centralized solution like OCLC's Local WorldCat?

These are difficult questions, and we have not yet answered them all. Although the fast-paced Library 2.0 skunk works team that came together around Blacklight was eager to move ahead at its own speed, working with the Library to confront these questions is leading to a more sustainable and more successful solution. We have not only received the green light to implement Blacklight, but the planning that went into this decision has generated other exciting changes in our organization:

+ we have started two weekly programming groups, one for library programmers who want to learn Ruby and one for staff who have never done any computer programming but want to learn;

+ we have shifted the responsibilities of several staff members in order to allow our programmers to work more closely with systems administrators, greatly improving response time and productivity;

+ while ultimately deciding to move ahead with Blacklight—starting with a smaller implementation (Blacklight DL) for our Fedora-based Digital Library system—we have also identified several other open-source OPAC efforts with which we hope to collaborate;

+ although we do not currently have the funding to create a full-time position dedicated to the Blacklight project, we have been able to use one-time funding to pay for outsourced development, building a fruitful working relationship with a local open source software development firm;

+ despite a current lack of funding to purchase dedicated hardware for the Blacklight project, we have built relationships with beTech, UVA's emerging community of programmers and systems administrators, allowing us to take advantage of their centrally-funded development servers (see http://betech.virginia.edu/);

+ and although we continue to assert that Blacklight is the greatest OPAC since sliced bread, we have also come to believe that there is no single right answer to the complex question of library information behavior. To that end, UVA is also considering OCLC's Local WorldCat, among several other options.

Future Plans

As of this writing, the latest version of Blacklight searches both our MARC records and most of the contents of UVA's rapidly-expanding Digital Library and electronic text collections. We are creating workflows to update Blacklight's circulation data incrementally through regular exports from our central ILS. We are also working with our Music Library to take advantage of rich but as-yet untapped metadata in the creation of a special Blacklight portal for music researchers. For example, we have enabled searching for sheet music according to the instruments required to perform any given piece, finally solving our music librarians' most frequently asked and frustratingly unanswerable reference question. In time, we hope to create similar customized interfaces for other specialized subsets of the UVA Library collection, such as material from our Fine Arts and Architecture library.

We are also solving the tricky problem of how to put a system like this into production without compromising our ability to modify the software easily, so that we can remain responsive to user requests. Finally, the Library's usability and graphic design teams are evaluating our rudimentary Blacklight interface before its next round of development, and have contributed CSS styling to let us match Blacklight to a recent Library Web site redesign.

Conclusion
A Two-Way Street
Both the information science community and the community of scholars served by NINES have realized benefits from the informal collaboration among UVA Library and Collex faculty and staff described in these pages. Our partnership began with a sense of shared interest in a narrow range of data-retrieval issues and continues in a broader common mission. Both Blacklight and Collex aim at open source solutions to problems—institutional as well as pragmatic—facing students and researchers who expect to access and contribute to increasingly rich, evolving collections of cultural and historical material through the participatory affordances of new media. Given the UVA Library's long-standing commitment to housing and supporting scholar-driven projects in digital humanities, it is not surprising that some practical and localized return on

investment would appear. To a great extent, Black-light exists because the Library generously offered office space to the Collex and NINES team, and because a culture of collaboration and mutual respect has evolved at our institution over the past fifteen years of digital humanities research development at UVA. Most of this has taken place in Library-based offices such as IATH (the Institute for Advanced Technology in the Humanities) and VCDH (the Virginia Center for Digital History).

The advantages of a Collex-inspired, Blacklight approach to problems of findability in library catalogs are clear. The strength and flexibility of Lucene indexing (and the simple addition of relevance ranking alone!) make it possible for our search results to meet the expectations of users weaned on Google's one-blank interface. But it is Blacklight's inherently faceted method of information browsing that most radically exposes the richness of our catalog, while simultaneously opening it up to user exploration in an intuitive way.

The benefits of Blacklight collaboration returned to Collex have been more difficult to quantify. In fact, for NINES, this venture has not been all beer and skittles, as our Collex development team is incredibly small (consisting of Nowviskie and Hatcher with the part-time assistance of freelance programmer Jamie Orchard-Hays), and the Blacklight effort has diverted time and energy from our primary duties to NINES. This has resulted in a shift in focus and loss of momentum that may be difficult to regain in light of the impending close of our grant funding in early 2008. Although we continue to use some NINES resources to support the Blacklight effort (including development hardware, an issue tracker for management of the project, and a wiki for documentation), we have consciously scaled back time spent during office hours on this side project.

The NINES steering committee agreed that our team could pursue Blacklight under the assumption that it would lead to concrete improvements and changes to the Collex faceted browsing model—and also because this work seemed to constitute a pragmatic way of thinking through issues involved in incorporating library catalog records into the NINES data set. So far, major generalizations of the faceted browsing model have *not* been deemed appropriate for contribution back into the Collex tool. NINES has, however, benefited from small-scale cross-pollination, in that some features, such as saved searches, have been prototyped in the Blacklight environment before being fully implemented and released in Collex, and the solr-ruby library developed by Hatcher as a result of his Blacklight work has streamlined Collex's interaction with Solr.

The NINES project has also used Blacklight's querying methods and index of MARC data to extract relevant UVA Special Collections records for indexing into Collex, radically expanding the virtual "holdings" of NINES. Thanks to Blacklight, it was a fairly trivial effort to formulate and tweak a query that returned 180,000 hits on rare books and manuscripts from the long nineteenth century, and then to map their Library of Congress genre headings to NINES-valid genres. NINES presently seeks a stable channel for bringing in catalog entries from a great number of other libraries with rich holdings in nineteenth century material. Unfortunately, because the support system for Blacklight is not yet firmly established in the UVA Library or elsewhere, Blacklight does not seem to us to be a sure enough bet as an intermediary between libraries and NINES. NINES will be exploring other options. That said, the education the NINES staff and steering committee has received in library standards and conventions will prove invaluable as we move forward in incorporating data from other institutions, such as the Bancroft Library at UC Berkeley, Indiana's Lilly Library, the Harry Ransom Research Center, and other libraries with prominent holdings in the nineteenth century.

Bringing Blacklight into the UVA Library system is an ongoing process and we remain, at this writing, in very early stages of the project. It is therefore difficult to assess any "lessons learned" or make valid generalizations from our experience. We do, however, see an interesting dynamic emerging between our scholar-driven research and development group and the library that hosts, nurtures, and serves it. In part, this dynamic replicates old assumptions that scholars and librarians may hold about their respective roles and partnership in the academy. It is the sense of the NINES group that the Library's current interest in Collex is narrowly confined to those faceted browsing features that were easily distilled into Blacklight. Clearly, as this book demonstrates, libraries are making great strides toward more participatory media and toward a greater understanding of the pressures and opportunities of the scholarly publication cycle. However, at this point, the social software and user-contributed metadata features so interesting to scholars do lie outside the scope of UVA's short-term OPAC improvement plan. The scholars who form the NINES collective, for their part, may well view work on Blacklight as pre-critical and service-oriented—outside the scope of the interpretive and analytical activity that is the scholar's domain.

Our collaboration implicitly challenges the assumptions scholars and librarians often hold about their respective roles in managing and interpreting information. Scholars must begin to engage at a much deeper level with the fundamental work of information representation and retrieval for which our increasingly networked and digitized cultural archive calls. That is to say, they must engage with the library and with librarians to a greater degree than ever before. And librarians must recognize that subjective response, multivalent interpretation, and new modes of discourse—the scholarly and pedagogical imperative manifested and made accessible through social software—constitute a critical and ever-expanding component of that very archive. In other words, the library must support and sustain new conversations and conversational media alongside those preserved in the printed word and its analogues.

Coda

"Well, I declare!" exclaimed Scarlett O'Hara. "This Library 2.0 OPAC is much easier to use. The bitsy info-graphics on the facets are just *darling*, and I love the way I can use this interface to narrow my search by media types, or locations, or Library of Congress descriptors, or even by languages. Fiddle-dee-dee, there's even a facet for call numbers and a way to save my little search!" Scarlett paused to fan her heaving bosom, and then frowned. "But how to incorporate journal holdings, commercial databases, and digitized multimedia files? And what about all those fascinating social software features that have yet to make their way from Collex into Blacklight? And how will those charming folks in Charlottesville extend the Blacklight collaboration to the greater benefit of scholars and librarians everywhere?" She snapped her fan and her laptop shut, with a double click.

> "Oh, well," sighed Scarlett, "I'll just think about that tomorrow. After all, tomorrow is another day!"

References

Alonso, Carlos. 2003. Crises and Opportunities: The Futures of Scholarly Publishing. *ACLS Occasional Paper* 57.

Antelman, Kristin, Emily Lynema, and Andrew K. Pace. 2006. Toward a twenty-first century library catalog. *Information Technology and Libraries* 25 (September): 128-139.

Beagle, Donald. 2002. Visualizing the digital commons. *The Charleston Advisor*, July.

———— 2003. Visualizing keyword distribution across multidisciplinary c-space. *D-Lib Magazine*, June.

Birchall, Alex and Roy Rada. 1995. The design of systems for learning and working in librarianship. Paper read at CAIS/ACSI 95: Annual Conference of the Canadian Association for Information Science, Edmonton, Canada.

Casati, Fabio, Fausto Giunchiglia, and Maurizio Marchese. 2007. Publish and perish: why the current publication and review model is killing research and wasting your money. *Ubiquity* 8 (January).

Delgadillo, Roberto and Beverly P. Lynch. 1999. Future historians: Their quest for information. *College and Research Libraries* 60 (May): 245-259.

Foster, Allen. 2004. A nonlinear model of information-seeking behavior. *Journal of the American Society for Information Science and Technology* 55 (February): 228-237.

Foster, Allen and Nigel Ford. 2003. Serendipity and information seeking: An empirical study. *Journal of Documentation* 59 (3): 321-340.

Gullikson, Shelley, Ruth Blades, Marc Bragdon, Shelley McKibbon, Marnie Sparling, and Elaine Toms. 1999. The impact of information architecture on academic web site usability. *The Electronic Library* 17 (October): 293-304.

McGann, Jerome. 2004. Culture and technology: The way we live now, what is to be done? *Electronic Book Review*. http://www.electronicbookreview.com/thread/electropoetics/rethinking.

Modern Language Association of America. 2004. *Tenure Summary Report*. MLA Executive Council tenure and promotion task force.

Morville, Peter. 2005. *Ambient Findability*. Sebastopol, California: O'Reilly.

Norman, Donald. 1988. *The Psychology of Everyday Things*. New York: Basic Books.

Ruecker, Stanley. 2003. *Affordances of Prospect For Academic Users of Interpretively-Tagged Text Collections*. Edmonton: University of Alberta.

Sadler, Elizabeth and Lisa M. Given. 2007. Affordance theory: A framework for graduate students' information behavior. *Journal of Documentation* 63 (1):115-141.

Schneider, Karen. 2006. *How OPACs suck, part1: Relevance rank (or the lack of it)*. http://www.techsource.ala.org/blog/2006/03/how-opacs-suck-part-1-relevance-rank-or-the-lack-of-it.html.

———. 2006. *How OPACs suck ,part 2: The checklist of shame*. http://www.techsource.ala.org/blog/2006/04/how-opacs-suck-part-2-the-checklist-of-shame.html.

———. 2006. *How OPACs suck ,part 3: The big picture*. http://www.techsource.ala.org/blog/2006/05/how-opacs-suck-part-3-the-big-picture.html.

Unsworth, John. 2003. Not-so-modest proposals: What do we want our system of scholarly communication to look like in 2010? Paper read at CIC Summit on Scholarly Communication, Park Ridge, IL.

Vicente, Kim J. and Jens Rasmussen. 1992. Ecological interface design: Theoretical foundations. *IEEE Transactions on Systems, Man, and Cybernetics* 22 (July/August): 589-606.

Waller, Nicole. 2002. Will libraries go to Antarcti.ca to transform the OPAC? *American Libraries* (June/July): 72-74.

Wikipedia. 2007. Skunk works. http://en.wikipedia.org/wiki/Skunk_works (accessed June 15, 2007).

Williamson, Kirsty. 1998. Discovered by chance: The role of incidental information acquisition in an ecological model of information use. *Library and Information Science Research* 20 (1): 23-40.

http://acrl.ala.org/L2Initiatives/index.php?title=Chapter_5/

Push and Pull of the OPAC

Daniel Forsman

Abstract

This chapter focuses on the work done by Jönköping University Library in Sweden to implement technical solutions associated with Web 2.0. These include developing the OPAC as a Web resource rich in content and features and fully integrated with the library Web site. Emphasis is placed on the technical aspects of Web 2.0 rather than the social features often discussed in the literature. In this chapter, we shall examine examples of spelling suggestions, dynamic help, search forwarding, linking to catalog content, and graphical and structural integration with his library's Web site, all implemented within the Ex Libris Aleph 500 system. The Jönköping University Library OPAC—JULIA—is not something we would describe as OPAC 2.0. There is still progress to be made, especially in the areas of social interaction. However, we are focused and determined to move forward.

Introduction

Library 2.0 is all about communication and interaction: interaction from person to person, person to organization, person to machine, and machine to machine. This chapter focuses on the technical aspects of Web 2.0 and options for a library's OPAC. By applying Web 2.0 technology to Jonkoping library-related services we are coming closer to achieving the status of Library 2.0. So far, our work has focused on creating a feature-rich environment for our users, linking library-related services together. By enhancing the OPAC we are serving the different needs of our users in a modern Web context. This could not have been accomplished had the library not been open to change. Changes to the OPAC were introduced one by one, features tested in production, some removed and others kept. The Library is now getting closer to a state of perpetual beta, in which constant change is both necessary and natural.

Imagine a vast ocean. Ships sail on its waters, visiting countries, small islands, and continents. Some of these are attractive tourist locations, while others supply the ships with goods for trade, boosting the economy. The trade between the most visited islands is huge and affects the entire way of life for those involved. Everybody knows who the key nations and traders are, and they are well respected and envied. The sea is bristling with activity. However, there are also other islands in the sea, small isolated islands without many visitors or any trade. Some tourists who stumble upon these islands love them. Our library OPAC is like one of these tiny islands, a place where few visit, cut off from the world, and with limited possibilities for contact with the outside world.

One might consider Web 2.0 to be a conceptual model that describes how we perceive usage of the Internet and its related services. As many have pointed out, the technical basis for 2.0 services is not entirely new. It is the way in which we regard the usage of these services that is new. The 2.0 mindset promotes the idea that social interaction adds value to the data, making it more interesting and valuable than in its original format. For example, a Web site can push data to other sites so that this data becomes more accessible.

Library technology has developed rapidly during the past ten years. Today libraries can offer

Daniel Forsman, Jönköping University Library, e-mail: daniel.forsman@bibl.hj.se

Web sites that take advantage of numerous options to create a complex, sophisticated product. The OPAC has usually not been a part of this trend. It has been cut off from the rest of the library services. Often the OPAC has its own server and domain, and its interface is outdated. The functionality of the system is basic, and little has been done to improve it.

Librarians have expressed their disappointment to vendors about this state of affairs. They have complained that the system is based on outdated architecture not suited for the modern Web. The OPAC of today was created yesterday; the technique used was valid then but does not work as well in the current information environment.

One may wonder if vendors are obliged to develop new functionalities as a part of their license agreements with libraries. I question whether it is reasonable for librarians to demand a new system architecture, rapid development, and quality control without paying anything more than the license fee. It is true that library systems are trailing in technological development. However, there are reasons why this is the case. An Integrated Library System (ILS) is a large, complex system that requires considerable effort to transform from the ground up.

Despite the innate complexity of the ILS, there are people in libraries with technical skills who are expanding the functionalities of their systems. Among others, I have found the work by the libraries of University of Huddersfield (http://www.hud.ac.uk/cls/), Plymouth State University (http://lamson.wpopac.com/library/), Groningen University (the LiveTrix project, http://livetrix.ub.rug.nl/), and the Ann Arbor public library (http://www.aadl.org/) very inspiring. Their work proves that much can be accomplished, given administrative drive and a skilled and motivated staff. An ILS need not be open source to be amenable to fundamental change. Librarians understand the workings of their catalogs. By combining this understanding with new service paradigms, the potential for enhancements is great. It just comes down to giving staff the mandate to explore and experiment with the system.

The future of the ILS lies in offering a flexible system that allows configuration options within a user-friendly administrative interface. For example, the Ex Libris X-server is a model that will work for many libraries. The X-server is a part of the ILS architecture that adds an XML-based presentation layer accessed through an Application Programming Interface (API) (Ex Libris). With the addition of the X-server, libraries have access to a functional system, and those who want to push forward are given a tool with which to work within the system.

When I started my employment at Jönköping University in the early fall of 2006, I was informed of its goal to raise the bar with the library's electronic services. There was interest in Web 2.0 technologies. The library administration was ready to explore what we could do to develop the tools we had, working within the framework of our licensed products. Drawing upon this mandate, I have started a long journey and exploration.

The Initiatives

This chapter describes examples of several initiatives with our ILS that promote the Library 2.0 notion of developing applications enhanced with several components to create a feature-rich online environment for users. The Jönköping University Library uses Ex Libris ALEPH as its ILS, along with the SFX link server and MetaLib. For those interested in technical details and code, please visit the wiki associated with this book.

The initiatives presented in this chapter include the following OPAC enhancements: embedding the graphical presentation of the OPAC into the library Web site, context-sensitive help, forward searching, permanent linking, using Amazon content, subject headings presented in a cloud view, and handling large result sets with post-search filters.

Embedded OPAC

One of the first projects I got involved with was the redesign of the Jönköping Library Web site (http://www.bibl.hj.se/). The project started out with brainstorming on how we wanted the site to look and to function. These ideas had to be adapted to the University's content management system. Working with that system was disappointing and led to the abandonment of many ideas. It also led, however, to the concept of expanding the library Web pages to external systems! The idea was to present external systems as a part of the structure and layout of the library Web site. It should be easy for the user to navigate from one system to another. After identifying which systems should be included, we started working on methods of applying the library Web site design to as many services and systems as possible including the design of the

Jönköping Library catalog, JULIA (http://julia.hj.se/).

The library Web site is usually described as a tool for finding information. We spend time thinking about navigation, structure, and content that can help our users find the information they want as easily as possible. We develop subject guides, link collections, a database of databases, tips, journal lists, etc. In the worst case, these carefully constructed systems are loosely connected by hyperlinks and shown without a consistent graphical presentation. This makes these tools harder to use and understand. By providing a common layout and structure, the library can help the user understand the conceptual differences between tools and navigate between them. This consistency also helps the user understand that the services are provided for them by their library.

Figure 1: The Jönköping University Library Website

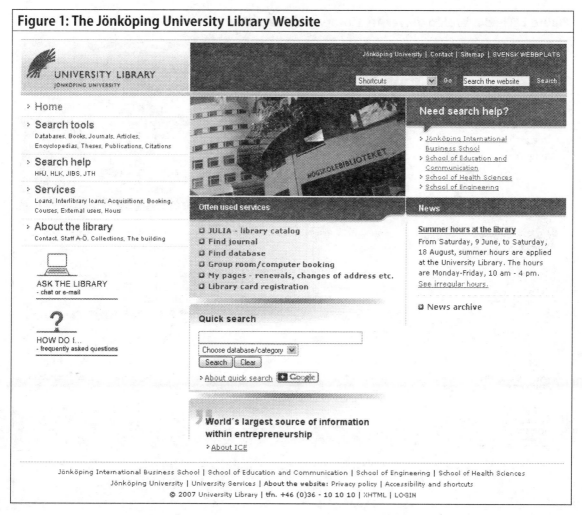

Through his Weblog "Self-plagiarism is style," Dave Pattern conducted an OPAC survey in 2007 (Pattern). 729 people related to libraries took part in the survey and there were some interesting results. One of the questions asked about features people would like to see in their OPAC. The embedded OPAC scored the highest. Offering an integrated OPAC is important and gives the library a chance to present its tools to users in a seamless way.

Because I had experience with other library systems, I was used to the notion of not being able to do what I wanted with the OPAC. Adapting an OPAC interface can be tedious and challenging. Having moved from one system to another, I came in with a fresh set of eyes and was determined to find new methods to make the system do what it needed to do. My ambition was to adapt the in-

terface and embed it into the library Web site so that users would not necessarily realize that they had moved from one domain to another. I found a method to re-work the way our OPAC was constructed, and integrated the OPAC with our main graphical profile.

There are those who worry about making changes to their systems, especially in the light of future upgrades. While these concerns may be valid, we cannot let them prevent us from adapting our systems to our needs. It is by doing so that we learn how our systems work. It is from this understanding that we can push the vendors into making real changes and becoming active partners with us. If we have an attitude that tells us to avoid modifications because we are afraid of the work involved, we will never get the systems we deserve.

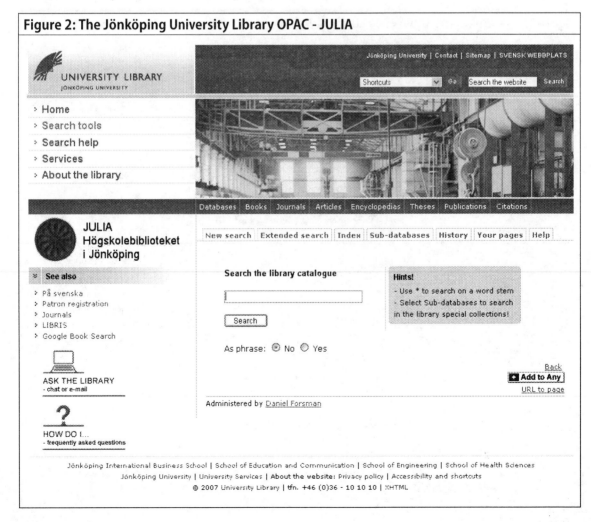

Figure 2: The Jönköping University Library OPAC - JULIA

Figure 3: An example of a help text being generated after the user has entered a search term

Results list

Free text= entrepreneurship

Hint!
The ICE special collection (with literature on entrepeneurship and small business) is located on the top floor of the library.

Showing 1 - 20 of 6238

`Go to #` [ ]

Sort on:
Author | Title | Year

#1 ☐ **Corporate entrepreneurship & innovation: entrepreneurial development within organizations / 2. ed.**
cop. 2008. Morris, Michael H.
BOOK
Show copy

#2 ☐ **Entrepreneurship /**
cop. 2008. Bygrave, William D., 1937-
BOOK
Show copy

Context-Sensitive Help

A core Web 2.0 value is that users should be able to influence and take part in the development of a Web service. Through user interaction and data enrichment, the value of the service being offered increases and makes it unique. When we talk about the users' role, it is usually in the form of direct influence and the ability to personalize. Another perspective on user influence is to study what people are doing on a site, monitoring their navigation on and interaction with the site. By studying user actions and correlating them with data in the systems, we can create added value by predicting needs for help and guidance.

At Computers in Libraries (CIL) 2007, Rich Wiggins from Michigan State University presented his work with a search log analysis (Wiggins). He proposed that the study of search logs is akin to having a discussion with the users of a site. In this case, Wiggins studied the university Web site and the logs for the search function. He drew upon the assumptions of Zipf's law (Wikipedia 2007e) and the Pareto principle (Wikipedia 2007b). Wiggins worked with mapping the most common search words entered into the search box of the Web site with the most relevant pages on the

site. During his presentation, I started thinking what his approach could mean for my work with the OPAC.

I had developed a method for catching search terms entered into the OPAC and matching them against a list of problematic terms. If any of the problematic terms were used during a search, a tailored help text was displayed in the OPAC. The idea was that library staff would define the terms and write the texts. The texts would be displayed in a meaningful context when the user needed help. For instance, if I search for *theses* in our OPAC, a short text will be displayed along with the search results. The text will give tips on where to find theses in full text and how to limit the search in the OPAC.

After CIL 2007 I started to perform quantitative studies on what users were searching for in our OPAC. I identified the most popular searches in the last two years. Even though my data does not come near to the numbers of the Pareto principle, I could see that some searches were being performed more often than others, and I could produce a list of those searches. From this list our librarians have reviewed the searches and designed help texts to match the queries.

The method for finding search terms is quite simple. The search terms in our OPAC are displayed in several places after a search has been initiated. One of these is in the URL. Using JavaScript, we read the URL and parse out the search terms. These are then passed on against the list of "marked" terms. If a term matches a marked term, then an appropriate help text or hint is displayed.

By combining the list of search terms and statistics of the most common searches, we are able to provide users with contextual help. As Wiggins noted in his presentation, looking at search logs is like having a discussion with users. If you are not listening to your search logs, you should start now.

Figure 4: Close up of a context-sensitive hint in JULIA .

Hint!

Are you looking for Master theses / Undergraduate theses? You can limit your search in JULIA! Master theses in fulltext are searchable through DiVA and Uppsök.

Forward Search and Linking

The OPAC is in many ways a dead end when searching for information. After you have performed your search, you are left to your own fate. The problem is that the OPAC is not the only source of information and users know it. We therefore leave it to users to understand the roles of the OPAC, free resources, and licensed resources. People use Google and then have a hard time finding their way to the expensive resources the library has acquired.

The OPAC needs to be put into context with other sources of information. Many databases offer a link back to the OPAC or link server. But how many OPACs link to databases and other search tools? The OPAC is just one tool and it is important to show users that there are other tools and that the library catalog is a part of a large pool of resources. Where this is meaningful, try to integrate and link between these tools and resources. By putting the free tools into the same framework as the licensed tools, we are making users aware of a broader range of tools. Today, in JULIA, we include links to Google Scholar, the Swedish national union catalog LIBRIS, the local public library, ebrary, and a quick search set in our MetaLib installation for some of the largest full text databases.

By allowing users to continue their search in other resources, the OPAC is put into a direct relationship with a wider range of tools. Users can see this relationship and benefit from it. By referring to Google Scholar, you are promoting Scholar over plain vanilla Google. By referring to licensed resources in the same context as Google, you are linking them all together and showing users that there are alternatives.

Library catalogs are not the holy grails of information. People will use other avenues for getting answers. It is important that we portray the OPAC as one alternative among others by allowing the search to be continued through additional resources.

The most primitive way to refer users to other databases or search services is through hyperlinks. When a service supports linking syntax for queries, hyperlinks should be generated with the search query as part of the URL. The construction of these is simple and uses the same method as parsing the URL for search terms as described earlier. A more advanced way to do this would be to perform the query in real time using a selection of services from inside the OPAC. When presenting the query-prepared link, the users can be shown the number of hits they will get if they click on the link. There are several ways to accomplish this. First, you need to obtain the search terms. Then you must pass the query to the external databases through a Z39.50 client or read an external Web file and parse/screen scrape it (in PHP, using fopen()).

Another method would be to use the services of a federated search engine. MetaLib from Ex Libris offers a set of Web services that you can use to

Figure 5: The option to forward a search to other search engines through a hyperlink

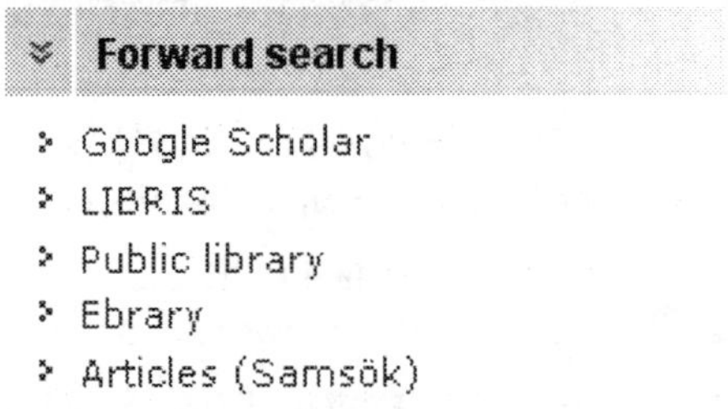

≫ **Forward search**

› Google Scholar
› LIBRIS
› Public library
› Ebrary
› Articles (Samsök)

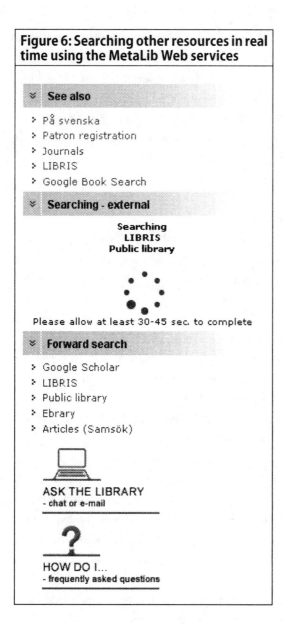

Figure 6: Searching other resources in real time using the MetaLib Web services

Figure 7: The hit counts from the external search are displayed with hyperlinks.

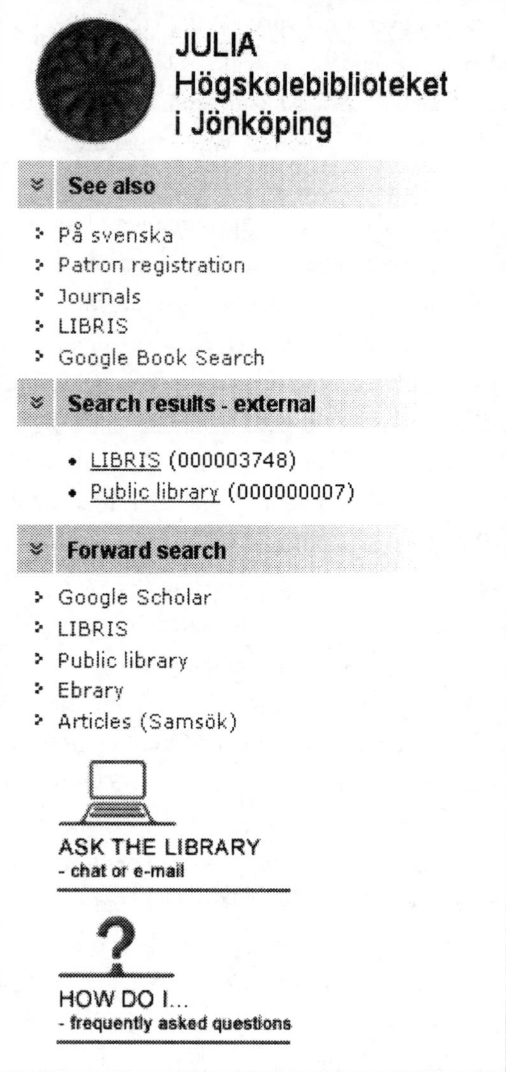

query databases and even call up records. By using these services, the OPACs can become a rough tool for federated searches. However, if you include all resources from MetaLib in your OPAC, then you might as well start the search in MetaLib. But to extract some of the sources in MetaLib and insert them in the OPAC while users are performing a search is to put the OPAC in a broader context. This helps users understand that there are other tools offered by the library.

Spellchecking

Most users today expect search services to check their search terms. The most common feature is offering spelling alternatives or a "did you mean" suggestion. There are different ways to construct a spelling control in a library catalog. You can use the words indexed in the database, install spelling software (such as Aspell, http://aspell.net/) on your Web server, or use a Web service to come up with the suggestions. A Web service is a software system designed to support machine to machine interaction over a network (Wikipedia 2007d).

Regardless of the chosen tool, you will need to find a method to capture search terms and pass them on to your spelling service. Google allows spelling suggestions through their SOAP API. SOAP is a protocol for exchanging XML-based messages over a network (Wikipedia 2007c). Basically, you send the Google SOAP API (http://code.google.com/apis/soapsearch/) a search term and the server responds with a spelling suggestion in an XML format. This communication is not meant to be read by the human eye but by the machines that handle the communication.

Unfortunately, Google has closed this service to new users and is now referring customers to its AJAX API. Spelling suggestions through Google is limited to 1,000 calls a day through SOAP. Yahoo! offers a similar service through REST (http://developer.yahoo.com/search/web/V1/spellingSuggestion.html), which allows 5,000 requests a day. Another interesting Web service for spelling suggestions is the Ockham Spell Web service (http://spell.ockham.org/about/).

We offer spelling suggestions for searches with zero hits and use the Google SOAP service. After studying the search logs, we came up with about 500 searches with zero hits a day. That leaves a safe margin to the 1,000 calls. We are now considering leaving the SOAP service and using another service that we can call upon as often as we want. This would allow us to provide a "did you mean" service even if the search results in hits. Most likely, this will move us to a solution with Aspell. From a technical standpoint, there are very few differences in using a server side solution from a Web service.

I believe we will see more controls performed on search terms. Functions to widen a search would be welcome, whereas today we focus on narrowing results. Another welcome service in a multilingual setting would be to translate search terms on the fly. There are some good Web services for translation, and it would be interesting to experiment with using them from within the OPAC.

Amazon

There are Web sites that are opening up their systems so that others can mine them for data. The most well-known example is Amazon, which offers a rich variety of Web services (http://aws.amazon.com/). The opportunity to use data from Amazon in conjunction with an OPAC is very exciting. Today Jonkoping University Library is retrieving book covers from Amazon and are in the process of exploring other services. We see no conflict in linking back to Amazon as a thank you to them for letting us use their data.

To use Amazon Web services for a specific book, you will need an identifier that works in Amazon. One suitable identifier is the ISBN. By using a Document Object Model (DOM) script, we can go through a record and capture the ISBN. DOM is a platform- and language-independent standard object model for representing HTML or XML (http://www.w3schools.com/htmldom/). Once the ISBN is captured, it is passed to a PHP script that queries Amazon, fetches the data, and brings it back to the OPAC using Asynchronous JavaScript and XML, known as AJAX. This is a method that can be used to update a portion of a page without refreshing the whole page (Wikipedia 2007a).

Linking

The Web is based on hypertext. This is a major problem if we cannot link to data within our system. Even if the OPAC offers the option to e-mail results, or to save records and search strings, this is not the same as linking. The URLs generated by

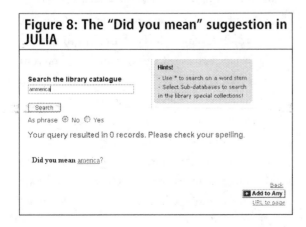

Figure 8: The "Did you mean" suggestion in JULIA

Figure 9: A cover being pulled from Amazon, displayed in the record view

our systems usually include session-specific data. Consequently, if a user saves the OPAC URL as a bookmark, it becomes useless after a while. By constructing permanent links, we are making it easier for users to connect to the content of our systems.

There are several on-line services that collect and manage bookmarks. To make our content visible, and convenient for our users to save, we must enable permanent links. By parsing the actual URL and stripping it of session data, the user has the option of finding and using a more stable link than the one normally found in the address bar. We also offer the option to use a URL aggregator service called "Add to any" (http://addtoany.com/). "Add to any" offers the user the ability to post a URL to different bookmark managers such as Del.icio.us (http://del.icio.us/), RSS readers such as iGoogle (http://www.google.com/ig), and other URL-based services such as Digg (http://digg.com/).

Library systems of today contain huge amounts of data. By studying the data in our database and understanding its nature, we can create new and interesting ways of preserving and presenting it.

Subject Clouds

The traditional descriptors generated by librarians add value to bibliographic records and that, together with user-generated descriptors (which Jonkoping University Library is not yet offering), yield a record rich in data. The problem today is that the library-generated descriptors are hidden in the record and presented in a way that makes it hard for users to understand what they are and how to use them.

Figure 10: A stable URL to the page and the "Add to any" feature

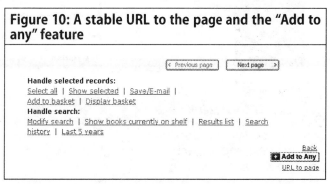

Figure 11: Close-up of the subject headings cloud in JULIA

> ⌄ **Subject cloud**
>
> *Afrika* Jordbrukspolitik
> Livsmedelsförsörjning Asia **Asien**
> **Africa** Gröna revolutionen Green revolution
> Agricultural policy Food supply

At the Jönköping University Library, we have found a way to display our descriptors graphically in subject clouds so that our users will notice them. The font size of a displayed descriptor is determined by its frequency in the catalog. The size really has nothing to do with relevance, as in many cases the smallest descriptor is the most interesting. For example, the general descriptor *Sweden* is very common and will always be displayed in a large-sized font, while a specific descriptor such as *AJAX* will be displayed smaller. However, the size of the descriptors is not the point. Our goal is to lift descriptors from the record and make them noticeable.

The foundation of the cloud view is a DOM script that fetches the record's unique system ID. From the system ID, we query the ILS Oracle database with SQL. The query counts occurrences and fetches the descriptors associated with the record. When the count is complete, the cloud view is generated and sent back to the OPAC using AJAX.

After finding a method for working with the HTML DOM in our OPAC, the library acquired a tool to work with the record and extract data from the OPAC presentation view. We can capture anything in our OPAC and pass it on to a script or a Web service.

We are now looking into what more we can do to exploit the data in our records. We are hoping to discover additional ways to enrich our records with data from other services and present the information in an attractive and useful way.

Handling Large Result Sets

Receiving large result sets from a query is more or less the typical experience with a search service. The amount of indexed words is constantly growing. For

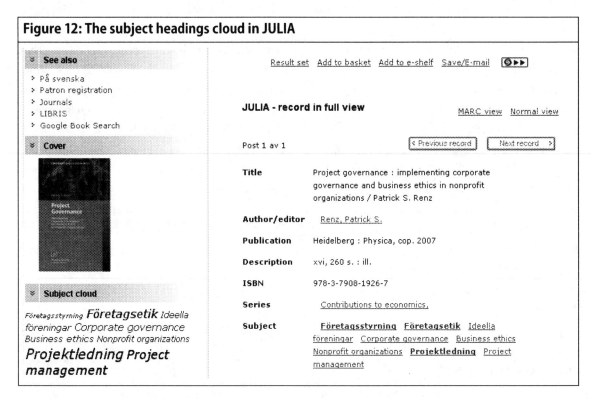

Figure 12: The subject headings cloud in JULIA

many users this is not a problem. They do not care if they get 100 or 1,000,000 hits. The typical behavior is to look at the first page or the first 20-30 records. The concepts of precision and recall, in which all librarians are drilled, is becoming meaningless since we can no longer judge the total number of relevant documents in a collection. A growing number of search services are focusing on providing methods to drill down through large results sets. The functionality that accomplishes this is not new, but usually the limit option is meant to be used before a search is initiated. Since the functionality already exists in the system, we can try to make it more useful, especially after a search has been performed.

We have started working with filters that can be applied to a result set. The filters are presented as hyperlinks to users. Today we can offer filters to remove books that are not on the shelf, in languages other than Swedish, and more than five years old.

Future Plans

Our future plans for the OPAC focus on refining our system. We aim to explore and exploit the system and work with the vendor to develop a better product. We are not satisfied with an out-of-the-box solution, but want a system that allows us to come up with new solutions, services, and presentations of the data as we see fit.

Recently we acquired MetaLib for federated searching. We plan to work with its rich set of Web services to improve the OPAC. We are aiming to customize MetaLib to the same graphical presentation as our OPAC so that this new tool will also be consistent with the library Web site.

We are looking forward to creating social space in our OPAC and are hoping to do this in collaboration with other libraries. This includes the formation of a Swedish consortia for handling user tags, reviews, ratings, and public and private comments. We will also explore what

types of RSS feeds we can offer. The future will be both complicated and challenging.

Conclusion

In many ways, library catalogs are isolated from the rest of the Internet. It is difficult to link in to catalog data and to continue your search out to the Web from within the OPAC. Often the catalog has its own graphical interface, distinct from the library Web site. This gives it the impression of being a dead end for the user. Library 2.0 is about networking and putting people in contact with other people, but it is also about putting machines in contact with other machines. We have many opportunities to connect the library catalog to the services that are associated with Web 2.0, and by doing so bring ourselves closer to Library 2.0.

Libraries are disappointed with ILS vendors and especially with the development of the OPAC. These libraries are entitled to demand that vendors develop their products. On the other hand, technical developments in recent years have been extensive. I question the fairness of demanding a new system architecture, developed rapidly with maintained quality control, while also selling at a low cost.

Libraries must accept the fact that vendors of library systems probably will never be in the front line of technical development. Libraries either need to wait for vendors to do their job, or try to solve issues on their own. Open source or APIs are usually described as the solution to deeper involvement with library systems. I am not in total agreement with this point of view. Libraries are used to being customers and letting others develop their systems. The systems in use today

Figure 13: Filters to handle large result sets in JULIA.

Handle selected records:
Select all | Show selected | Save/E-mail |
Add to basket | Display basket
Handle search:
Modify search | Show books currently on shelf | Results list | Search
history | Only swedish titles | Last 5 years

are in many ways open and accessible. It is possible to work with them and create modern features. There are plenty of examples of people who are developing their systems to get what they want without the benefit of open source or APIs. It all comes down to an investment in people who have the right mindset and are driven to get results, and giving them the trust and time they need. The competence gained from tweaking and developing features for the ILS makes libraries stronger partners for vendors. Through leading by example, we can force change. Once this happens, we will have real use for API's or open source components in the ILS.

Jönköping University Library recently decided to work more actively with its library-related systems to refine them in order to better meet user needs. During the Web site redesign, we chose to enforce the same design and structure on the OPAC so that it appears to be fully integrated with the site. The same concept was applied to other systems, such as the SFX A-Z list, proxy server, etc. The objective was, where possible, to provide users with a coherent structure and interface of the tools offered by the library.

In the OPAC itself, we are now catching problematic search terms in order to give dynamic help. We have also created exits from the OPAC so that users can continue their search in other services on the Web. By doing external searches in real time, the OPAC can become a small tool for federated searching. By looking at what other data providers offer and trying to incorporate them into our own system, we aim to create a richer and more functional catalog.

The ability to construct links into the OPAC is crucial on the Web today. The Web is navigated by hyperlinks. Catalogs that offer no chances to link to its resources are more or less invisible on the Internet. By creating stable links, we are giving users a chance to make our resources visible in multiple environments.

By processing the data in the library system, we can find new ways to present information and make the user notice valuable information. We have started working with cloud representation of descriptors with the purpose of making them more visible. We have also worked with the limit functions of the system, making them available as filters that can be applied after a search.

In the future, we aim to continue developing our online services, especially our own catalog. We can use the experience of working with the ILS to put pressure on the vendor to develop a more flexible and modern system. It is of strategic importance for the library to invest in people who are willing to push library services forward so that we are not left behind.

References

Ex Libris. Aleph - architecture. http://www.exlibrisgroup.com/aleph_architecture.htm.

Pattern, Dave. 2007. Self-plagiarism is style—OPAC survey results. http://www.daveyp.com/blog/index.php/archives/category/OPAC-survey/.

Wiggins, Rich. 2007. Search analytics: Conversations with your customers. http://www.slideshare.net/richwig/search-analytics-conversations-with-your-customers.

Wikipedia. 2007a. AJAX. http://en.wikipedia.org/wiki/AJAX (accessed June 11, 2007).

Wikipedia. 2007b. Pareto principle. http://en.wikipedia.org/wiki/Pareto_Principle (accessed June 11, 2007).

Wikipedia. 2007c. SOAP. http://en.wikipedia.org/wiki/SOAP (accessed June 11, 2007).

Wikipedia. 2007d. Web service. http://en.wikipedia.org/wiki/Web_services (accessed June 11, 2007).

Wikipedia. 2007e. Zipf's law. http://en.wikipedia.org/wiki/Zipfs_law (accessed June 11, 2007).

UThink: Library Hosted Blogs for a University-Wide Community

Shane Nackerud

Abstract

UThink: Blogs at the University of Minnesota Libraries began in April 2004 and is now one of the largest, if not the largest, academic blogging sites in the United States. UThink began with these goals: to promote intellectual freedom, to help build communities of interest on campus, to investigate the connections between blogging and the traditional academic enterprise, and to help retain the cultural memory of the institution. This chapter discusses how well the University of Minnesota Libraries has met these goals through the UThink project. It also focuses on the project as a whole, from its inception to its current iteration. The future of the project is also discussed.

Introduction

Web blogs, or blogs, have become an important part of many libraries' communications and outreach efforts. In fact, many times blogs are the primary means by which a library makes its first foray into the world of Library 2.0. Today, libraries of all types are utilizing blogs to quickly publish news concerning new acquisitions, library tips and help, library events or programs, and information about specific subjects. In numerous academic libraries, library patrons are thrilled with these developments since the blog format is something they readily recognize, and sometimes even expect, to stay current with their informational needs outside of the library. Obviously, many library patrons also maintain their own blogs which discuss their daily lives, views on national and world events, and also their expertise (and bias) concerning a wide variety of topics.

What is the value of bringing these two types of blogs, library and patron, together? Is there any value in encouraging library patrons to blog and even providing the hosting mechanism to do so through the library? These are the questions that the University of Minnesota Libraries is seeking to answer through the UThink blog initiative (http://blog.lib.umn.edu/). With UThink: Blogs at the University of Minnesota Libraries, the Libraries hosts blogs for the entire University of Minnesota, including all four coordinate campuses. There are well over 80,000 potential users including faculty, staff, graduate students, and undergraduate students at the university.

UThink launched in April 2004. As of the writing of this chapter, UThink hosts well over 4,600 individual blogs and over 65,000 individual entries, and has well over 10,000 registered users. This level of usage makes UThink one of the largest, if not the largest, academic blogging sites in the United States. This chapter will discuss the reasons why the University of Minnesota Libraries decided to host this initiative, goals of the project, technology, use metrics, and future plans for expanding the functionality of the system.

The Initiative

In the spring of 2003, the University of Minnesota Libraries were in the midst of a process to determine how we could better serve our undergraduate population. As part of that process,

Shane Nackerud, University of Minnesota Libraries, e-mail: snackeru@umn.edu

Figure 1: UThink: Blogs at the University of Minnesota

the libraries conducted a series of focus groups in which we asked students to tell us not only about their research needs and how they currently use libraries, but also what frustrates them most about the University in general. We were struck by the thankfulness of the student participants; they literally thanked us for giving them an opportunity to tell us what they thought. We soon realized that it was important to find a way in which students could easily share their opinions on a regular basis. Blogs seemed to be a perfect fit, especially given their blossoming popularity among students.

As we conducted more research into the possibility of hosting blogs for students, we quickly came to the realization that blogs could have a much wider impact than just giving students a forum for voicing opinions. Some believe that, thanks to blogs, academia is having a bigger influence on public discourse than ever before. Blogs offer faculty, staff, and students a freedom of tone impossible in scholarly journals or even the student newspaper. Blogs offer an immediacy of publishing unheard of in academia, as well as an easy, and sometimes, fun way to do it. Blogs also put faculty, students, and staff on an even playing field; essentially your opinions are judged on the merits of your writing and arguments, not your standing in your academic field. Blogs offer a medium for rapidly discussing opinions, issues, and ideas, and allow people from across the country, and campus, to connect with each other. They are also lowering the cost of publishing while at the same time raising public awareness of academic issues (Glenn 2003).

It also became clear that blogs can complement a more formal "institutional repository" by giving University faculty, students, and staff a place to share both polished and unpolished opinions, research, and views on a wide variety of topics. In

many cases, students, faculty, and staff are already blogging using off-campus services such as Blogger, LiveJournal, or Xanga. Some of this content is of questionable academic merit, to be sure, but it is obvious that a great deal of important content is being freely given to off-campus services with possibly suspect commitments to preservation, or services that do not share the research mission of the institution. At the University of Minnesota Libraries, we concluded that by hosting blogs we could retain much of this content and as a result potentially a unique slice of the cultural memory of the University.

Blogs can also be used as a classroom tool to enhance and promote learning. Blogs can replace tra-

Figure 2: The Movable Type interface

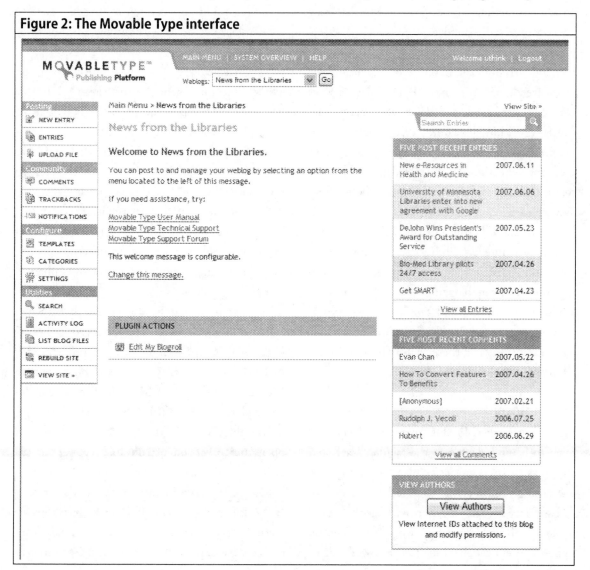

ditional course Web pages through instructors using them to post class notifications, readings, and recently found Web sites related to course content. Blogs can also help organize class discussions. Instructors can create a single class blog, with all students attached as authors, or assign each student the project of creating his or her own blog to use for essays and class participation. Successful use of blogs in a classroom setting has been well documented, with instructors who have taken the plunge reporting high satisfaction with student interest, learning, and commitment to this relatively new learning tool (Downes 2004).

Finally, while it is true that blogs can provide an easy means of expressing an opinion or sharing an idea, sometimes these ideas or opinions may be controversial. Libraries traditionally believe passionately in the principles of intellectual and academic freedom and in our role as advocates for those freedoms. Academic libraries have always collected, preserved, and defended controversial content. Within this context, the University Libraries became convinced that blogs would be an excellent opportunity to further demonstrate our role as defenders of intellectual and academic freedom on campus.

In summary, UThink began with these goals: to promote intellectual freedom, to help build communities of interest, to investigate the connections between blogging and the traditional academic enterprise, and to retain the cultural memory of the institution. After three years, how well has UThink met these goals? This question is addressed later in this chapter.

Technology

UThink uses the Movable Type publishing platform to bring blogging to the faculty, staff, and students of the University of Minnesota. Two overriding requirements dictated our choice of software: we needed a software package that could make use of the University of Minnesota's central signon/authentication mechanism, and we needed a

software package that could host multiple blogs on a single installation of the software. In September of 2003, when we were making our decision, there was a limited number of blogging tools that could meet our needs. After inspecting other blogging software packages such as Manila (http://manila.userland.com/) and Roller Weblogger (http://rollerweblogger.org/), we eventually decided on Movable Type. This decision was based on a number of factors:

+ At the time, Movable Type was free for educational institutions.

+ Movable Type was open source software in the sense that we could alter the code to make use of the University of Minnesota's Central Authentication Hub.

+ We could also configure Movable Type to create blogs on the fly without any administrator intervention.

+ Movable Type could host multiple blogs on a single installation of the software. Again, this was extremely important given the potential for UThink to host thousands of blogs.

+ The software is written in Perl and uses MySQL as its backend database of choice, two tools with which we had some expertise.

+ Movable Type had a large user base, possibly the largest of any tool at the time in terms of installed blogging packages, and an active development community regularly submitting enhancements (plugins).

Almost immediately after UThink launched in April 2004, Movable Type changed its licensing structure to a commercial, for-profit model. Needless to say, this was very troubling, but we had already locked into Movable Type as our delivery platform. Thankfully, Six Apart, the maker of Movable Type, has decided to again release an open source version of Movable Type 4 in Fall 2007 (http://www.movabletype.org/).

Due to the experimental nature of the project, UThink began on a relatively weak server architecture. According to a February 2004 study from the Pew Research Center, at least 2% of Internet users had their own blogs (Bruner 2004). When we designed our architecture, we considered students to be our primary audience. With approximately 50,000 students enrolled at the University of Minnesota—Twin Cities campus (the first campus UThink served), we decided we needed to build a system that could handle between 1,000—2,000 users. The server we built was a SunFire v120 with 650MHz, 2 GB RAM, and 120 GB of disk space.

For the first two years of the project, this architecture performed well. However, as the number of blogs and users climbed, and as the Movable Type software upgrades became more complex, the system began to respond very slowly. In November 2006, we upgraded our hardware to an IBM eserver BladeCenter HS20 Blade, with 3.4GHz and 4GB SDRAM. Our disk space is now hosted by the University of Minnesota SAN network, which in theory has an unlimited amount of space.

Because of the capacity of the SAN network, individual UThink users have no restrictions on uploading images, videos, audio, and other media formats. The only constraint is that individual files must be 65 MB or less. However, users may upload as many 65 MB files as they wish.

Users with a University of Minnesota Internet ID and password can quickly create a new blog on UThink In fact, blog creation takes less than a minute for most users and requires no administrator intervention. This functionality, the connection with the University of Minnesota central authentication system and on-the-fly user blog creation, required custom programming and modifications to the Movable Type code. Figure 3 illustrates the blog creation screen a user sees after logging in for the first time. In addition to this functionality, we have added a number of enhancements to UThink over the years based on user requests. Most of the improvements have come in the form of freely available Movable Type plugins. For example, we have installed:

+ StyleCatcher—Gives users more than eighty pre-made blog designs to choose from.

+ MT-Enclosures—Adds the necessary enclosure tags to RSS feeds to create podcasts.

Figure 3: Adding a new blog to UThink

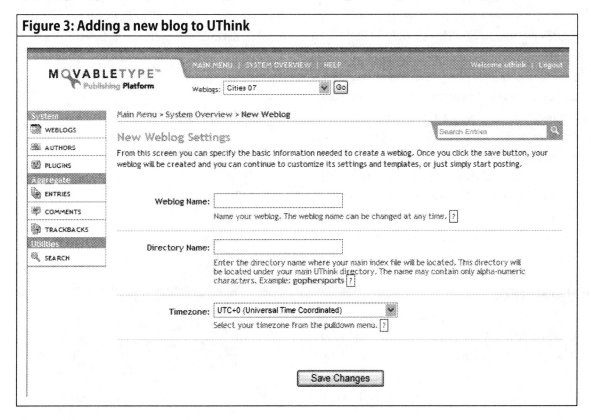

♦ CAPTCHA—Gives users another important tool to fight comment spam.

♦ MT-Blogroll—Assists users in creating a list of links, or blogroll, on their blog's home page.

These are just a few of the plugins we have installed on the system. We have also implemented mechanisms that allow blog owners to attach additional authors to their blog(s), including users not affiliated with the University of Minnesota. Anyone with a University of Minnesota Internet ID can be attached to a blog as an author, including guest University of Minnesota Internet IDs created through the University of Minnesota Portal system "MyU" (http://www.myu.umn.edu/). Some UThink blogs have as many as eighty authors. A number of on-campus conferences have used UThink to create blogs and attach non-affiliated users as authors. This includes a recent Committee on Institutional Cooperation (CIC)/Big Ten Library conference blog (http://blog.lib.umn.edu/CICLib07/).

In addition, we have created a UThink frequently asked questions wiki through which any user at the University of Minnesota can add topics or modify existing articles (https://wiki.umn.edu/twiki/bin/view/UThink/WebHome). A number of articles have been posted on such topics as Movable Type templates, comments, adding authors, password protecting blogs, and podcasting. Many of these articles were submitted by users of the system rather than UThink administrators or librarians.

We are excited about what we have been able offer through the UThink service in terms of technology and incremental improvements. Further enhancements and planned improvements will be discussed later in the chapter.

Use Metrics

UThink has seen steady growth since its launch in April 2004. As of June 2007, there are over 4,500 blogs. What has been most interesting, however, is the changes in how the system has been used over the three years of the project.

When UThink first launched, it was assumed that personal blogging, or blogging about personal opinions, stories, and ideas, would be the dominant form of blogging. This was certainly true in the beginning, but over time the system has become more academic in nature than expected.

How UThink is Being Used

In April 2005, we attempted to determine how the active blogs on the system were being used. We defined an active blog as any blog that had been updated within the last three months. Each active blog was inspected and placed into one of four categories:

♦ Personal - where the subject matter was of a personal nature

♦ Class-based - blogs used in conjunction with a particular course

♦ Work-related - blogs used in relation to a department or college on campus, or blogs by individual authors for work-related topics

♦ Testing - blogs created to test the system

Of the approximately 500 active blogs in April 2005, we found that 57% of the blogs were personal in nature, 23% were class- based, 13% were work-related, and the rest were just there to test the system.

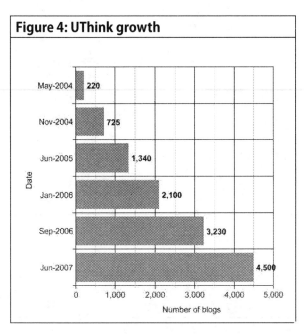

Figure 4: UThink growth

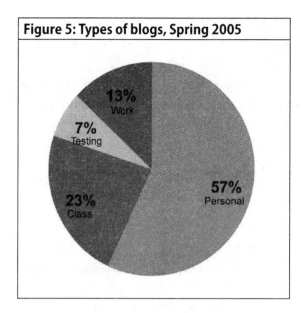

Figure 5: Types of blogs, Spring 2005

13% Work

7% Testing

23% Class

57% Personal

This breakdown was not a surprise. We expected personal blogging to be the dominant form of blogging. In fact, at the beginning of the project, there was a slight worry on the part of library administration that the system would not be "academic" enough. When UThink began, blogs had a reputation for being less than scholarly. As the project has matured, we have begun to see a shift in the main type of blogging on the system. In Spring 2006, out of approximately 700 active blogs, personal blogging dropped to 41% and class-based blogging jumped to 33%. This is not necessarily a huge shift, but we were excited to see the system being used more prominently in a classroom setting.

This shift continued in the fall of 2006, as class-based blogging became the primary type of blog on the system. Of the approximately 1,000 active UThink blogs in the Fall 2006 semester, 55% of were class-based. A number of reasons might account for this shift. For one, blogging as a classroom tool has received a great deal of attention both in popular magazines and scholarly journals relating to education. The rise in course-related blogging in UThink certainly coincides with this increased attention on the potential use of blogs as an educational tool. Second, over time UThink itself has received more attention at the Univer-

sity of Minnesota as the service has gotten larger and more well known. Discovered through word-of-mouth and advertising on campus, professors seeking new mechanisms to engage students have found and utilized the UThink system. In addition, tools such as MySpace and Facebook have increased in popularity during the same time period that UThink has been in existence. Many people at the University of Minnesota, and the world, have flocked to these tools for their personal, as opposed to their educational, networking needs.

It is possible that the primary reason for the more academic nature of UThink derives from the fact that blogs on the system are not anonymous. When a blog is created, the first directory in the new blog's URL is the University of Minnesota Internet ID of the user that created the blog. Understandably, many users that may want to write about a controversial topic, or about a personal opinion, have shied away from the system. This is not to say that controversial topics are not posted on UThink. That is far from the truth. However, the lack of anonymity has had an impact on the type of blogs that are created on the system. Many potential users have commented to UThink administrators that the lack of anonymity forced them to choose other platforms to host their blogs, especially personal blogs. Note that there are ways

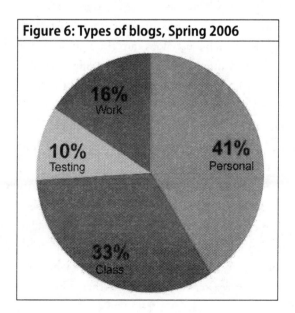

Figure 6: Types of blogs, Spring 2006

16% Work

10% Testing

41% Personal

33% Class

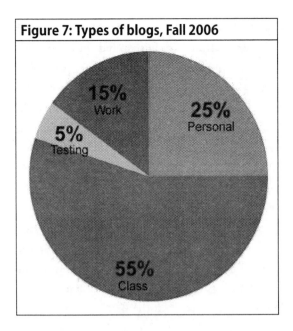

Figure 7: Types of blogs, Fall 2006

to make students attached to a course blog anonymous in compliance with the Family Education Rights and Privacy Act (FERPA).

Who Uses UThink

UThink has a potential user base of over 80,000 faculty, staff, graduate students, and undergraduate students. Over the past three years, over 10,000 Internet IDs have been registered in the system. Registration itself is very easy. All a potential user needs is a University of Minnesota Internet ID and password. This is the same Internet ID and password they use to access their e-mail account or the University of Minnesota registration system. When a user logs into the system for the first time, information from the campus central authentication database is imported into the Movable Type database. In this way, users do not fill out any forms asking for personal information, and registration and initial blog creation are done in under a minute.

Of the 10,000 registered users, we can identify 8,127 University of Minnesota affiliated users. The discrepancy can be attributed to non- University of Minnesota users on UThink, possibly some alumni, and possibly some users who—for whatever reason—no longer use their University

of Minnesota Internet ID and have been deleted from the system. As a result, these users no longer have access to UThink.

Of the users we can identify, 56% are female and 44% are male. In the overall blogosphere, the breakdown is 50% male and 50% female (Lenhart and Fox 2006). Interestingly, the gender breakdown for UThink corresponds with the trend many universities and colleges, including the University of Minnesota, are seeing in higher enrollment numbers for females. Of these users, we can determine the following University of Minnesota status: 60% are undergraduate students, 20% are graduate students, 15% are staff, 3% are faculty, and 2% are guests/unknown.

Finally, of the students (graduate and undergraduate) using the system, approximately 626 majors and disciplines are represented within UThink. We are excited by the wide variety of majors and disciplines on the system. The following majors and disciplines have the most registered UThink users. Note that UThink allows users to create as many blogs as they wish, so many of these users have multiple blogs on the system.

1. English B.A.: 213 users
2. Psychology B.A.: 189
3. Political Science B.A.: 140
4. Journalism B.A.: 135
5. Sociology of Law/Criminology/Deviance B.A.: 89
6. History B.A.: 84
7. Animal Science B.S.: 84
8. Sociology B.A.: 74
9. Applied Economics B.S.: 74
10. Teaching M.Ed.: 70
11. Communication Studies B.A.: 69
12. Architecture B.A.: 68
13. Graphic Design B.F.A.: 67
14. Biology B.S.: 60
15. Art B.A.: 59
16. Mathematics Ph.D.: 55
17. Foundations of Education: Elementary B.S.: 50

18. Family Social Science B.S.: 50
19. Spanish Studies: 49
20. Public Policy M.P.P.: 48
21. Environment and Natural Resources B.S.: 48
22. Global Studies B.A.: 47
23. Environmental Science B.S.: 46
24. Nutrition B.S.: 46
25. Sociology Ph.D.: 45

Some expected degree programs appear at the top of the list, such as writing intensive disciplines like English, journalism, and history. In fact, the top ten majors and disciplines on UThink are mostly within the arts and humanities and the social sciences. This gives the University Libraries a unique marketing opportunity. At the University of Minnesota, new investments are being made in the liberal arts, and there is a renewed commitment to writing within the curriculum. Blogs can be marketed as a tool to help students master the art of writing. Blogs also help in the writing process because they give users a means of receiving feedback in the form of comments. It appears that some majors and disciplines are already making this connection and using UThink to help students learn about the writing process.

We have noticed other interesting details about how our users are utilizing the UThink system. For example, while undergraduate students are the dominant type of user on the system, as a group they usually use UThink only when it is part of a class-based assignment. Most classes on the system require that a student either create a blog and post about a variety of set topics or post entries to a course blog created by the professor. In the latter case, a professor or instructor can make the attached authors anonymous in compliance with FERPA. There are undergraduates who use UThink for personal blogging, but this is not typical. In fact, from what we can tell, most personal blogs on the system are written by graduate students. Apparently, most undergraduates are using such tools as MySpace or Facebook for

their personal blogging and/or networking needs. It also appears that faculty use UThink primarily for courses they teach, while staff use UThink for work-related blogging. Further analysis of these usages is needed.

UThink Goals Revisited

At the beginning of the chapter, our goals for UThink were defined as: to promote intellectual freedom, to help build communities of interest, to investigate the connections between blogging and the traditional academic enterprise, and to retain the cultural memory of the institution. How has UThink fared in meeting these goals?

Promotion of Intellectual Freedom

Libraries in general are the traditional defenders of intellectual freedom in our society. This should be no different on a university campus where it is recognized that the principles of intellectual and academic freedom must be maintained. Besides the breadth of our collections, however, academic libraries may not have many opportunities to demonstrate a commitment to intellectual freedom. UThink offers the University of Minnesota Libraries a very explicit example of these principles in action.

When the idea of UThink was being promoted to the University community, the libraries received some startling suggestions and questions. For example, a professor in the law school asked if we could ban law students from having access to the system. He was concerned that students would write negative comments about law school professors. We refused to ban law school students. A business professor asked if we would monitor the system to make sure that only entries of a certain quality were published. This request was especially troubling within the context of a teaching university where students are learning how to write and may not quite be able to do so at a high level of "quality." In addition, how would "quality" be determined? The University Libraries are not interested in censorship of content in any form. This includes the "quality" of that content. We informed the professor we would not be monitoring the content at all.

During the first three years of UThink, controversial entries have been published and we have been asked to remove specific content. Surprisingly, though, requests for the removal of content have been sporadic. We have received perhaps five removal requests in the last three years. For example, on one occasion a student blogger wrote some negative comments about a local business. The student's blog entry soon reached the top of Google's search results for a search for that business. The business demanded that the entry be removed and threatened potential legal action. In compliance with university policy on academic freedom, the University Libraries refused to remove the content and the threatened legal action proved to be a bluff. The University Libraries have never been forced to take down content by anyone from either within or outside the university. As guardians of intellectual freedom, the University Libraries have encouraged people to write what they want, and when they want, without fear of institutional restraint. We have backed up our users when necessary.

Building Communities of Interest

Most people who write blogs hope that other people will read what they write and maybe even comment on those writings. Whenever a person creates a blog, s/he is entering the community of the blogosphere. Whenever a person creates a blog about a topic, and remains diligent in writing about that topic, that person is also attempting to create a community around that blog or to enter an existing community of topical blogs.

Bloggers and blogs on UThink are no exception. There have been many popular blogs on the system throughout the three years of the project, blogs that have certainly built their own communities. Perhaps the most popular blog to appear on

the system was "Mr. Cheer or Die's Viking Underground," a blog about the Minnesota Vikings football team. This blog was written by an adjunct faculty member in the Pharmacy department, and accounted for the majority of traffic on the system for two years. It has been abandoned and is no longer updated. Another extremely popular blog called "Oil is for Sissies" built a large following by expertly covering the Minneapolis-St. Paul biking scene. This blog was written by a graduate student in the Physics department, and has also been abandoned. In fact, the student left the university to start his own bike shop.

There are also scholarly examples of UThink blogs that have helped build communities of interest. A journalism professor created a successful blog called the "Schwitzer Health News Blog" which critiques health related stories in print and TV news. A graduate student in the department of Family and Social Sciences created a blog called "Six Impossible Things Before Breakfast" which documented her efforts to write her dissertation on African-American adoption. The Center for Studies of Politics and Governance has created a blog called "Smart Politics" which looks at national and local politics and elections. An astronomy graduate student created a blog called "EGAD" which he used to document his studies in Israel, as well as his views on the Israeli-Palestinian conflict. A staff member in our academic computing department created a blog called "Around the Campfire" in which he posts his science fiction writing. A faculty member in the department of Gender, Women, and Sexuality has created numerous blogs for herself and her courses to discuss issues surrounding feminism and female hip-hop culture. All of these blogs are read regularly by university community members and people around the world. The list could go on and on.

Overall, the biggest and most successful community created on UThink is the general community that uses and reads UThink blogs and the main UThink site itself. We have created a number of mechanisms to help people find UThink blogs by title, by subject (through blog post categories), and by searching. We also list most recently updated blogs on the UThink home page, and we provide feeds from local news sources (the Minneapolis *Star Tribune*, Minnesota Public Radio, local TV stations, etc.) as well as national news sources to help keep people informed about news happening close to campus and around the world. It is our hope that UThink can help coordinate a University of Minnesota-flavored response to local, national, and world events, and that people on campus will come to UThink to get this kind of content.

Blogging and the Traditional Academic Enterprise

As noted above, UThink has uniquely positioned the University of Minnesota Libraries to be able to deliver blogging as a new tool to contribute to teaching and learning on campus. We are very excited that UThink is being used in this way so heavily, and future enhancements to UThink will focus on how we can make this connection stronger and more beneficial to the professors and instructors that use the system. We also feel that our efforts with UThink fit nicely within the ACRL Information Literacy Competency Standards for Higher Education (2000). In particular, Standard 4 states: "The information literate student, individually or as a member of a group, uses information effectively to accomplish a specific purpose." Within this standard there are a number of desired outcomes that blogging helps deliver for students such as, "Maintains a journal or log of activities related to the information seeking, evaluating, and communicating process," and "Uses a range of information technology applications in creating the product or performance." We are excited to be able to promote UThink within the context of these outcomes and information literacy standards.

Class-based blogging is also one of our best examples of building community within UThink and of promoting collaboration among blog au-

thors. This is especially true when an instructor creates a single blog for a class, and then attaches all the students in the class to the blog as authors. There are some wonderful examples of classes using UThink to encourage class-based discussion and promote dialog among students.

In addition, thanks to UThink the University Libraries are now considered to be the blogging experts on campus. As a result, we have given numerous presentations and workshops to individuals and departments at the University of Minnesota about using blogs in a class-based setting. This has created new relationships for the University Libraries with departments, instructors, and professors. UThink has provided us with a new way of reaching out and serving the University community.

Retaining the Cultural Memory of the Institution

One of the traditional roles of the University of Minnesota Libraries is to retain the cultural and historical memory of the institution. We currently perform this function through our collections, for example those housed with the University Archives. Blogs offer the Libraries another opportunity for preserving University history. They will be a source of rich content about the life of the University to future researchers..

Before UThink, the only blogging options for the University of Minnesota community were commercial services such as Blogger or LiveJournal. Because these services were hosted off campus, much important University content was being given away. UThink has helped us keep that content on campus. It has provided us with a unique method of encouraging our community to give us content that would have been difficult to preserve in the past.

For example, one of the more challenging tasks for University archivists is to preserve the history and cultural memory of the students of the University. This is typically achieved through the preservation of yearbooks, the student newspaper, and materials relating to student government, clubs, groups, and committees. What has been difficult to track, however, has been student opinions and reactions to what is happening around them. UThink gives us the opportunity to collect this important information. For example, UThink blogs include student reactions to local politics over the past three years, the 2004 presidential elections, the Iraq war, and recent, controversial reorganization issues at the University of Minnesota. Although students still put a lot of this content on off-campus services such as Blogger, Facebook, and MySpace, we are very excited to have the information that UThink offers.

Our methods of archiving and retaining this information are still somewhat in flux. One of our strategies is to treat UThink as a "living" archive. In other words, we are leaving all the content on the system in perpetuity. Rather than moving abandoned blogs to a separate archive, we are just leaving them in place to be searched and read. We are also using Archive-It, a subscription service of the Internet Archive (http://www.archive-it.org/). We started using Archive-It in January 2007, and we are currently archiving the UThink site on a quarterly basis. As a part of this program, we are also archiving other selected University sites. We will unveil this Web archiving program August 2007 as part of the rollout of the University of Minnesota Digital Conservancy, our institutional repository effort (http://conservancy.umn.edu/). UThink will be available in the Conservancy as a part of the University Archives.

Interesting Details

Since we unveiled UThink in April 2004, some interesting, surprising, and unexpected details have emerged about the service.

Site Statistics

According to our server statistics software, UThink is the most heavily hit site maintained by the Uni-

versity of Minnesota Libraries. Our main Web site, www.lib.umn.edu, averages about 140,000 hits and 52,000 page views per day. The UThink system, blog.lib.umn.edu, averages about 197,000 hits and 130,000 page views per day. We were quite surprised by these statistics.

There are a number of possible explanations. For example, the UThink system contains a far larger number of Web pages than the main library Web server. Each new entry into the UThink system generates an individual Web page. This means there are at least 65,000 Web pages on the UThink system, and probably two to three times more when all the Movable Type archiving and templating mechanisms are taken into account. Search engines index all of UThink, and this activity, including crawler indexing and hits coming from search results, probably accounts for a large amount of the hits coming into the server. The presence of UThink blogs on Web search engines presents the library with a unique marketing opportunity. Thousands of people around the world are searching for and ultimately reading content provided through the University of Minnesota Libraries.

Google PageRank

Google gives UThink blogs extremely high page rankings. For example, when a department at the University creates a blog, that blog is usually the top search result for a query about that department. This means that the UThink blog will sometimes rank higher than the departmental home page itself. Why this happens is unknown, but we have speculated that Google must automatically give pages it considers as coming from a library ("blog.**lib**.umn.edu") a higher page rank. This has caused some frustration on campus, but it has also created some interesting opportunities. For example, the ranking phenomenon is also true for individuals who blog on the system. If a student uses UThink to blog, that blog is usually at the top of a Google search for the student's name. This could be marketed as an opportunity for students to better manage their virtual identity. We have all heard the horror stories of potential employers seeing inappropriate pictures or reading less than flattering stories about applicants based on Google searches. Students might conceivably put their best foot forward by using UThink blogs to post a resumé, or samples of their best writing, or pictures of their graduation. Given UThink's high page rank, future employers may see these student blogs first and develop a good first impression about a student or recently-graduated applicant.

Non-traditional Usage of Blogs

We have also been surprised by the variety of non-traditional ways in which the University community is using blogs. Many campus departments are using UThink RSS feeds to populate content on their departmental Web sites, for example a "What's New" section. The Department of Sociology is using UThink blogs to help maintain faculty profiles on their site. Faculty in this department use UThink as a mini-content management system to update their online profiles, and the RSS feeds from UThink populate their profiles on the departmental We site. The College of Liberal Arts is using a UThink blog as a database to maintain a huge list of grant opportunities. With UThink, the college can easily categorize and search for potential grants and keep track of those they have applied for. These are just some of the interesting ways in which the community has extended the functionality of UThink blogs.

Multimedia Through UThink

The Libraries are not only in an excellent position to meet the blogging needs of the University of Minnesota campus, but we are now also highly regarded for our abilities to deliver other media, such as podcasts and video files. As mentioned above, UThink allows for file uploads of up to 65MB and unlimited space for individual blogs. It was also noted that we have installed the MT-Enclosures plugin which automatically adds the necessary "enclosure" tags that make podcasting and

vodcasting possible. Many courses and departments have started to use UThink to deliver this type of content, including the School of Public Health, the department of Gender, Women, and Sexuality, and University Relations, among many others. Due to UThink, the University Libraries are now one of the first places people go on campus not just for blogging, but also to deliver these newer audio and video based technologies.

Support

UThink support usually entails at least two hours a day from one full time employee. We strongly believe that the support the University Libraries offers for UThink is one of the most important aspects of the service. Whether we like it or not, UThink is in competition with off-campus blogging services, and these services move at a very rapid pace to deliver upgrades and new features. One area in which UThink betters these services is through the support we offer to users of the system. While we have endeavored to make the system as easy to use as possible, questions do arise. We try to answer these questions quickly, pleasantly, and comprehensively. This level of support is something that other blogging services do not provide. We hope that our efforts encourage the continued use of the UThink service and that satisfied customers spread the word concerning what we are able to offer.

Future Plans

UThink frequently changes as we add new features and plugins. UThink will most likely upgrade to Movable Type 4 shortly after it becomes available in the fall of 2007. Moving to version 4 will help keep UThink current and better able to compete with other blogging services. Along with this upgrade, we hope to add these enhancements to the system:

♦ Based on the heavy use of UThink for class-based blogging, we would like to expand the system's functionality to make the creation of class related blogs easier. We hope to attach UThink to the University of Minnesota course registration system so that professors can easily create course blogs and attach registered students to them. Currently, professors and instructors must do this by hand.

+ To better comply with FERPA, we hope to make it easier for blog owners to password protect entire blogs or individual blog entries. Currently is possible to password protect a blog, but the blog owner must have a certain level of technical expertise to make it work.

+ We also hope to enhance the file management features of the system. File uploading is available in Movable Type, but the software expects a certain level of server access to properly manage the uploaded files. Movable Type comes with the ability to easily upload files, but we have had to further customize the software to allow people to see their uploaded files and delete them if necessary. In order to better serve users making podcasts or videos, we hope to improve our file management functionality in the future.

+ Along those same lines, other University of Minnesota departments have begun to create new applications to help faculty, staff, and students manage and distribute multimedia files on campus. This includes systems like Media Mill from the College of Liberal Arts (http://mediamill.cla.umn.edu/mediamill/) and GopherTV (http://gophertv.micro.umn.edu/gophertv/). It is our hope to strengthen our ties with these systems by allowing for quick publishing of multimedia files from these systems to UThink, and allowing UThink users to upload large multimedia files to these systems for better file management capabilities.

We would also like to better tie UThink to traditional library services. UThink access has been built into our implementation of SFX, allowing for the posting of OpenURL citations to individual blogs. Many librarians have used this functionality in blogs that deliver news about subject areas and liaison work. We hope to explore further how UThink can help librarians deliver research assistance, and help individual researchers manage and deliver their research output.

Conclusion

The University of Minnesota Libraries are very happy with the success of UThink. In essence, UThink is a story of taking a chance. Before the concept of Library 2.0 was coined, UThink took a chance with the idea that users could contribute something valuable to the library's information environment. In that regard, UThink has been very successful and has prompted the University of Minnesota Libraries to consider other tools that feature user trust.

How long can UThink compete with the larger world of Web 2.0? We have come to the conclusion that this question may not be as important as the concept of taking a chance, pushing the envelope, not being afraid of failure, and changing peoples' perceptions of what a library can deliver in terms of technology and library services. With UThink we are happy to serve the users that want to be served, and through that support we stake our claim in the larger world of Web-based technologies. As UThink is possibly the largest academic blogging site in the United States, clearly our users have responded favorably to our efforts.

UThink has changed perceptions at the University of Minnesota concerning what the University Libraries can offer to the University community. The project has opened doors, created relationships, and convinced many people on campus that the library can be a player in terms of new and exciting technologies. Some people question the value of creating a tool like UThink when there are so many other larger blogging tools to choose from on the World Wide Web. UThink was created when the idea of using blogs in an educational setting was still in its infancy. As a result the system made it possible for the University Libraries to play an important role on campus in demonstrating the potential of blogging as an educational tool. UThink has also allowed the University of Minnesota Libraries to uniquely serve our academic audience in ways that other commercial services cannot. We can offer a much deeper level of support to our faculty, staff, and students, customize our blogging software to better meet the needs of our institution, and through our efforts we can create relationships that connect the libraries to our clientele in different and exciting ways. The vision statement of the University of Minnesota Libraries asserts that the libraries will provide "extraordinary information experiences" for the University of Minnesota and beyond. Through UThink, we feel that we have provided "extraordinary information experiences" for our users, and we look forward to continuing to do so throughout the life of the project.

Acknowledgements

The author would like to thank Bill Tantzen, the University of Minnesota Libraries Web applications programmer behind the magic that is UThink. Without Bill's work customizing Movable Type, there would be no UThink project. In addition, the author would like to thank Paul Bramscher for helping put together the section on UThink's usage statistics.

References

Bruner, Rick E. 2004. Blogging is booming. *iMedia Connection*, April 5. http://www.imediaconnection.com/content/3162.asp.

Downes, Stephen. 2004. Educational blogging. *Educause Review* 39 (September/October): 14-26.

Glenn, David. 2003. Scholars who blog. *Chronicle of Higher Education* 49 (June): A14.

Lenhart, Amanda and Susannah Fox. 2006. Bloggers: A portrait of the internet's new storytellers. *Pew Internet*, July 19. http://www.pewinternet.org/PPF/r/186/report_display.asp.

http://acrl.ala.org/L2Initiatives/index.php?title=Chapter_7/

Discussing Student Engagement: An Information Literacy Course Blog

Gregory Bobish

Abstract

Student discussion in a one-credit information literacy course at the University Libraries at the University at Albany was flagging, with one or two students making most of the contributions. In order to stimulate discussion and broaden participation, a course blog was developed. This blog functions both as a clearinghouse for course information and last-minute announcements as well as a forum for discussion. Most importantly for student engagement, students are required to comment on several information literacy-related blog postings as part of their homework. This not only means that every student has to process and respond to course material in writing, but also enables each student to see what his or her peers have to say and ensures that everyone is ready for class discussions. Students have been very receptive to the initiative, participating more often and in more depth than is required. With each semester, new assignments and new technologies have increased the effectiveness of this flexible tool.

Introduction

This chapter describes my implementation of a blog in my section of a credit-bearing information literacy course at the University Libraries at the University at Albany. There are several instructors at the University Libraries who use blogs in their classes to one degree or another. In this chapter, I discuss my particular use of the tool, and how it has evolved and been integrated into my class since its creation in 2006.

Motivation

Instruction librarians at the University Libraries have been teaching our one-credit information literacy course for seven years. Each new class is an opportunity to improve and update course content and the techniques for conveying it. Course sections meet once a week for seven weeks, for two hours per session. The course is based on the Information Literacy Competency Standards for Higher Education developed by the Association of College and Research Libraries (ACRL). While the practical aspects of information literacy (such as learning the available tools and skills necessary to narrow a topic to find relevant information, and evaluation of resources) are obviously quite important and comprise a major portion of the course, students in my classes have been more likely to see the personal relevance of issues raised under the umbrella of Standard 5:

The information literate student understands many of the economic, legal, and social issues surrounding the use of information and accesses and uses information ethically and legally (Association of College and Research Libraries 2000).

Focusing on copyright, file-sharing, privacy issues, the rise of online communities, and other current topics has generated some of the best class discussions and brought a depth to the course which is sometimes difficult to create in only seven class meetings. Unfortunately, while some discus-

---

Gregory Bobish, University at Albany, SUNY, e-mail: gbobish@uamail.albany.edu.

sions have been wonderful, others have been less so. Class dynamics, personalities, and even the weather can determine whether everyone is awake and eager to share their opinions or half-asleep and barely willing to say "yes" or "no".

Faced with the opportunity to engage students in productive discussion of fascinating issues, but frustrated by not knowing from one day to the next whether it would happen, I was constantly on the lookout for possible solutions. My search was even more compelling because I knew from homework assignments that some of the most intelligent students in the class were not participating.

During this time, I had been reading widely about Library 2.0 and Web 2.0. I wanted to incorporate what seemed to be a group of great community-generating technologies and ideas into a course that was based around finding, sharing, and creating information. Since the 2.0 technology with which I was most familiar was blogs, mostly through reading/commenting on others', but also through a little experimentation of my own, this was the route I decided to investigate.

Examining types of motivation can help to explain why some students participate more than others. Encouraging intrinsic motivation (the genuine desire to learn) is more desirable than stimulating extrinsic motivation (reward/punishment) in many instances because it encourages students to go beyond what is strictly required for an assignment or a grade, and to look more deeply into subject matter. Unfortunately exercises and curricular elements that tap intrinsic motivation often require more class time than is available in a short course (Jacobson and Xu 2004, 3-19). In a required general education course, much of the motivation at the beginning tends towards the extrinsic (grades). Using a blog to communicate with students outside of class would be one way to address motivation issues and to increase student-instructor contact time.

Another factor that increases student engagement is a sense of autonomy (Jacobson and Xu

2004, 87-99). When students feel that they have a role in choosing what or how to learn in a class, they are more likely to "buy into doing it" (Crow 2007, 49-50). Since blogs are by nature flexible, I felt it would be relatively easy to find opportunities for student choice.

What I found most intriguing about using a blog as a course tool was the opportunity for interaction. Creating interpersonal rapport and a positive learning environment goes a long way towards getting students interested in a class, through teaching behaviors such as "encouraging questions and comments", and "assuming equality" (Jacobson and Xu 2004, 55-64). Comments are the very essence of a blog, and all comments appear on an equal footing, ranked only by time of posting. By using a course blog, I hoped to develop an atmosphere of open and equal communication amongst students as well as between students and the instructor.

Would it be Feasible?

According to the Pew Internet and American Life Project, 57% of online teens have created some form of content for the Internet (Lenhart and Madden 2005), so I could reasonably assume that most students would be familiar with the blog format and would not need extensive technical assistance in its use. With a couple of exceptions, this has proven to be the case. Blogs also help to support different learning styles through the use of multimedia and interactive content, and by allowing students to actively produce information (Richardson 2006), all of which encourages broader participation in class discussions. One of the questions often raised by those contemplating the use of classroom blogs is how likely students are to participate (Coulter and Draper 2006). This may be more of an issue in one-shot instruction sessions or ungraded classes, as there are examples of longer or graded courses in which participation was quite lively (Downes 2004; Glass and Spiegelman 2007).

In addition to the practicality of blogs as a tool, there is also something to be said for jumping in and using the tools students are using more and more in their own lives. One of our roles as librarians, particularly user education librarians, is arguably to be "instructors about society's information environment" (Cohen 2007). If we accept this role, then it makes sense to help students gain proficiency in effectively creating and retrieving information in as many formats as possible, from print-based sources to the latest online tools, and to point out the benefits and drawbacks of each.

2.0 Trends

In the past, the Web presence for the course had been limited to a static Web page. While informative, this was a very one-sided medium. Essentially, I could put the information up, and students could read it. In the 2.0 world where user participation is the name of the game, communication channels need to be at least two-way, if not more. By creating a course blog as a one-stop clearinghouse for course information, last-minute announcements, and homework assignments, I have been able to implement several Library 2.0 concepts: radical trust/librarians cede control, taking the library to users, and perpetual beta. Briefly addressed below, more detailed examples will follow in the main section of the chapter.

Radical Trust/Librarians Cede Control

Students (and theoretically anyone who stumbles upon the blog) are able to post comments freely, with no approval from the instructor necessary. This was not done immediately, as it opens the blog to the usual risks of trolls and spam. Eventually, however, students pointed out that they were never sure if their comments had been posted, and often they sent comments repeatedly before realizing that approval was pending. This, coupled with the fact that they wanted to see what others had already written, prompted me to open comments for immediate posting when the next session of the course began.

Taking the Library to Users

Students are accustomed to Web 2.0 and they want more than just something to look at; they want to participate. A blog enables two-way communication. When students start responding to one another's comments, the discussion becomes even more complex.

With everything from the syllabus to homework to information about snow cancellations in one place, students can access the course when and where they are ready. This is true not only for course materials, but for instructor assistance as well. By adding an easily-created instant messaging widget to the main page of the blog, I have enabled students to get real-time help. While I make no guarantees of availability outside of normal business hours, I am happy to respond if I happen to be online and notice a student e-mail or instant message. The student is usually surprised and appreciative to hear from me at her or his point of need.

Perpetual Beta

As is appropriate to the experimental nature of many 2.0 initiatives, this course blog is a work in progress. Student feedback comes in, colleagues offer contributions and suggestions, my personal skill with 2.0 technologies increases, and the blog becomes richer and more integrated with the rest of the course. One of the great benefits of blog technology, as compared to static Web pages or more complex course management tools, is its ease of use and the opportunities it presents to quickly post new materials. Mere minutes from the beginning of a class, I can have an idea for a new exercise, or find an interesting link, and barring any major network catastrophes it will be posted and available to students immediately. Sometimes this does not go entirely as planned, but even the failures often lead to interesting discussions.

The Initiative

During the summer of 2006, in preparation for the coming fall semester, my focus was on student engagement. As I reviewed the ACRL standards for information literacy, the more practical points lent themselves to in-class exercises and homework assignments. Students can begin to learn how to use a certain database to find relevant materials or how to evaluate Web resources by simply trying it, getting feedback from the instructor and/or peers, and trying it again. Students are generally willing to do these sorts of exercises, provided they are sufficiently interested in the associated research project.

Unfortunately, many students are less likely to participate in class discussions that focus on the broader implications of the way information is created and shared. Bringing up the topic of illegal music downloading might get their attention and a few chuckles initially, as they wonder what the instructor's reaction will be to the fact that none of them will admit to having purchased a song in any format. After this superficial interest, however, there is rarely much interest in going deeper into why this state of affairs has arisen, or whether it is a positive or a negative development.

I knew from discussions with students after class that they did hold opinions but were often uncomfortable sharing them in class. Written assignments allowed me to see some of these opinions, but what I really wanted was to facilitate discussion among students, rather than to read a student's approximation of what I might want to hear.

Enter the blog. During the breaks in class, my students IM friends, check MySpace and Facebook pages, and comment or read comments in various online environments, including blogs. Some even seem to be typing something during lectures, when their screens are blank. If this form of communication engages students to such a degree, I reasoned that it must somehow be useful as a learning tool.

Starting the Blog

The first step was to learn how to create and manage such a tool. I had tried more complex course management systems in the past, and for a course

that only meets seven times, they had proven to be more than was necessary. Static Web pages did not allow for the amount of interactivity required, while a wiki would have required a more thorough redesign of the course than I was looking for at this point. Based on my previous experiences with blogs, I had an idea that this was the technology that would meet current needs and be expandable if necessary.

So, one day at the reference desk I created a blogger.com account for the course, and began to play around with the design and content. Our Library 2.0 guru happened to walk by during this first try, and mentioned that we had just gotten a number of additional licenses for the Libraries' Movable Type blog installation. She suggested that this course blog be hosted locally. For the past several months, the University Libraries had been running its own in-house blog program, but I had not known that accounts were available for course-related blogs (University Libraries). We had a talk about the advantages of local hosting: expert help on site, in-house guarantee of the application, more flexibility in administering the blog, and not least the opportunity to participate in a new library-wide 2.0 initiative. As a consequence of this talk, I drafted a brief proposal and submitted it via a Web form. Soon after, the course blog was set up and waiting to be developed.

Since it was summer, I was able to experiment widely with the appearance of the blog, and had fun with some remarkably ugly designs before settling on a fairly plain look. This experimentation enabled me to learn how the pages were structured and which parts of the code affected what. This knowledge came in very handy later on when I began to try out various widgets. Many of my experiments with the code had quite undesirable results, but this was a very important part of the process. I made most of my mistakes when nobody was looking at the blog, so that there were very few embarrassing moments once students were using it for class.

First Try

Once the appearance and general functionality of the blog were in place, it was time to figure out just how to use this tool to generate the discussion and engagement I was hoping for. I made one important determination: the blog would not be just another place where students would have to remember to go. The blog was to be the central repository for everything information literacy-related. To make this a reality, links to the syllabus, library Web site, citation style guides, and the general information literacy pages are all available at the top of the page. Since students are always online, the course would go where they were!

On the first day of class, the first posting went up: *Welcome to UNL 205, Information Literacy.*

This posting provided basic information about the purpose of the blog, a link to the syllabus and to that day's PowerPoint slides, as well as links to library maps. It also came with the following warning: *Please refrain from posting irrelevant or offensive material, as it will not **get approved** for posting, and will not be credited toward your homework grade.* Student comments would be held for moderation before appearing on the blog. At this

---

Figure 1. The blog homepage

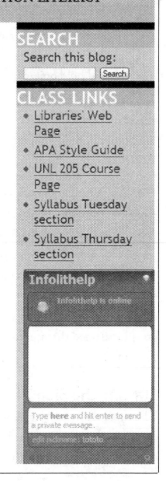

Information Literacy

THIS IS A PAGE FOR STUDENTS IN UNL 205 -- INFORMATION LITERACY

SEPTEMBER 11, 2007

ATTENTION: There are 2 different sections of this class

There has been some confusion about due dates.

When looking for your homework assignments, find the Categories section on the right hand side of the page.

If you're in the Tuesday section, click Tuesday Homework.

If you're in the Thursday section, click Thursday Homework.

This should hopefully clear up any confusion about due dates.

Also, starting this week, the assignments are not the same for different sections, so please be sure you're looking at the right section. The day the section meets will be part of the title of all homework posts.

Any questions, please ask!

Posted by GB at 10:38 AM | Permalink | Comments (0)

Week 3 Assignment - TUESDAY CLASS

1. Find 1 SCHOLARLY, 1 POPULAR, and 1 NEWSPAPER article on your topic, and complete the 3 ARTICLES WORKSHEET, including citations and annotations.

2. NONE OF THE 3 ARTICLES MAY BE FROM THE PERIODICAL'S

SEARCH

Search this blog:

[   ] [Search]

CLASS LINKS

- Libraries' Web Page
- APA Style Guide
- UNL 205 Course Page
- Syllabus Tuesday section
- Syllabus Thursday section

Infolithelp

Infolithelp is online

Type **here** and hit enter to send a private message.

edit nickname: tototo

beginning level, I was not very "radically trusting" or "ceding control." In fact, looking back on it, the first class with the blog was in some respects just written assignments handed in online — just barely 2.0.

Students could comment, but would they? Well, they would at least comment on the assignments that required it. Students are required to comment on three postings, always on something related to the social, legal, or ethical implications of the use of information. Sometimes these postings come before the class discussion of the subject, sometimes after. There is always a choice of two or three topics for each assignment, in case one of the topics is not of interest to them.

The first "blog assignment," as they came to be known, was simply the class discussion topic post-ed to the blog. The assignment was either to react to some privacy issue we had already discussed in class that day, or to share a personal experience that related to the topic. Some students were fairly blasé about it, and had faith that banks, businesses, or the government would implement the needed safeguards. Most students expressed some concern, however, and a number shared stories of compromised personal information. The first student comment provides a window into privacy issues outside of the United States:

> The lack of privacy is becoming a serious problem. In Eastern Asian countries such as Korea and Japan, there is a personal cell phone tracking service, similar to the GPS navigation system of the united states. However, the difference is that any person can track the location of another just by typing in their cell phone number. Once the number is entered the service will provide the exact location of where that phone is located.

> This summer I was tracked by a friend that I was trying to avoid at the time. Just by typing in my number, he was able to find my present location. The most alarming aspect of this system is that the system can track one's present location. This is a clear invasion of privacy.

Another student shares a family experience:

> My parent's identity was stolen multiple times. Now in order for them to use their credit cards over the phone they need to provide a lot of additional information. It is really amazing how easy it is to steal someone's identification, especially over the internet. I recently read an article on the subject and they explained how the thieves would set up exact replica sites of (lets say)

Figure 2. Blog Assignment 2

« Week 3 Assignment - Periodical Articles | Main | Week 4 assignment - Websites »

| Blog assignment 2

There are 2 links below that deal in one way or another with information ethics issues. Comment on one or both of them. Offer your opinion, reaction, or questions raised by the links in a few sentences.

Or, if you see or experience something else related to the issues we discuss in class, you can comment on that too.

1. This is a (very) short story set in the near future. Bonus: there are references to at least 2 popular songs in here - the first person to post a comment identifying one or both of them gets one bonus point on your final grade for each song you name.

Bruce Sterling story

2. Cell phones in Kenya - Africa has the fastest growing population of cell phone users in the world. Think about how this easy access to each other and to information might affect a rapidly developing society. What are the implications of this trend?

Why Africa?

You must post your comment before class on October 3, 2006.

Song/Poem references: THE BONUS POINT CONTEST IS NOW CLOSED - THANKS FOR PLAYING!

The two I was looking for were:

The Sound of Silence - Simon and Garfunkel - Found by Elizabeth, Areji, Marie, and James
Suedehead - Morrissey -Found by Areji

BUT- people found several other interesting things

Howl - a poem by Allen Ginsberg - Found by Areji and Shun
I should be allowed to think - They Might Be Giants -Found by Cassie
The Spirit of Radio - Rush - Found by Diane

ebay and tricked them into willingly giving their credit card information out.

An unexpected benefit of these first postings was that as each student shared an experience or information about their own experiences, all students (and the instructor) were provided with a list of twenty-three different privacy issues *connected to personal, everyday experience*. When I had previously asked the same question in class discussion, on a good day one or two students would share a brief anecdote. This was encouraging!

The next blog assignment asked students to comment on either the Bruce Sterling short story *"I saw the best minds of my generation destroyed by Google"* (Sterling 2006) or on an article about the growth of the cell phone market in Kenya (Massachusetts Institute of Technology 2007).

Comments ranged from the brief, but honest:

No joke, the Bruce Sterling story was weird. When i first sat down to read it, i got through the first paragraph and i thought the person who wrote this must have been on crack. I read it a second time and still found it too strange for my liking and i didnt catch the songs in the article either. I am actually going to ask a friend if he can find them though.

to several longer, intelligent considerations of the pros and cons of the issues raised such as this one:

(1)   Bruce Sterling Story
If our minds and lives are totally controlled by the information world, but not by ourselves, it would be a disaster for all human beings. As we don't use our brains to think, we won't have our own ideas, opinions and innovation. Also, an emphasis on on-line communication among people rather than face-to-face communication would make the relationships worse as many psychologists

point out that the latter is the better way of communication. If we live as mentioned in the story, we are like robots which have no their own thinking. We are then no longer human beings.

(2) Why Africa ?
The growing uses of mobile phones in Kenya may contribute to its economic development and enhance the literacy of its people. First, a mobile phone user needs to have a basic level of literacy in order to text messages (SMS) and read information through the mobile phone. Besides, the easy access to market information through mobile phones would also help the increase of trades throughout the country. The fastest growing mobile phone market in Kenya would help its technological and economic developments.

Every student in the class commented — many on both of the topics, even though the assignment only required them to read one of the articles. This was quite heartening, since for previous in-class discussions it was clear that many students had not read anything at all. We had briefly discussed related issues in the class before this assignment, but not these particular articles.

In the next class, we followed up at the beginning with a few examples from the comments, and students were actually more comfortable talking in class when they saw that their peers were coming up with similar types of comments online. This particular assignment included an additional option which proved popular and a source for discussions. The Bruce Sterling story includes references to a number of popular songs and a poem, so I offered one extra-credit point for each reference students could find. Some students found one or another of the songs I had found, or the poem. A few also found references to songs I had not known about. Some pointed out songs that referenced the songs referenced in the story. This led to a discussion of how culture feeds on itself and then into the original intent of U.S. copyright law to offer an incentive for creativity as well as to protect the rights of copyright holders. One student found some of the song lyrics misquoted on a lyrics Web site, and this led to a discussion of what would be the most reliable source for song lyrics - the CD case? the band's Web site?

Several students pointed out that because comments had to be approved, many were not available until just before class. This had resulted in a number of repetitive comments. This issue was one of the first things I addressed before the next seven-week session of the class began.

Second Seven-Week Session

Based on student requests during and after the first seven-week session of the course, I decided to open the comments for immediate posting, rather than holding them for approval. This was a little nerve-wracking, since it meant that anyone could post offensive or at least irrelevant material. So far, however, this has not happened. Radical trust has been rewarded with excellent comments. There has been an added benefit: once students realized that I trusted them to contribute valuable information to the class online, they were much more willing to participate in classroom discussions.

Another factor that has contributed to student engagement has been the use of multimedia content such as Flash movies, videos, and online games. I had previously used several online movies as examples in class, but the only way students could access them afterwards was by typing the URL into their browsers. This is not a difficult thing to do, but even that small extra step was sometimes enough of a roadblock to discourage much follow-up discussion. With the blog, every type of material is a click away. Students have commented both online and in class that they like these materials and have even shown them to friends outside of class. It certainly helps that much of this material is humorous, and taken

from popular culture, such as *The Daily Show* and various animated shorts. Connecting information literacy topics to real life is one of the best ways of engaging students I have yet found. It also creates a common ground where students and instructor can meet, thereby encouraging the sharing of opinions and ideas.

Use of the class blog as a communication tool started off slowly, but has increased in frequency and complexity. Originally, students could submit a comment to ask a question, and the comment would be directed to my e-mail account in addition to being posted on the blog. Although this eliminated the problem of students losing my e-mail address, there was one aspect that was less than ideal. During business hours, students could expect a response within a couple hours at most, but outside of that, particularly on weekends, it might be a few days before they heard from me. This was better than waiting for a once-a-week office hour, to be sure, but still not the 24/7 situation students are used to in many other aspects of their lives. I would not dare to suggest that I intend to be available 24/7, but I did want to improve the situation somewhat. As I explored other blogs and various Web sites, I was on the lookout for something that might help.

Eventually I stumbled upon the Meebo IM widget (http://www.meebome.com/). Meebo.com is an instant messaging Web site that allows you to check several IM accounts at once, from any computer, without having to install instant messaging software. The Meebo widget is a small instant messaging window that can be embedded in any Web page, in this case the course blog. This is done by pasting in a few lines of code provided by Meebo. If visitors have a question or comment, they can type it into this window and it will immediately be seen in my meebo.com account. I had given out my IM screen name before, with little success. What was appealing here was the convenience for students. By installing the Meebo widget directly

Figure 3. Meebo instant messaging widget

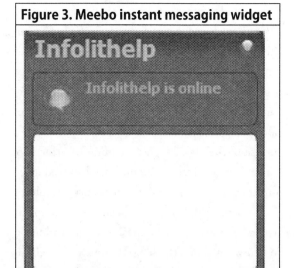

on the main class blog page, students looking at an assignment would be able to ask me a question without leaving the page. I would then receive the question wherever I was logged on to a computer and be able to respond immediately. When I briefly explained this new box on the blog, I told the class that whenever I was online, I would be logged in to the account and willing to answer questions.

While it is not quite true to say that there was an overwhelming response, several students immediately began using this tool to ask questions, often while they were in the library less than 100 yards from my office. Some asked questions during the day, but the greatest usage was in the early to mid evening, when I would answer questions from my home computer. Most of these questions were more in-depth and focused than I was used to getting in person. Even though not every student uses this means of communication, I consider the addition of the widget an absolute success.

Spring 2007

The winter break of 2006 was spent in consideration of the blog experiment. In most ways, it was successful. The general formatting of the blog and the way it was integrated into existing course content had reached a point where only minor tweaks were necessary. At this point the novelty of the tool was wearing off a bit and I had the luxury of thinking more about the blog assignments themselves. Issues of privacy, file sharing, and other information ethics issues still predominated, but I wanted to steer at least some of the discussion towards self-examination. How could I get students to look more closely at their own information seeking and processing behaviors in addition to examining what others were doing? Partly, this was being accomplished in the general discussions and reactions to news stories, but these were not deep enough. Two attempts to address this in the Spring Semester 2007 are detailed below. One was more successful than I could have imagined, the other...less so. I will begin with the less successful attempt.

I have been exploring the use of online games to enhance learning, partly inspired by the success of the song-finding contest described above. Among the issues we discuss in class are the ways information creators might try to influence your perception of a given topic. Often these ways are obvious, for example using attractive people to make what they are doing/selling seem attractive as well. On the other hand, sometimes the methods can be more insidious, for example subliminal marketing or intentionally leaving out relevant information.

In my online wanderings I discovered a game based on the "Stroop effect" (Manuel). This is the idea that one task can delay the processing of another (Wikipedia 2007). The game is simple: words such as "red," "green" and other colors come at you, but they are printed in a color other than the one the letters spell. The game is to click as fast as possible on the correct color of the type, rather than the word.

The aim of putting this on the blog as an in-class exercise was twofold. First, playing the game would be a quick break after a fairly long lecture about using online databases. Second, it would lead to a discussion of the brain's information processing behavior and how it can be used to influence our perception of a message. The first aim was entirely fulfilled. Students loved it, and a contest developed, with one of the quietest students in class utterly demolishing the scores of everyone else. The second aim did not work as well as it might have. After five minutes or so of gaming, I attempted to introduce the idea that producers of information might exploit, if not this particularity of the human mind, then other similar ones, in order to influence our reception of their message. A few students seemed to get the gist of it, and brought up the idea of subliminal messages, and the "Young Girl-Old Woman" illusion (Weisstein 2002) as examples of the type of thing that might happen. Most students, though, did not quite see the connection. As a result of my over-exuberance, I had attempted the exercise without adequate preparation and did not have much background material to support myself. The possibility of posting something you have discovered thirty minutes before class is both a blessing and a curse. It may be that the "perpetual beta" mindset was a bit too strong in me that day.

After the partial failure of the Stroop game exercise, I wavered a bit in my intention to open up the last blog assignment of the semester, but went ahead anyway. Instead of responding to a specific article or video, students were asked to reflect on the course and on information literacy in general, and to comment on how they thought the course could be improved, or to suggest something that they would like to learn about. Concerned that I would get too many "This teacher is great" comments hoping to influence grades, I made this final posting optional, for two points of extra credit. I was surprised that about half of the class posted something, when there had been easier opportu-nities for extra credit that nobody took advantage of. There were still some comments that seemed grade-related, but there were also several excellent, well thought-out comments that went beyond what was required. One example is remarkably creative:

The 'Internets 2.0' has created an environment where information is so readily available and in such abundance that it's totally changed the way we learn and interact as a culture.

Sure, it's great to be able to hop onto a computer and find video of a fat kid playing with a light saber, a few addictive and pointless games like Line Rider or 50 States, or maybe even comment on your favorite fan Web site or update your personal blog, but what do we do when we really need to know things?

CNN?
Wikipedia?
Google?
As students we must be able to discern the garbage from the gems, a difficult task in an InterBlogoSphereWebNets 2-Point-Pwns-Yur-SOULZ where nothing is dated, signed, or copywritten.

So we cross our fingers and hold our breath when we say that John McCain won the presidential debate, because Mit Romney and Ron Paul are both claiming the same honor on their Web sites.

This class proves that we need to be careful, fastidious, methodical and thorough when gathering information. And that's a good enough lesson to get out of college.

In the information age, it's best to get the right information.

Another examines an entire lifetime of research experience:

> Reminiscing all the way back to my grade school days, I feel it is amazing how far the internet has come. In grade school, when a project was due, we would be taken to the library and have to do our research using the books available to us. As I advanced into middle school and high school, the internet was gaining mass popularity and acceptance throughout the world but not in schools. I clearly remember my teachers repeatedly stating we are forbidden to use the internet as a research tool for our projects. My teachers felt it was not proper to get information on a specific subject as quickly as the internet provided us. Instead, according to them it would be to our advantage to use the library and search the collection of books for the more time we put into the project, the better it would turn out. Coming to college, I noticed that the internet being used as a research tool was much more accepted then it was in high school. However, attacks on using such Web sites as Google, Yahoo, and Wikipedia were common throughout my courses. Yet, I found it quite interesting that this class embraced those Web sites and focused on them as well. In none of my classes was I ever allowed to use Wikipedia as a source until this course. I feel this class has taken the first step into internet modernity and could set a great example for other courses. Information is information. It should not matter whether it is retrieved from a book or a Web site, as long as it is accurate. We should accept the internet and the information for what it is and not censor it.

This was in response to the following assignment: "Free choice topic — anything related to anything we've discussed in class, or observations or sugges-tions you have about this class, the blog, or library use in general." A student *chose* to analyze all of his previous research techniques. Wonderful.

Future Plans

Perpetual beta will continue. There will probably be more "Stroop" effects, but it is hoped that these will be few and balanced by many insightful comments. There will be more interactivity such as games and Flash interactions. These are the things that have engaged students the most, so I will continue to search for relevant materials that require interaction, and will use the flexibility of the blog to make them available both in and out of class.

Student participation will continue to increase. One thing I will try next semester is to have students write an entry on which other students will comment, rather than everyone just commenting on my entries. This might increase the risk of unfriendly comments, but radical trust has richly rewarded me in the past so I am sticking with it. I hope to see opinions expressed to other students which might not have been expressed to me as an instructor.

Currently there are four instructors in the University Libraries who maintain information literacy course blogs, and there is one blog dedicated to information literacy-related current events to which we can all contribute. We share ideas and technical tips on an informal basis, and encourage each other as we venture into the unknown. As our program develops, a local "information literacy instructors who blog" wiki might be a future place to share successes.

I also occasionally check to see what is going on in the wider world of information literacy blogs to keep up with new developments. Although most publicly available information literacy blogs that I have found seem to be more librarian-oriented than course-related, I have recently discovered a number of interesting blogs that are integrated with information literacy classes to varying degrees. I plan to keep up with these blogs, and hope that the wiki accompanying this book will become a central place for instructors to share our ideas and experiments.

Now that the course blog has proven to be a success, I plan to experiment with other 2.0 technologies. Wikis are attractive as a vehicle for group work, and the University Libraries may be implementing this technology soon. Our User Education department has been developing podcasts and other multimedia projects. Involving students in the production of these materials as part of the course would be interactivity at its best, and will give them an opportunity to deal directly with issues such as copyright involved in producing information for publication.

Conclusion

…This blog system also made me more interested in this class and kept me wanting to read and learn more about how to research the right way. Thank you for this class experience. — Student Comment

As evidenced by the comment above, and numerous other online and in-person comments, students are appreciative of the way the blog works within the class structure. Since the main goal of this initiative is to engage students in discussion, it is an almost unqualified success. Students participate more deeply in discussions, both online and in class. The opportunity to add content to the course blog encourages more of a give and take atmosphere in the class and exposes students to many different perspectives on the issues at hand.

Figure 4. Blog usage statistics

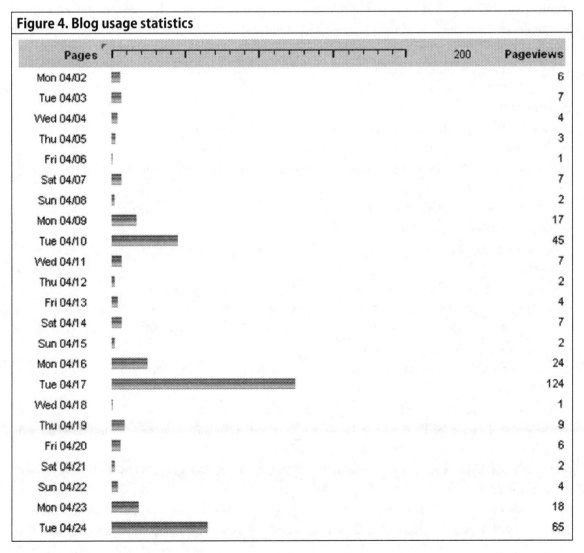

Pages	200	Pageviews
Mon 04/02		6
Tue 04/03		7
Wed 04/04		4
Thu 04/05		3
Fri 04/06		1
Sat 04/07		7
Sun 04/08		2
Mon 04/09		17
Tue 04/10		45
Wed 04/11		7
Thu 04/12		2
Fri 04/13		4
Sat 04/14		7
Sun 04/15		2
Mon 04/16		24
Tue 04/17		124
Wed 04/18		1
Thu 04/19		9
Fri 04/20		6
Sat 04/21		2
Sun 04/22		4
Mon 04/23		18
Tue 04/24		65

Students ask more complex questions through the IM widget after class and during office hours. In fact, for the first time, a student came back a month after the course ended and sought out my help for a large research project.

Starting in the second semester, usage statistics became available, and I am now able to see quantitatively when the blog is being visited. It should be apparent from the chart below which day of the week the course met, but even on other days a few students were stopping by.

Technical issues were largely nonexistent, due entirely to the decision to use our local blog server and its concomitant local support. When a rare issue arose (for example, accessing the administrative module from off-campus), it was resolved within a day. Students had no problems whatsoever understanding the functionality of the blog, presumably because they were so accustomed to using similar tools outside of class.

An unanticipated benefit of the blog was the opportunity to go over student postings and reflect on what worked and what did not. I was able to do this after the course ended, and even sometimes while the course was still in progress. This has given me a new way to create or redesign exercises based on all of my students' points of view on the topics discussed, rather than only those few expressed verbally in class.

This initiative is one of those happy occasions in which the tool fits the job perfectly. Where a one-time instruction session might not require a Web presence at all, and a full semester-length course might benefit from a more robust course management system, our information literacy course is of a medium length. The class blog has proven to be just flexible enough to contain relevant course information and communication tools without overwhelming students (and the instructor) with unnecessary features.

References

Association of College and Research Libraries. 2000. Information literacy competency standards for higher education. http://www.ala.org/ala/acrl/acrlstandards/informationliteracycompetency.cfm.

Cohen, Laura B. 2007. Academic libraries and 2.0. http://liblogs.albany.edu/library20/2007/08/academic_libraries_and_20.html

Coulter, Priscilla and Lani Draper. 2006. Blogging it into them: Weblogs in information literacy instruction. *Journal of Library Administration* 45 (1/2): 101-115.

Crow, Sherry R. 2007. Information Literacy: What's motivation got to do with it? *Knowledge Quest* 35 (March/April): 48-52.

Downes, Stephen. 2004. Educational blogging. *Educause Review* (September/October): 14-26.

Glass, Richard and Marsha Spiegelman. 2007. Making their Web 2.0 space an information literacy space. Presented at the 39th conference of the SUNY Librarians Association, Throggs Neck, NY. http://polar.sunynassau.edu/~rmweb20/ppt/sunyla3.pdf.

Jacobson, Trudi and Lijuan Xu. 2004. *Motivating students in information literacy classes.* New York: Neal-Schuman Publishers, Inc.

Lenhart, Amanda and Mary Madden. 2005. Teen content creators and consumers: More than half of online teens have created content for the internet; and most teen downloaders think that getting free music files is easy to do. http://www.pewinternet.org/PPF/r/166/report_display.asp

Manuel, Rob. Click the colour (and not the word) by Rob Manuel [B3TA : WE LOVE THE WEB]. http://www2.b3ta.com/clickthecolour/.

Massachusetts Institute of Technology. 2007. EPROM - Why Africa? http://eprom.mit.edu/whyafrica.html.

Richardson, Will. 2006. *Blogs, wikis, podcasts and other powerful web tools for classrooms.* Thousand Oaks, CA: Corwin Press.

Sterling, Bruce. 2006. I saw the best minds of my generation destroyed by Google. *New Scientist.* September 15. http://www.newscientisttech.com/article/mg19125691.800;jsessionid=OPEGCJHNALIL?DCMP=ILC-OpenHouse&nsref=mg19125691.800INT.

University Libraries. University at Albany. LIBlogs. http://liblogs.albany.edu/.

Weisstein, Eric W. 2002. Young girl-old woman illusion. From MathWorld—A Wolfram Web resource. October 28. http://mathworld.wolfram.com/YoungGirl-OldWomanIllusion.html

Wikipedia. 2007. Stroop effect. http://en.wikipedia.org/wiki/Stroop_task (accessed October 16, 2007).

Building Library 2.0 into Information Literacy: A Case Study

Susan Sharpless Smith, Erik Mitchell, and Caroline Numbers

Abstract

This chapter describes a pilot program at Wake Forest University's Z. Smith Reynolds Library that was designed to revitalize our information literacy instruction through the introduction of Library 2.0 concepts. The pilot explored new methods and technologies that can be used to engage students in a collaborative environment. The goal was to produce a class that is more relevant to how students learn through using current information issues, collaborative social software, and information management applications. Included is a discussion of conventional information literacy program standards and educational theories that informed the framework of the pilot's structure.

Introduction

After three years of teaching a one-credit information literacy elective at Wake Forest University's Z. Smith Reynolds Library, the authors saw a need to revitalize our class to make it more compatible with student approaches to research. We saw that students were coming to the class with a set of core information seeking practices that they have adopted through their use of the Internet for personal and previous academic work, and that trying to teach them to abandon those practices in favor of the traditional idea of the "right" way to conduct research was unsuccessful. By approaching information literacy from their existing skill set, we hoped to demystify information management and research methods, assist students in bridging technology skills, and inform them of current information issues.

Students have become more proficient at conducting research over the last several years as technological advances have become increasingly available to them. The landscape of available information now includes both library resources and a wide variety of freely available electronic resources. When taking this "new world" into consideration, we began to re-think the way we were teaching the course "Accessing Information in the 21st Century." In doing this, we questioned the foundations of our information literacy curriculum with respect to current methods over traditional methods, and the relevance of our own approaches to information discovery, access, and evaluation.

The course modules emphasized the various information tools that students use socially as the foundation for discussing information literacy concepts, and encouraged students to use these tools in other information seeking contexts. In re-formatting course content, we endeavored to utilize Library 2.0 concepts in the framework of accepted information literacy standards and educational theory.

Information Literacy Standards

It is generally accepted that an information literate citizenry is an essential goal in today's global world. A customary description of information literacy is "the set of skills needed to find, retrieve, analyze and use information" (Association of College & Research Libraries 2007). But, with the proliferation of information sources and availability today, this definition seems a bit one-dimensional. A more

Susan Sharpless Smith, e-mail: smithss@wfu.edu; Erik Mitchell, mitcheet@wfu.edu; and Caroline Numbers, numbercj@wfu.edu, all of Wake Forest University.

comprehensive definition of information literacy is "the ability to locate, manage, critically evaluate, and use information for problem solving, research, decision making, and continued professional development" (Orr, Appleton, and Wallin 2001).

Information literacy instruction has been designed to equip people with the critical skills necessary to become independent lifelong learners. Although many K-12 schools are incorporating this type of instruction into their curriculum, higher education is still the primary location for this education to occur.

There are various information literacy models in existence today that institutions can use to develop their programs. Prominent ones include the Big6, Shapiro and Hughes' Information Literacy as a Liberal Art and, ACRL's Information Literacy Competency Standards for Higher Education.

Big6 (http://big6.com/) is a model developed by educators Mike Eisenberg and Bob Berkowitz that is processed-based. Students are taught to approach problem-solving via six stages: task definition, information seeking strategies, location and access, use of information, synthesis, and evaluation. This can be accomplished consciously or not and does not have to be done in a linear fashion. Its goal is to teach students to focus on the entire research process and not just resources and location skills. Originated in the late 1980's to meet needs in the K-12 arena, the model has been adopted in higher education settings as well (Hagan Memorial Library 2007). Students who learned the Big6 in K-12 have carried the skills with them into their college years and utilize them in their academic careers. The standards listed by ACRL and those in the Big6 complement and strengthen each other (Story-Huffman 2002).

Information Literacy as Liberal Art approaches information literacy by defining different categories of literacy skills as opposed to defining specific actions or processes. Jeremy Shapiro and Shelley Hughes maintain that information literacy is a new liberal art which includes technical and critical skills required to access information. They argue that "critical reflection on the nature of information itself, its technical infrastructure and its social, cultural, and even philosophical context and impact" (Shapiro and Hughes 1996) are components of the literacy process. They frame a curriculum that consists of sets of literacies, consisting of:

+ Tool literacy—ability to understand and use the practical and conceptual tools of current information technology

+ Resource literacy—ability to understand the form, format, location and access methods of information resources

+ Social-structural literacy—understanding the social nature and production of information

+ Research literacy—ability to understand and use the IT-based tools relevant to the work of today's researcher and scholar

+ Publishing literacy—ability to format and publish research and ideas electronically

+ Emerging technology literacy—ability to adapt to, understand, evaluate and make use of the continually emerging innovations in IT

ACRL's Information Literacy Competency Standards for Higher Education: Five core information literacy competency standards were developed by ACRL (Association of College & Research Libraries) in 2000 (2000). These have become the standard that has provided the foundation for most information literacy curriculum in higher education. Their purpose is to establish a framework that can be used to assess students' ability to effectively manage information seeking skills.

The five standards are:

1. The information literate student determines the nature and extent of the information needed. (know)

2. The information literate student accesses needed information effectively and efficiently. (access)

3. The information literate student evaluates information and its sources critically and incorpo-

rates selected information into his or her knowledge base and value system. (evaluate)

4. The information literate student, individually or as a member of a group, uses information effectively to accomplish a specific purpose. (use)

5. The information literate student understands many of the economic, legal, and social issues surrounding the use of information and accesses and uses information ethically and legally. (ethics)

A review of many information literacy (IL) syllabi and course Web sites points to the use of the ACRL standards as the prominent structure around which courses are built. The bulk of curriculum time in most syllabi is spent on the first performance indicators in Standard #2—Accessing Needed Information. Performance indicators for this standard include such skills as "selects the most appropriate....information retrieval systems for accessing the needed information", "constructs and implements effectively-designed search strategies", "retrieves information....using a variety of methods" (use of search systems and classification schemes), "refines the search strategy," and "extracts, records, and manages the information and its sources" (includes the need for citation skills) (Association of College & Research Libraries 2006).

Typical modules of instruction that meet ACRL competency standards are often " how-to" or "activity-based" in nature:

+ Choosing a Topic
+ Identifying Types of Information Sources
+ How to Find a Book (Use the Online Catalog)
+ How to Search a Database to Find Articles
+ Keyword vs. Controlled Vocabulary Searching
+ Classification Systems
+ Complex Search Construction (Boolean Searching)
+ Source Citation
+ Internet Search Engines
+ How to Evaluate Information Sources
+ What is Plagiarism?

Overview of Information Literacy Approaches

In the higher education arena, one can find a variety of approaches to delivering information literacy instruction (ILI). Traditionally, "one shot" classes were the staple. These are also known as BI (bibliographic instruction) sessions and preferably are course related and integrated. With the explosion of online distance education, Web-based tutorials are also popular for their 24/7 access and consistent presentation.

Librarians have long recognized that "one shot" classes fall far short in teaching literacy skills. Many institutions have developed formal free-standing information literacy courses that range from non-credit to credit-bearing, from required to elective, from core curriculum to discipline specific. Because these typically cover multiple sessions, more opportunity is afforded for in-depth exploration and learning. Some schools have taken the next step and have integrated information literacy instruction into the overall curriculum (Kasowitz-Scheer and Pasqualoni 2002).

No matter which approach is selected, ILI planners strive to incorporate as many of the "best practices" to meet their missions. These include such components as relevance to course goals and curriculum, formation of partnerships between faculty and the library, scalability, and the use of student-centered, active, and collaborative learning (Kasowitz-Scheer and Pasqualoni 2002).

Overview of the Z. Smith Reynolds Library Information Literacy Program

Wake Forest University, a private institution located in Winston-Salem, NC, is a liberal arts institution with undergraduate, graduate, and professional programs. Undergraduate enrollment is 4,300 with a graduate and professional school population of 2,400. Z. Smith Reynolds (ZSR) Library is the largest library on the two campuses, with a mission "to support the current and future instructional and research needs of the faculty and students of the College, the Calloway School, the Graduate School of Arts and Sciences, and the Divinity School of Wake Forest University, as well as the information needs of the administration and staff of the University." (Z. Smith Reynolds Library 2007)

In the spring of 2003, ZSR Library piloted a one-credit information literacy elective, "Accessing Information in the 21st Century." It was well-received and was permanently incorporated into the university curriculum that fall, filling nine sections. Topics covered in the fourteen-class course included how to: select a research topic, prepare a search strategy, select the best information, use search engines and print material, determine scholarly information, and decide if one is looking at misinformation. It also covered copyright, plagiarism, and freedom of information. A curriculum template was developed within our University Blackboard course management system by the Information Literacy Librarian. The template was designed to standardize and streamline the instruction process, and included a suggested syllabus, content modules, class exercises, and assignments. In the beginning, instructors followed this set "script" so that each section covered identical subject matter.

The course has continued to fill up to eleven sections each semester since 2003. Course work involved a series of research exercises centered around student-selected topics, ultimately resulting in an annotated bibliography comprised of a series of resource types including reference resources, books, journal articles, and free Internet resources. Students were allowed to self-select topics that they have been assigned to research in another class, or ones that had caught their interest. During the course, individual assignments became building blocks toward the final producible: an annotated bibliography that required a specified number of resource types (reference, books,

journal articles, free Internet sites) and then addressed why each resource selected was the most appropriate and valuable.

Instructors came from the Information Services team and interested librarians from different departments in the library. As the various instructors gained experience in leading the classes, it was inevitable that different teaching approaches have been incorporated. Some of the approaches highlight different types of library resources, methods of evaluation, and levels of electronic vs. print emphasis. Despite these differences, a majority of instructors continue to focus on traditional research skills and on the production of the annotated bibliography as the final project.

Because the authors are technology-oriented due to our "regular" assigned responsibilities on the Library Information Technology team, it was natural that our section was one of the early adopters of a more technical slant to the subjects being taught. We included print resources, of course, but we focused more on electronic solutions to information retrieval and management. As soon as the university got a site license for the reference management software EndNote, competence in the use of this software became a core skill in our section. After this was incorporated, we found, through our course evaluations, that EndNote was a highly rated part of our section's curriculum. Students' evaluations on components of the course that we shared with the other sections were consistent: to them, the least useful modules were classification systems, using print monographs, citation syntax, and Library of Congress Subject Headings.

The realization that students were tuning out on traditional information literacy topics and were engaged with the prospect of mastering a research management tool started our conversations. How could we modify our class to become more relevant to our students' perceived needs, while ensuring they acquire the skills they need? It was evident to us that there was a major gap that could be bridged with the right approach.

The Initiative

ILI and Library 2.0

During the summer of 2006, a group of our ILI librarians met weekly to dissect our program's curriculum and to explore how it could be updated. There was a consensus that we had to find new "hooks" that would engage the students in a more participatory fashion and teach them skills that not only would be valuable in their academic careers but that also would travel with them beyond their school years. It quickly became apparent that we were talking about the need to weave in many Library 2.0 concepts: introducing social scholarship and radical trust in an environment where we offer a higher level of student control of course direction. In the spring of 2007, the authors developed and delivered a course which focused on these ideas.

In this approach to information literacy, course content focuses on helping students to recognize the skills they already have rather than emphasizing skills which have only limited relevance in their information environment (such as complex catalog searching). This approach included

  • drawing parallels between commonly known applications and information issues (privacy, access, management)

  • introducing a number of tools and approaches for discovering, acquiring, managing, and evaluating information

  • student driven discussion of information issues

We emphasized approaches over specific applications and methods, and encouraged students to try a number of avenues for information discovery and management. As a result, several modules typically found in other information literacy courses, including complex Boolean logic and resource centric classes (such as "Books" or "Reference Resources"), were replaced with more general topics which focused on the research process, information management, and organization techniques. This meant that we emphasized research management tools (in our case EndNote) over memorizing proper citation styles. In following with current education approaches including active learning, problem-based learning, and information technology literacy, this course used technology and instructional approaches which emphasized group learning and student engagement with information literacy issues.

Students were not given prescribed assignment formats to complete, but rather were expected to create content based on their concept of what the assignment entailed. Course assignments focused on both individual and group-work, and a conscious effort was made to have students provide the content and direction for at least two of the twelve classes. Instead of covering social information issues as part of course content, students were assigned one of these issues as their research area for the semester. Students were then given time to present their findings during class and relate their experiences with the rest of the class.

Instructional Methods

When planning the re-design of the information literacy curricula, the authors wanted to base course pedagogy on student-driven instructional models. In addition, while course content was largely based on what the instructors considered to be most relevant to current information literacy, it was also important to structure content in an optimal way to pique student interest.

This discussion of course methods includes an overview of the constructivist approach to learning, techniques for applying inquiry/problem based learning in the classroom, and a review of specific methods organized around Shapiro and Hughes' Information Literacy Model.

Constructivist Learning

While constructivist learning techniques have been popular in educational circles for many years, their use in information literacy has lagged behind. Constructivist learning is based on the idea that students learn and create meaning through an individual/social interaction with information. As a result, a constructivist learning environment enables students to explore the boundaries of a topic as opposed to a strict, focused curriculum. This often includes challenging students to ask their own questions, find their own answers, and use multiple sense-making techniques to learn.

In their book *In Search of Understanding: The Case for Constructivist Classrooms*, Brooks and Brooks lay out the basis for modern constructivist classrooms. They detail five principles of constructivist classrooms (Brooks and Brooks 2001).

1. Teachers seek and value their students' points of view

2. Classroom activities challenge students' suppositions

3. Teachers pose problems of emerging relevance

4. Teachers build lessons around primary concepts and "big" ideas

5. Teachers assess student learning in the context of daily teaching

These principles underscore the idea that students learn through creating individual understanding by grappling with new information and perspectives. They also introduce Library 2.0 concepts by encouraging students to take control of the course, add/modify content, and drive course direction.

These ideas, while simple enough, can prove difficult to adhere to, particularly in the face of an undergraduate population being presented with admittedly dry material. By turning the approach to information literacy on its side and persuading students to think about it in terms of information skills that they already had, the instructors hoped that students would become more engaged with course content. By employing open-ended, loosely-structured assignments which encouraged students to determine the scope, format, and content of their work in the course, it was expected that students would have to make full use of evaluation and critical thinking skills.

Instructional Techniques and Classroom Approaches

Inquiry (or problem) based learning (IBL) uses constructivist foundations to lay out a mechanism for encouraging students to define and solve their own learning problems. IBL techniques focus on providing students with open-ended problems which encourage them to define the boundaries of the work and direct their own information seeking. IBL began in the medical field in the 1970s. Over the last thirty years, it has been adopted in other fields (Savery and Duffy 1995).

IBL is often contrasted with traditional classroom approaches which emphasize lecture, direct factual memorization, and simple quantitative evaluation. Dave Knowlton discusses learning techniques related to IBL as including open inquiry and student centered learning, collaboration, self-directed learning, and active participation. (2003). Katherine Steeves expands this list to include in-depth questioning, integrated knowledge and skill learning, and time for reflection (2005). Brooks and Books point out that teachers should encourage student autonomy, allow students to drive both lessons and course content, encourage dialog and collaboration, and provide students time in class to create group relationships (2001).

Collaborative work is often a key component of IBL approaches. Lutz & Huitt outline four components of cooperative learning approaches (2004):

1. There must be cooperative interaction among groups.

2. Group incentives must be provided.

3. There must be individual accountability.

4. There must be an equal opportunity for all students to earn high scores and contribute to the group effort.

Cooperative learning includes both group participation and student contribution back to the course. This idea, that students direct course content, is key to providing students the authentic environment of inquiry discussed by Brooks and Books. One important aspect of this is the requirement that the instructors serve as a model collaborative group for the students to follow. By sharing course load, contributing to discussions during class time, and evaluating student work together, the authors attempted to create a visible collaborative environment.

Student Centered, Group Created

The Library 2.0 framework emphasizes user control, radical trust, flexibility, and user autonomy. These ideas are common to the constructivist and IBL teaching philosophies and merge well with the information literacy guidelines discussed above. Further, the goals of lifelong learning, evaluation, and critical thinking are central to the ACRL information literacy guidelines.

In relation to Library 2.0, the Web 2.0 application framework creates software which emphasizes user control, flexible use, and rapid development. The information landscape of the typical college student includes real-time and asynchronous communication, social networking sites, and multi-media applications. While students are specifically familiar with these technologies, the course instructors suspected that they did not automatically generalize these skills into larger information consumption skills. An initial survey of the students in the course revealed that all of the students were familiar with social networking sites in the form of Facebook and MySpace but did not connect those skills to other social networking software including blogs, wikis, and RSS feeds.

Social Software

The goals discussed above required new instructional tools (as opposed to Blackboard, PowerPoint, Word documents, and printed handouts). Social software applications were able to satisfactorily fill many of these roles. They permitted rapid development of course content and served as a collaborative space for students. They served as a bridge between common information literacy skills with

which the students are familiar and the skills that are considered essential in an information literacy environment. Further, social software embraces Library 2.0 concepts such as radical trust and user driven content and creates an environment where students can explore collaborative research models. Much has already been written about the uses of wikis, blogs, and social networking sites in courses, and the approaches used for course management in this case were not much different. In this course, a wiki, hosted on the MediaWiki platform, was used as the primary Course Management System (CMS) and contained course structure/content, student assignments, and contact information. All content created by the instructors and students was open to editing and deletion by all participants. Other social software employed included Flickr (for an information organization class), social tagging sites, and mashup applications that demonstrated information harvesting possibilities and how new knowledge is built from the work of others.

In addition to social software applications, a number of common free and commercial applications were used. Freemind (http://freemind. sourceforge.net/wiki/index.php/Main_Page), an open source mind-mapping application, was used to organize and present class content, MediaWiki extensions were used to embed Freemind, YouTube, and other multi-media content into the course wiki, and openly available applications from Google and other information discovery and distribution sites (employing saved searches, RSS feeds, and TOC services) were used. The specific uses of these applications are discussed in a later section.

The instructors debated the benefits and drawbacks of having students complete assignments in an open wiki. While students are comfortable learning in social environments, it was decided that privacy in evaluation should be guaranteed. For this reason, e-mail and Blackboard were used to provide feedback on assignments. While a wiki was our chosen application, other social software applications may be more suited to other goals. In selecting the social software application to use a number of questions should be asked:

- What educational outcome am I trying to achieve?
- What tools exist (both hosted and local) which could be used easily and securely?
- What level of privacy and security are required?
- What timeline do I have for development?

Rapid Course Development

In order to introduce timely information literacy issues, and base content on student needs, the course employed a rapid development framework. This involved constructing a complete template for the course at the beginning of the semester which facilitated the modification of elements based on current events and student feedback. For example, a flare-up issue with Wikipedia in the spring of 2007 met with popular coverage on The Colbert Report. Course content was shifted to include this event. Social software applications allowed a great deal of functionality and flexibility with minimal development, included feeds and current awareness topics (RSS feeds), and facilitated student feedback for current topics.

Applying an Information Literacy Model

The model proposed by Shapiro and Hughes in their 1996 article includes not only traditional literacy instruction but also other literacy components. This approach differs from the ACRL model (Association of College & Research Libraries 2007), which emphasizes general activities around the information use process as opposed to the specific activities suggested by Shapiro and Hughes. Similarly, the model of the Big 6 differs in that it emphasizes processes over the facets of literacy defined by Shapiro.

While each of these models brings many of the same skills together, Shaprio and Hughes' approach is used to discuss the various components of this information literacy course. Their model underscores the idea that information literacy is not about a process but rather is a multi-faceted approach to consuming information. This model seemed to fit well with the socialized nature of the course structure and provided a framework to include or exclude content.

Tool Literacy

Early in the course, students were encouraged to grapple with automated information discovery through the use of RSS feeds, e-mail alerts, TOC alerts, and saved searches. These automated discovery techniques made it possible for students to work within their own schedule and to refine searches through result evaluation over time, and promoted ongoing information management techniques. The theme of tool use continued as students began to work with EndNote, the course wiki, and social software sites.

Resource Literacy

In many other information literacy courses, resource literacy is a central theme. By shifting away from traditional components such as complex searching, database-specific skills, and resource-centric retrieval methods to more general concepts such as information organization processes, how Google works, and the information timeline (Meriam Library 2007), students were encouraged to think more globally about the information discovery and retrieval process. When students focused their research on one of four large information literacy issues, they were encouraged to discover resources using a variety of free, fee, scholarly, and non-scholarly approaches.

Socio-Structural Literacy

The emerging interactive nature of the Web, information creation in a social context, and social software means that social participation in the creation of knowledge is a much more integrated component of knowledge today. It is with this purpose that students were asked to reflect on their use of social network sites with an eye towards thinking about the use of categorization, knowledge building, search, discovery, management, and information privacy within the context of the course wiki.

Research Literacy

Two concepts were taught in relation to research literacy:

+ Ideas such as the research/information seeking process and the information timeline were used to give students frameworks for approaching their work in the course.

+ Research management applications were used to demonstrate techniques for using automation tools to enhance and simplify the research process.

Research management applications included a number of features such as the citation database, digital document storage, import/export functionality, note taking, and embedded citation ability. These functions allowed students to store information found during research, and permitted them to harvest this information in a number of ways, particularly during the paper creation process. While EndNote was the application of choice in this course, a number of other research management applications exist, including RefWorks, Procite and an open source application, Zotero (http://www.zotero.org/). Each of these applications has its own strengths and weaknesses but offers students the ability to engage with information management issues on an individual level.

Emerging Technology Literacy

Emerging technology was a key component of this course. Much has been made of the familiarity of Millennials with technology, but it became clear early on that these students had an imbalanced exposure to technology in which their experience was centered on popular culture technologies. By understanding that the underlying technologies in their social networking sites also exist in other Web services (for example, RSS feeds), students were able to employ technology on a wider basis. This is one reason that wiki software was used as a learning platform. By using the wiki, students had the opportunity to work with popularly used social software and participate in the culture of publishing on the Web.

Critical Literacy

Evaluation is a critical component of information literacy courses. While the core ideas of evaluation, synthesis, and critical review have not changed, the specific questions that must be asked given various information formats are addressed by different criteria. By learning to think critically, not only about the information that they find but also about the alternative methods for locating traditional information, students become flexible information consumers.

A major drawback with the annotated bibliography final product used by most sections in the program related to the level of engagement. While students were allowed to select their own research topics, they were not required to complete the actual research for another course. This tended to result in superficial critical evaluation of the resources. By shifting the assignments to focus on applied research and class presentations, students were required to connect with the material and be prepared to discuss their findings with their classmates.

The Shapiro-Hughes model served as a foundation for making sure that the appropriate types of literacy instruction were included in the course. By framing modules around these themes, the instructors were able to create an environment which defines tangible objectives for course content.

Course Structure

In restructuring this course, and in keeping with the ACRL standards, our goals included the incorporation of technology that our students could use and understand to teach proper research and citation methods. The class was designed around the concepts of group work and open academic collaboration. Some core tenets of this approach included open discussion, course content Web publishing, significant group participation, and a willingness to experiment.

This section contains a review of student responses during pre- and post course surveys, an overview of the course structure and wiki, discussion of course modules and student assignments, and a review of student work.

Course Learning Systems

At the center of the course was a wiki, to which both students and instructors contributed. The basic wiki served a similar purpose to Blackboard, housing the course syllabus, upcoming classes, and

assignments. We chose to use Blackboard to post grades, since it is a secure service, but that was its only purpose. Although 69% of the students had never used a wiki, over 88% of them believed that wikis could have a use in research.

This approach required some up-front learning by both students and instructors but ultimately facilitated

  • easy collaboration and contribution to the syllabus and course materials by instructors

  • embedding course content (Freemind files, YouTube videos, and Flickr pictures) into the wiki by instructors

  • on-the-fly modification and revision of items by both students and instructors

  • creation of a flexible, digital environment for students to create and submit assignments

**Figure 1: Course Wiki
(http://wiki.zsr.wfu.edu/infolit/index.php/Lib100D_Spring2007/Main_Page)**

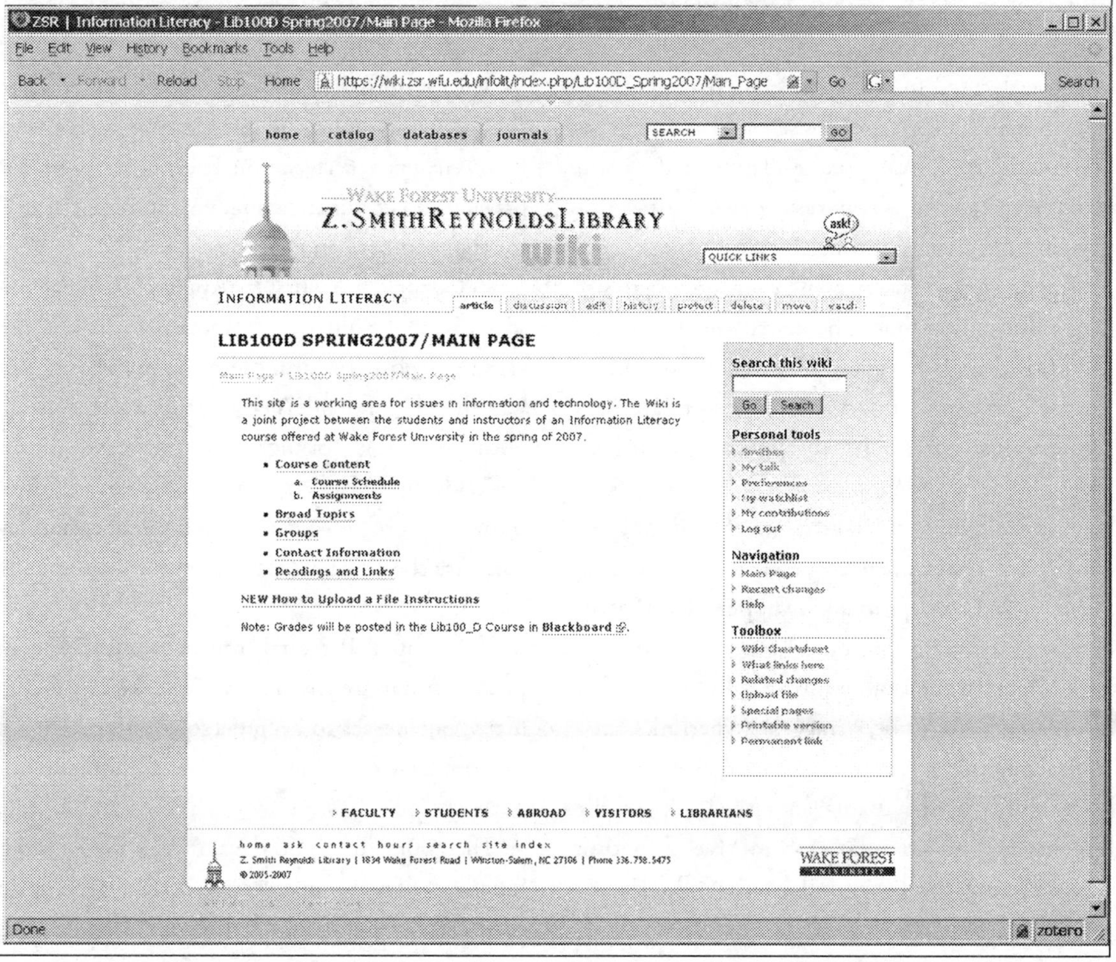

The use of a wiki was important because the traditional CMS typically does not allow instructors to easily collaborate on documents, revert to previous versions, or allow students to contribute to the course process. In the same vein, using a course wiki permitted students to:

+ collaboratively build assignments
+ engage in discussions in an electronic environment
+ take ownership over course content and contribute back to the discussion
+ take part in the creation of a Web content and knowledge building exercise

Because students had little previous experience creating or editing wiki pages, we spent half of a class session training the students on the use of the wiki. Student adoption of wiki editing appeared to be strong. They all successfully created and edited pages, and added links to other sites and documents. The authors believe that one reason that students used the wiki so extensively was that we decided to make the class paperless. All course materials, class exercises, and assignments were completed, evaluated, and returned to students electronically. This resulted in a great savings in time during grading and class time.

In addition to encouraging the students to use new information tools, the instructors used non-traditional tools for content presentation. In this course, Freemind mind-mapping software was chosen as an alternative to applications such as PowerPoint because it allowed rapid development and organization of class content, and did not emphasize a linear teaching style. Freemind is an XML-based concept mapping application that allows you to create a graphical representation of a mind-map. In addition, it provides the

+ ability to embed images, hyperlinks, and digital objects
+ ability to be displayed either within the Freemind application, as an html tree, or within a wiki using the Freemind MediaWiki Extension

+ ability for instructors to assemble class materials and lecture notes into a single context-sensitive space

Given the ability of Freemind to create a student-browsable environment, students were able to access course materials at their own pace and easily target specific content areas.

Curricula Structure

The sixteen students were divided into four groups for the duration of the course. The instructors created a list of broad information literacy issues, put each in a hat, and asked each group to draw for the issue that they were to research for the extent of the class. The broad subject areas that were offered were:

+ social networking
+ digital divide/net neutrality
+ gaming in education
+ Internet privacy
+ identity theft

The four broad issues selected were narrowed to the following topics and questions by each group:

+ Group 1: Privacy on Facebook: How does privacy affect future employment opportunities for the members on Facebook?
+ Group 2: Ability to Apply to Colleges for High School Students: As more colleges and universities move toward online applications, how will the digital divide/net neutrality affect the application process for high school seniors?
+ Group 3: Effects of Video Games in Education: How are video games used in education and what are the advantages of video game use to education?
+ Group 4: Personal Information and E-commerce: What are the steps being taken by e-commerce businesses to keep personal information of consumers from being used for fraudulent purposes?

The course met two days a week for a total of fourteen fifty-minute sessions. The agenda for each class was posted on the wiki. Class discus-

Figure 2: Freemind Presentation on the Internet, the Web, and 2.

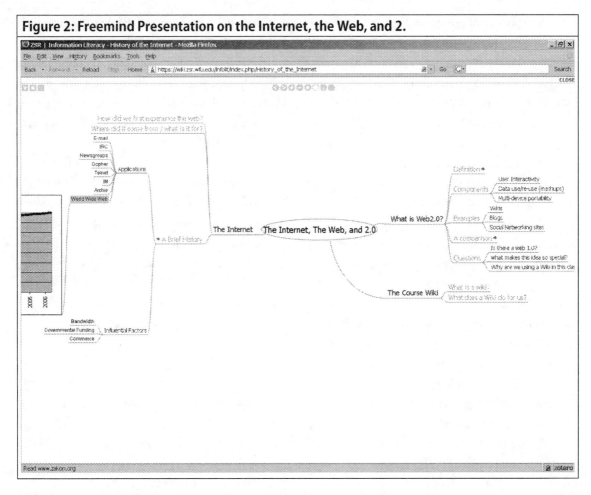

sions were organized around a Freemind presentation. This was an experimental approach, but became a very useful in-class tool. Since students were required to bring their university-issued laptops to class, each had access to the presentation mind maps during class. They took advantage of this access without being asked to do so, following along during the class with the mind map open on their own computers. We found that student access to the maps during the discussions led them to greater involvement with the wiki and class content.

Classes typically included an overview of the day's topic, class discussion, and an in-class exercise or group work time.

Course Modules

In redesigning the course, modules were shifted from format-based to literacies-based classes. This meant that classes often included the common themes of discovery, access, and evaluation along with the introduction of a specific technology tool. For instance, scholarly resources were discussed within the context of content, not within the context of availability or print/electronic format. Because students were given the task of researching and presenting current information literacy issues, the coverage of this subject matter was left for the last two classes via group presentations. Following is a summary of the class modules:

Class 1 – What Is Information Literacy?/Initial Survey/Information Literacy Issues

• Overview of the course; ideas surrounding information literacy; overview of the course wiki; brief introduction to current issues in information literacy

Class 2 – Getting To a Research Question/The Research Process

♦ Assignment of groups and group topics; the research process; topic refinement; question creation

Class 3 – Social Software and The New Web/ Introduction to the Wiki

♦ History of the Web; Web 2.0 applications; introduction to the course wiki; creation of individual and group pages

Class 4 – Managing Your Research, Automated Discovery and Distribution (RSS)

♦ Web tools for research: RSS feeds, RSS readers, live bookmarks, search alerts (e-mail & RSS); discussion surrounding Wikipedia issues

Class 5 – Getting Acquainted With Your Topic, Introduction to Research Tools

♦ Tools for finding overview information; role of reference resources; differentiating sources (scholarly vs. popular); print vs. electronic: benefits and drawbacks; evaluation techniques and tools

Class 6 – Building On the Work of Others, Remix Culture and Citations

♦ Remix culture: sampling, bastard pop, and mashups; attributing through citing; intellectual property

Class 7 – Research Management Applications, Introduction to Endnote

♦ Configure EndNote, learn basics of building citations and managing references, introduction to Cite While You Write

Class 8 – Knowledge Organization and Searching

♦ Discussion of organization methods; comparison of controlled vocabularies vs. folksonomies; relationship to discovery; discussion of popular discovery tool features (in Amazon, Google, and licensed databases); exercise using Flickr to describe and retrieve pictures

Class 9 – Finding and Evaluating Scholarly Resources I

♦ Types of library resources (books, journals); scholarly vs. popular; discovery tools; third party tools (Amazon, Google/Google Books, Worldcat. org)

Class 10 – Finding and Evaluating Scholarly Resources II

♦ Review of the research process; finding scholarly resources (via library tools and on the Web); impact on searching; research management tools (export/import, attaching digital object, taking notes in Endnote)

Class 11 – Using the Open Web for Research

♦ Types of information on the Web; publishing models; finding licensed resources on the Web; impact on evaluation and use; citing in EndNote

Class 12 – You on the Web: Privacy

♦ Personal information on the Web; privacy; types of social networking sites; communication mechanisms; what is too much information?

Class 13 – Class presentations

Class 14 – Class presentations & Evaluations

Assignments

Students were given five assignments which included a final presentation of their research findings and the development of their topic wiki pages. Of the five assignments, three were group assignments and two were individual assignments.

An effort was made throughout the course to de-emphasize the format of resources and emphasize their utility. It seemed inappropriate to require students to find a set number of books, journal articles, and Web sites when the relationship and use of specific formats varies from topic to topic. We saw this as one of the shortfalls of the annotated bibliography assignment that was previously used as the culminating project.

On the last two days of the course, the groups presented their research findings. They were given twenty minutes in front of the class and were told that they could choose any presentation method that they would like. Each member of the group was asked to take on a speaking role of some sort. The group was also asked to show its wiki pages and a list of its properly cited resources. Three of the four groups used PowerPoint to present their research findings, creating PowerPoint templates from scratch. For example, the group that presented on Privacy on Facebook developed a template in PowerPoint to make its presentation look as though it were being given through Facebook. The group that did not use PowerPoint in its presentation relied on its wiki as the presentation method. All of the groups did an exceptional job with their presentations and answering their research questions.

Student Surveys & Feedback

The course design was tentatively established, but a pre-course survey was done to identify gaps in additional subject area coverage that would need to be addressed. On the first day the class met, the sixteen students enrolled in this course were asked to participate in an introductory survey (see Appendix 1). The survey was designed to assess the students' familiarity with information management tools, social networking technologies, and information sources.

We found was that around 90% of the class had regular or frequent use of half of the technologies we planned to use in this class (social networking sites in particular). The second half of the technologies, including wikis, RSS and EndNote, were recognized (but not used) by about 60% of the class. Over 90% of the class thought books, journals and newspapers, Web sites, databases, and people/experts were important to their research needs, and 69% of the students claimed that they would turn to journals and newspapers first to start research.

At the end of the course, we conducted a post-course survey to assess any differences in student responses (Appendix 2). The students' perspectives changed greatly over the course period about what would be useful for scholarly research and what they would use in the future. One of the most interesting findings was that the students decided that all resources are important depending on their research needs, and that no one resource

	Type	Goal	Producible
Table 1: Course Assignments			
1	Group	Narrow the broad topic assigned to the group and formulate a research question	Create a wiki page which includes the narrowed topic and research question along with supporting materials
2	Group	Discover introductory material to support the group research question and define the parameters of the investigation	Enhance the wiki page created in assignment 1 with supporting background and scope information. Include a list of consulted resources
3	Individual	Become familiar with discovering, accessing, and evaluating licensed scholarly resources	Create a wiki page which presents the resource selected along with a critique of the resource and its relation to the group research question. Create an entry in EndNote, export it in APA style into Word; upload the Word document with the exported citation to the wiki
4	Individual	Become familiar with discovering, accessing, and evaluating openly accessible scholarly resources	Create a wiki page which presents the resource selected along with a critique of the resource and its relation to the group research question. Create an entry in EndNote, export it in APA style into Word; upload the Word document with the exported citation to the wiki
5	Group/ Individual	Become comfortable with being a collaborative researcher and participating in the creation of information in a social software environment	Present findings from research to class, edit and organize wiki pages to represent a cohesive answer to the research question

stood out as most important. Also, the students indicated that they preferred the use of the wiki over Blackboard as the course delivery system.

Along with our post-course survey, students were asked to complete a course evaluation administered for the University. Our students indicated that the aspects they found most valuable were the use of EndNote and the wiki. They liked having the course material online and accessible at all times. Additionally, they enjoyed contributing to the class through the wiki. They also appreciated learning how to evaluate resources and determining whether something was scholarly. Some of our students did not enjoy group work and would have preferred to create wiki entries as individuals. This was not unexpected, since not all students like group work. All indicated they would recommend this specific class to others. One student even indicated that his job requires the use of a wiki, and that he now feels more comfortable with this technology because of our class.

When comparing our survey results to other sections of the information literacy courses that were taught during the spring semester of 2007, most students found the technology aspects of the classes taught most useful (EndNote, wiki), along with classes involving searching, use, and evaluation of online resources. Students deemed least useful classes to be those involving books and print resources, how to locate resources in the library, how to use the catalog, and how resources in the library are organized by call number.

Future Plans

While it proved difficult to compare student achievement between this information literacy class and others offered at the university, we plan to design a quantitative study over the next academic year. The results of this study will be posted on the post-publication wiki that supplements this book.

The successes identified in this new approach are being adopted in part by other instructors in our library's information literacy program:

+ incorporation of a wiki to replace Blackboard

+ structuring group work as a component of course assessment

+ movement from manual citation to an automated method

+ change of final project from annotated bibliography to a research essay and presentation

Other social software applications are being investigated for their potential use in this course. One course section is looking at blogging software as a discussion forum while others are exploring alternative electronic citation methods. The instructors are also evaluating scholarly resource tagging sites such as CiteULike (http://www.citeulike.org/) as a method for collaborative resource gathering.

Conclusion

This class contained a number of new educational methods and included substantial new content. Student and instructor feedback was overall positive but also indicated the need for improvement in a few areas.

+ Balance class time between learning technology tools, investigating research skills, and participating in collaborative work.

+ Build additional student presentations into earlier class discussion. Have students present an overview of their research question during one of the first few class sessions.

Shifting from the annotated bibliography project, which tended to be resource driven, to a research and report project which emphasized discovery, access, and evaluation skills, produced better overall projects and resulted in more student participation in the course. Further, by utilizing group work and allowing the students free reign over the specifics of content, format, and work assignments, we found that groups collaborated together to fill in each others' knowledge gaps.

In attempting to approach information literacy from a Library 2.0 framework, the authors found that employing constructivist teaching methods and social software created a classroom environment that was more effective at delivering information literacy skills. In short, the Library 2.0 information literacy classroom:

+ creates an information literate person who has technical and evaluation skills which can be re-used in changing information environments

+ creates an environment where there is no "correct" approach to discovering, evaluating, and managing information; solutions are as personal and unique as our students and patrons

+ dispels the notion that technology is a separate component of information; students should grapple with technology as part of their information literacy process because doing so enables them to find new paths through information

+ creates an information literate person who is capable of employing inter-disciplinary and diverse approaches to information seeking and who can apply critical and evaluative frameworks to information based on the required need and origination

If nothing else, a Library 2.0 focused information literacy course should reflect the information environment that we are trying to teach. The goal of creating information literate students is more easily met when the tools and approaches are embedded in every aspect of the course from the syllabus to assignment creation and professor/student communication.

References

Association of College & Research Libraries. 2000. Information literacy competency standards for higher education. http://www.ala.org/ala/acrl/acrlstandards/informationliteracycompetency.htm.

———. 2007. ACRL information literacy. http://www.ala.org/ala/acrl/acrlissues/acrlinfolit/informationliteracy.htm.

Brooks, Jacqueline Grennon and Martin G. Brooks. 2001. *In Search of Understanding: The Case for Constructivist Classrooms.* Columbus, OH: Prentice Hall.

Hagan Memorial Library. 2007. Information literacy. http://www.ucumberlands.edu/library/course/literacy.html.

Kasowitz-Scheer, Abby and Michael Pasqualonil. 2002. Information literacy instruction in higher education: Trends and issues. *ERIC Digest.* http://www.ericdigests.org/2003-1/information.htm.

Knowlton, Dave S. 2003. Preparing students for educated living: Virtues of problem-based learning across the higher education curriculum. In *Problem-Based Learning in the Information Age,* Knowlton, Dave S. and David C. Sharp, eds. San Francisco: Jossey-Bass.

Lutz, Stacy T. and William G. Huitt. 2004. Connecting cognitive development and constructivism: Implications from theory for instruction and assessment. *Constructivism in the Human Sciences* 9 (1): 67-90.

Meriam Library. 2007. Information timeline. http://www.csuchico.edu/lins/handouts/info_timeline.html.

Orr, Debbie, Margaret Appleton, and Margie Wallin. 2001. Information literacy and flexible delivery: Creating a conceptual framework and model. *The Journal of Academic Librarianship* 27 (November): 457-463.

Savery, John R. and Thomas Duffy. 1995. Problem based learning: An instructional model and its constructivist framework. *Educational Technology* 35 (September/October): 31-38.

Shapiro, Jeremy J. and Shelly K. Hughes. 1996. Information literacy as a liberal art. *Educom Review* 31 (March/April). http://www.educause.edu/pub/er/review/reviewArticles/31231.html.

Steeves, Kathleen Anderson. 2005. History, uncovering the past through inquiry. In *Integrating Inquiry Across the Curriculum,* Audet, Richard H. and Linda K. Jordan, eds. Thousand Oaks, CA: Corwin.

Story-Huffman, Ru. 2002. Big6 in higher education: Considering the ACRL standards in a Big6 context. http://www.big6.com/showarticle.php?id=431.

Z. Smith Reynolds Library. 2007. Library mission & vision. http://zsr.wfu.edu/about/mission.html.

http://acrl.ala.org/L2Initiatives/index.php?title=Chapter_9/

Appendix 1: Pre-Course Survey

1. To what extent are you familiar with/have used the following information management tools?
   a. Wikis
   b. Blogs
   c. RSS Feeds
   d. Bibliographic Management Software
   e. Podcasts
   f. Facebook/MySpace (social Web sites)
   g. Text Messaging
   h. E-mail

2. Which of the following technologies do you think have use for research?
   a. Wikis
   b. Blogs
   c. RSS Feeds
   d. Bibliographic Management Software
   e. Podcasts
   f. Facebook/MySpace (social Web sites)
   g. Text Messaging
   h. E-mail

3. Rank the order of importance these tools in terms of your research.
   a. Books
   b. Journals/Newspapers
   c. Web sites
   d. Databases
   e. People/Experts
   f. TV
   g. Radio
   h. Other Sources

4. In beginning your research which information resources are you most likely to turn to first?
   a. Books
   b. Journals/Newspapers
   c. Web sites
   d. Databases
   e. People/Experts
   f. TV
   g. Radio
   Other, please specifyAppendix 2: Post Course Survey

1. Indicate the extent to which you will continue to use the following resources:
    a. RSS Feeds
    b. Search Alerts
    c. EndNote
    d. Wikis
    e. Blogs
    f. Find a Journal
    g. Find a Database
    h. WFU Full Text Options
    i. Library Subscription Databases
    j. Library Online Catalog
    k. Web Search Engines (ie Google, Yahoo!)
    l. Web Accessed Information (ie resource reviews, Wikipedia articles)

2. Based on your experience in this class, rank the importance of the following skills
    a. Finding search terms
    b. Ability to write good citations
    c. Understanding of Library of Congress Classification System
    d. Familiarity with ZSR Library
    e. Performing comprehensive searches
    f. Automating research via search alerts/RSS feeds
    g. Managing research references in EndNote
    h. Using print resources
    i. Using electronic resources
    j. Using social network sites (Facebook, Flickr)
    k. Knowledge of emerging technologies
    l. Familiarity with Information Literacy issues
    m. Ability to distinguish types of resources (books, journals, Web sites, etc)
    n. An understanding of the research process
    o. Ability to evaluate information resources

3. Rank the order of importance of these tools in terms of your research
    a. Books
    b. Journals/Newspapers
    c. Web sites
    d. Databases
    e. People/Experts
    f. TV
    g. Radio
    h. Other sources

4. When beginning your research, which information source(s) are you most likely to turn to first
    a. Books

    b. Journals/Newspapers

    c. Web sites

    d. Databases

    e. People/Experts

    f. TV

    g. Radio

    h. Other sources

5. Based on your experience with the wiki in this course and Blackboard in other courses, which course tool would you rather use?

    a. Blackboard

    b. Course wiki

6. What did you think about using the wiki to create and submit assignments?

7. If you have a preference between the Course wiki and Blackboard, can you tell us why you would prefer one tool over the other?

8. Did you ever use other student generated content in class to help guide your own work? (Yes or No)

9. Rate the usefulness of the class topics

    a. Definition of Information Literacy

    b. Orientation to class wiki

    c. Defining the research process

    d. Selecting and Refining a research question

    e. History of the Internet

    f. Overview of Web 2.0

    g. E-mail Alerts/RSS Feeds

    h. Resource Evaluation

    i. Differentiating scholarly and popular resources

    j. Finding Web resources

    k. Remix culture and citations

    l. Using Endnote

    m. Information Organization / searching

    n. Using library tools to find resources (online catalog, Find a Journal, Find a Database, WFU Full Text Options)

    o. Privacy Issues

    p. Presentation of group research findings

10. Do you have other comments or suggestions for future courses?

IMplementing IM @ Reference: The GW Experience

Deborah Gaspar and Sarah Palacios Wilhelm

Abstract

This chapter details the development of the Instant Messaging (IM) Reference service at The George Washington University (GW). The authors include a brief literature review exploring the characteristics of 21st century college students as well as the uses of IM. Information on software selection, including an examination of downloadable versus Web-based IM applications, is provided. Other considerations addressed include staffing models, advertising, and training. Librarians at the University focused on the question: how do we serve students in their preferred medium of communication? When seeking information, students have many options available to them. The librarians wanted to shape reference services to place the library and credible information within the students' selected mode of communicating. Students use IM to receive and share information. The library can take advantage of this and use the IM tool to communicate with students.

Introduction

During the 2005-2006 academic year, librarians at GW piloted and introduced an IM reference service. The theories and concepts embedded in Library 2.0 informed the decision process for this new venture. Librarians crafted this new service using a patron selected communication tool, solicited patron input, and continue to alter the service in response to patron feedback. This chapter details the steps, challenges, and progress of this new initiative. GW is located in the heart of Wash-

ington, D.C. and serves a diverse population that includes 9,700 undergraduate students and 12,400 graduate students. The main campus is home to Gelman Library which serves both graduate and undergraduate programs. A smaller satellite campus featuring classrooms, school athletic fields, and many freshman dormitories, is located three miles from the main campus. This campus is home to Eckles Library which primarily serves freshmen. Both libraries are members of the Gelman Library System (GLS).

Most GW undergraduate students rely on Instant Messaging as a mode of communication. A quick scan of library workstations confirmed that students had moved beyond e-mail and toward the more immediate instant messaging. Reference services might better serve these students by offering the option to use IM. Since customer service is a

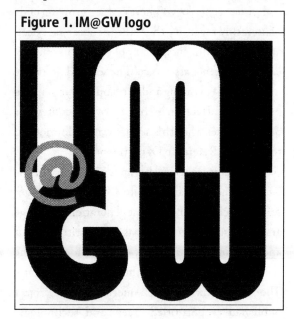

Figure 1. IM@GW logo

Deborah Gaspar, Ed.D., e-mail: dgaspar@gwu.edu, and Sarah Palacios Wilhelm, e-mail: palacios@gwu.edu, both at Gelman Library at The George Washington University.

core value for both Gelman and Eckles librarians, staff members from both libraries formed a working group to study the feasibility of providing IM as an additional form of reference service. The IM Group focused on the question: how do we serve students using their preferred medium of communication? When seeking information, students have many options available to them. Members of the GLS Reference Department wanted to shape services to place the library and credible information within the students' selected mode of information finding and communication. Students use IM to receive and share information and the library could potentially use this same tool to communicate with them.

Literature Review: Library Pioneers Who Went Before

Since the task of the IM Group was to explore the potential for IM as a new mode for reference service, the first step was to conduct a literature review. There is much written about the "Millennials," many of whom now comprise the current generation of college-age students who work, network, and communicate with friends using computer technology. There is also a growing body of literature regarding the future of library services, and IM is prominent in many of the discussions related to reference assistance. The selected literature informed the planning and decision-making. It also proved critical later on in that it provided context for our colleagues when this service was recommended to the GLS Reference Department.

The literature review began with a focus on the patron, since the aim was to inform a customer service decision. The present generation of college and high school students has been written about and scrutinized extensively, but the focus of the review was their use of technology and the library. The Pew Internet and American Life Project published a report titled "Teens and Technology: Youth are leading the transition to a fully wired and mobile nation" (Lenhart, Madden, and Hitlin

2005). This often-quoted report is rich in self-reported data and is essential to understanding the library's current users. Of particular interest was the pervasive use of IM technologies by teenagers: 75% regularly online, use IM. Almost half of teens surveyed chose IM over e-mail for communication. Furthermore, IM assumes a seamless part of their homework and computer time, as the teens report that they do other online activities while conversing via IM.

Abram and Luther asserted that since this generation grew up with technology, they are comfortable multitasking, have no strong attachment to any particular format, and are more collaborative than previous generations. The authors specifically noted that IM held potential for interactive remote reference service (Abram and Luther 2004). Lippincott provided a holistic view of library services relevant to students from the "Net" generation. Her discussion touched on Google, difficult database interfaces, and IM as a reference service suited to students' communication preferences (Lippincott 2005).

The IM Group also reviewed literature in order to explore the practices, successes, and challenges encountered by other libraries already providing reference service via IM. Schmidt and Stephens likened IM reference service to telephone reference. The authors attested to its usefulness for serving undergraduates and suggested that IM reference services would not only appeal to the new generation of patrons, but also enhance the service for returning patrons (Schmidt and Stephens 2005) .

Foley's case study was particularly informative as she detailed the implementation, successes, problems, and results of the pilot IM reference program at State University of New York at Buffalo (Foley 2002). Two of Gelman library's target populations were the same as those identified in Buffalo: distance education students and on-site students who would be reluctant to relinquish their seats in crowded computer labs.

When the IM Group began its study, the Reference Department had been providing Virtual Reference (VR) together with other schools in the local consortium for four years. VR services utilized vendor supplied software to respond to off site patron queries. The software provided a form of chat and the ability to co-browse with the patron. Issues arose, however, if the patron's computer preferences included a firewall or pop-up blockers. Only 1.5% of GW students took advantage of the VR service because interacting with the VR software became a barrier. Houghton and Schmidt's article, "Web-based chat vs. instant messaging: who wins?" compared the opportunities and challenges associated with the two service modes including speed, cost, consortia, and training. The authors noted that IM is much faster than VR, making IM far more attractive to our undergraduate patrons (Houghton and Schmidt 2005). This was an informative introductory article that formed the basis for the final recommendation to the Reference Department advocating the switch to IM.

The Initiative

Members of the working group determined that IM reference would meet the needs of GW undergraduate and distance education students better than the VR service. An important supporting argument for the switch to IM was the fact that undergraduate students already used IM for communication and collaboration. The recommendation to the Reference Department included drafts of an implementation plan, policies, and procedures. The plan was approved, as were the IM names: GelmanInfo and EcklesInfo.

Software Selection and Security: AIM, Yahoo!, MSN, GAIM, or Trillian?

There is a multitude of instant messaging protocols available. Each of these services provides a downloadable and/or Web-based client that allows users to communicate with other users via a single service. Some of the most popular of these single-client services include AOL Instant Messenger (AIM), Yahoo! Messenger, Windows Live Messenger (MSN), Jabber, ICQ, Skype, and Google Talk. For an initial pilot program, the IM Group decided to limit IM reference to the AIM service because it was the most popular service at the time in the United States, although recent studies indicate that MSN has gained popularity (Comscore 2006). Future plans include adding other services such as MSN.

Running multiple single-client IM protocols is not efficient. For this reason, we examined several multi-protocol platforms that are available for free and that would facilitate future expansion. Multi-client protocol platforms offer several advantages over single-client platforms. They allow users to streamline the IM process by consolidating multiple service protocols into one application. As a result, the training process is also simplified because new users only need to become familiar with a single interface. Additionally, it was determined that multi-client software featured cleaner interfaces with less advertising, including intrusive pop-ups. Many of these third party multi-client applications also provide greater security from Internet viruses and spyware. Furthermore, these clients often offer customizable features that allow users to change the appearance of the interface or how the application functions. In the process of selecting an IM application, the IM Group looked at a variety of solutions including downloadable, open source, and Web-based options. The applications were examined using nine key criteria, based on the library's needs:

1. Interface, ease of use (auto start, auto login)
2. Tab chat windows for multiple conversations
3. File sharing options (if allowed, can it be blocked?)
4. Chat room capabilities for conferencing with multiple students or librarians
5. Whiteboard/co-browsing features
6. Pop-up blocker and embedded advertising
7. Transcript logging/history capabilities

8. Security and encryption capabilities (possible interaction with the University's firewall)

9. Performance of Web-based vs. downloaded applications

Examination of downloadable multi-protocol clients began with Trillian (http://www.ceruleanstudios.com/), which allows users to connect to AIM, Yahoo!, MSN, ICQ, and IRC services, the most popular IM services. Other open source applications considered include Pidgin (http://www.pidgin.im/), formerly called GAIM, and Miranda (http://www.miranda-im.org/), which allows simultaneous access to between ten and sixteen services, including all those covered by the Trillian client. For Mac users there is Adium (http://www.adiumx.com/), which works with sixteen different services.

The only Web-based multi-client application considered was Meebo (http://www.meebo.com/). Meebo permits users to sign on to AIM, Yahoo! Messenger, Windows Live, Google Talk, Jabber, and ICQ with a single login. Meebo also offers a widget that allows users to embed an IM window into a Web page. Several additional software-based clients offer Web-based programs that require no downloads, including AIM Express, Web Messenger (MSN), ICQ2Go, YA-HOO! Messenger for the Web, and Google Talk. One drawback is that the automatic logging features for each of these programs are usually not as efficient as those available in the downloadable programs. Another drawback is the limited customization that is available through Web-based programs.

The staffing models were an important consideration as the IM Group reviewed the available software. The service was initially staffed from multiple desks, thus requiring installation of the software on individual workstations. This proved to be a time- consuming process of setting individual preferences and increased the demand for troubleshooting. As the project progressed, a shared network drive housed a preset version of the software that could be copied onto individual computers. The library has since moved to the current model, staffing the service from the Reference Desk which requires software installation on only one computer. This has eliminated the need for multiple setups. Using the automatic log function, all logs are collected in a single file, providing group members with remote access to the transaction logs. The only drawback to this model is that the program is inaccessible when the shared network is down; however, this has been a relatively rare occurrence. In the event that the networked drive is lost, a second version of the Trillian application is kept on the local hard drive as a fail-safe.

The Trillian client was selected largely in response to security issues. All library computers are connected to a shared network and downloading software from the Internet raised serious questions about network security. Based on discussions with the IT Department and the technology librarian, it was determined that the Trillian software offered the greatest security because it had been in development and its code tested longer than the other available open source clients.

Training: Transferring our Best Practices

Though IM software is easy to use, it was necessary to introduce something new to busy colleagues in a careful manner. Each librarian in the Gelman Reference Department has other duties as well: instruction, collection development, government documents, or Web site design and maintenance. Hence, beginning a new service utilizing unfamiliar software had to be a well-planned process. The librarians unfamiliar with IM received copies of articles from the literature review and the following description to provide context: "Use of the instant messaging client is a tool for short, fast questions or communications. Patrons get a response more quickly than an e-mail and in a less intrusive fashion than phone calls. Furthermore, away messages can help users know what to expect regarding response times or availability of the staff they are attempting to contact" (Maldonado 2006).

During the Fall 2005 semester, one of the IM Group members installed Trillian on each librarian's personal computer and other group members then assisted individual librarians with creating their personal screen names and accounts. Some librarians had already established accounts, and this eased the process as they were willing to assist their colleagues. Once the software was in place and personal names were established, Reference Department members received step-by-step instruction on accessing and using Trillian. This information was accompanied by supporting graphics to facilitate learning. Reference librarians were encouraged to use IM for internal communication and received a weekly survey inquiring about any issues or problems encountered with the software.

After Gelman reference librarians developed familiarity with the software and learned how to send messages among themselves, formal training for providing reference via IM began. Working in an electronic classroom, librarians paired with members of the IM Group to practice answering reference questions using the Trillian interface. Translating normal face-to-face practice to abbreviated yet descriptive text is challenging. Even seasoned IM veterans found the transition somewhat cumbersome.

In addition to full-time librarians, at Eckles Library student workers staffed the IM service. The students were already adept with IM software and protocols. They were not, however, fully trained to provide reference services. Hence, portions of the reference training document designed for incoming librarians were adapted for student staff. The students needed to understand the policies and work of the Circulation Department, to learn how to locate the various formats of periodicals, and to demonstrate competence with key databases. Students were also taught how to conduct a reference interview and how to deal with a difficult patron.

Important to student training was understanding when to stop trying to answer a reference question, i.e., knowing when and how to refer the patron to the appropriate subject specialist.

Reference librarians and student staff were also provided with the following Etiquette Guidelines focused on the immediate nature of IM.

IM Etiquette

When covering GelmanInfo or EckelsInfo, staff members are representing The George Washington University. It is important that staff members remember that they are speaking to patrons and should show online patrons the same respect and regard that they would show in-person patrons. This includes, maintaining a professional tone at all times and providing the same level of service online as would be provided to in-person patrons.

1. Professional tone

As stated before, patrons contacting the library though IM should be treated in the same way in-person patrons are treated. This means that some conversational tones, styles, and remarks commonly used in personal online communications should not be used when covering GelmanInfo or EcklesInfo. Library staff members should avoid using slang or acronyms in online conversations, just as they would in an in-person conversation. All procedures should be explained as clearly and concisely as possible. Staff members should remain courteous at all times; edgy or sarcastic comments should be avoided.

2. Handling rude patrons

Maintaining a professional tone may be difficult if the patron is being rude, aggressive or otherwise inappropriate. If the patron makes an inappropriate comment, you can ignore the comment and move on or you can inform the patron that the comment is inappropriate and the conversation should focus on the conversation at hand. Example: "I don't feel comfortable responding to that comment, why don't we focus on finding what you need." If the patron continues to be inappropriate you can block the patron and e-mail your supervisor regarding the incident.

3. Handling in-person patrons at the same time

If a patron approaches the desk and you are the only staff member on duty, let the online patron know that you must assist another patron and then assist the in-person patron. If the in-person transaction will take several minutes to resolve, let the online patron know that you will return shortly and offer to e-mail a complete response later. If the online patron can be assisted quickly, it may be appropriate to inform the in-person patron that you are assisting an online patron and complete the transaction.

4. Handling multiple windows at the same time

If you receive more than one patron inquiry at one time, inform both patrons that you are helping another patron at the same time and that there may be a slight delay. Most patrons will understand.

Well-planned training addressed most difficulties before they came up in practice. For example: detailed step-by-step procedures for transferring a patron to a subject specialist were provided. This entails maintaining contact with the patron via the department IM account, while simultaneously sending an IM to the colleague using a personal account.

The Reference Department has established standards for person-to-person transactions that include conducting a thorough reference interview and providing the patron with the requested information, all the while delivering excellent customer service. Similar guidelines exist for telephone reference. These documents served as the basis for a Best Practices document for IM:

Best Practices

1. Greet patrons when beginning a chat session. Open with a salutation and an offer to help; also consider greeting them by name.

2. Using your own discretion, consider providing personal contact information (e.g., your name and telephone number or the Reference desk number, 202-994-6048) while chatting with a patron in order to establish rapport and ensure the patron can reestablish contact in case of technical problems.

3. Strive to provide the same service as you would in a face-to-face or telephone Reference interview. For example:

- Ask patrons when they need the information they're seeking.
- Ask patrons where they have already searched, and what they have already found.
- Restate the patron's question.
- Include keyword search strategies within the text of the chat session so the patron can retrace your steps.
- Cut and paste URLs within the text of the chat so the patron can revisit sites later.
- Explain things step by step. Whenever possible, have patrons initiate searches under your instructions, since this will increase opportunities for instruction.

4. When referring patrons to a specific database, use the same name as listed in ALADIN (this is GW's portal to available databases) for clarity.

5. Make sure the patron understands the concepts and vocabulary you're using in the transaction (e.g., "article database" or "coverage").

6. When answering a second or third IM, let patrons know you are helping more than one patron. At your own discretion, consider limiting the number of patrons you help at once (perhaps no more than three or four) in order to ensure good IM Reference service. If the service is too busy and you are unable to assist a patron, refer him or her to another person or Department or offer to contact the patron later.

7. When referring patrons to another person or Department, include contact information.

8.   When ending an IM session, be sure to invite the patron to check back with the service

or with the Reference desk if they have additional questions.

Pilot Program: How Do our Students Communicate?

The IM service was introduced using a pilot program in two phases. This provided reference librarians and student staff with experience as well as input into designing the new service. The pilot also provided opportunities to solicit feedback from patrons. We continued to focus on the question: how do we serve students using their preferred medium of communication?

The first phase of the pilot began during the exam period of the Fall 2005 semester. This is a period of declining student research as their focus is on final exams. Yet, it is also the time when students who are stressed might try a new service rather than take time to physically come to the library. This initial offering ran for ten days, during which time the IM Group finalized the design for an advertising campaign and tested the Web page links for an extended Spring pilot. The following message was posted on the IM page to inform patrons that librarians would keep a log of transactions:

"In order to evaluate the service we are providing, we may examine the content of our interaction with you for questions and answers. This information will be used ANONYMOUSLY. All identifying information will be removed from the message before we use the content to evaluate our responses to your question."

The initial phase of the pilot also provided time to finalize the log and feedback form that librarians would later use to report IM transactions. This was a critical opportunity to assess the efficacy of the training sessions and to identify any further training needs.

The second phase of the pilot lasted throughout the Spring semester of 2006 and reference librarians continued covering the IM reference shifts from their desks. This staffing model allowed the librarians to focus solely on these transactions, very important during this learning period. Colorful posters announced the new service and instruction librarians included information about GelmanInfo and EcklesInfo in their lessons. During this semester, reference librarians carefully documented student use by maintaining logs and keeping statistics.

As reference librarians saved the record of each transaction, they also determined the nature of the transaction, either Reference or Directional as established by the Association of Research Libraries (ARL) statistical surveys. Reference questions are: "an information contact that involves the knowledge, use, recommendations, interpretation, or instruction in the use of one or more information sources by a member of the library staff. The term includes information and referral service. Information sources include (a) printed and non-printed material; (b) machine-readable databases (including computer-assisted instruction); (c) the library's own catalogs and other holdings records; (d) other libraries and institutions through communication or referral; and (e) persons both inside and outside the library. When a staff member uses information gained from previous use of information sources to answer a question, the transaction is reported as a Reference transaction even if the source is not consulted again." The majority of IM submitted questions fell into the Reference category. Others were Directional questions as defined by ARL: "an information contact that facilitates the logistical use of the library and that does not involve the knowledge, use, recommendations, interpretation, or instruction in the use of any information sources other than those that describe the library, such as schedules, floor plans, and handbooks" (Association of Research Libraries 2004-2005).

Throughout the pilot, students were invited to provide feedback. Statistics revealed that students used the service most between 2:00 and 5:00 in the afternoons. Yet, when asked, students suggest-

Figure 2. Promotional poster

ed that the service be available during late night hours, particularly after the Reference Desk has closed. Tuesday was the busiest day of the week, closely followed by Wednesday. Saturday and Sunday saw the least transactions. The students agreed that this usage pattern accurately reflected the days when they would use the service. Students from the United States confirmed that AOL was the service of choice, though international students preferred MSN. The IM Group immediately implemented one student suggestion: inserting the AOL running man logo as an online indicator on the library Web page. Students can immediately tell whether EcklesInfo or GelmanInfo are available to take questions. Initial concerns about copyright were addressed by America Online's Trademark Information Web page (AOL 2007). Also as a follow-up to students' suggestions, an "away" message was drafted to alert online patrons

that responses could be delayed slightly if the librarian was currently busy.

Point of Connection is Everywhere: Reaching Patrons

Marketing played a key role in the successful implementation of the IM reference service. While much could be said about marketing to the millennial generation, the essential goal was to get the library's IM ID on the patron's buddy list. To this end, the marketing strategy was focused primarily on advertising at the point of need. This involved placing marketing materials where students study or seek research assistance. Posters and table tents were posted in library

Figure 3. Promotional bookmark

and campus computer labs. Bookmarks advertising the service were also placed at the circulation desk. Online indicators, that activate when the library is signed onto IM, were added to the Ask A Librarian section on the library's homepage and the service was advertised in a revolving image space also on the homepage.

Course instructors also play a critical role in reaching students at the point of need. Students are likely to approach their instructors for research assistance, so it is critical that instructors are aware of the library services available to patrons. Faculty members have been encouraged to include the library's IM ID on the course syllabus, along with a librarian's contact information. Additionally, instruction librarians emphasize IM

Figure 4. Snapshot of the online indicator

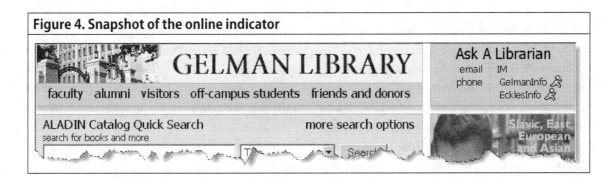

along with the other services available during their instruction sessions. This strategy has been particularly effective among required freshmen writing courses.

IM reference allows the library to move out of its physical space and into the community. Hence, a second marketing strategy has been to advertise the service outside of the library. Mini-posters were used on the student commuter shuttle and an ad was placed in the student newspaper. IM outreach initiatives have also included special campus events called "Feed, Read, and Ride" that allow university organizations to highlight their services to students commuting to and from the satellite campus, along with serving breakfast refreshments. The IM reference service has also sponsored special library events. For example, during cancer awareness month a campaign titled "Research Saves Lives!" advertised an art exhibit related to cancer and IM reference service together. This initiative included a "Feed, Read, and Ride" event, posters, and bookmarks.

A third approach has been to broadcast the IM ID among particular patron groups, such as incoming students, freshmen, and writing classes that have librarian partnerships. Special effort has been made to reach incoming freshmen students during freshmen orientation by including the IM

Figure 5. Promotional poster for the "Research Saves Lives!" event

ID on promotional materials, such as Frisbees, pens, and highlighters.

Successful IM marketing campaigns will produce dividends for the library and can even be a secondary marketing tool for the library as a whole. Due to the nature of the buddy list, if a student adds the library as a buddy during his or her freshmen year, it is very likely that the library will remain a buddy throughout the student's academic career at the university. This places the library in the unique position of always being present in the student's life while not imposing.

Keeping Track of Success: Stats, Logs, and Assessment

One benefit of an IM reference service is the ability to capture the complete transaction, a functionality not usually available at a traditional reference desk. During the initial pilot phase of the project, when librarians staffed the service from their individual computers rather than a shared computer, librarians were asked to submit logs via a Web-based form because it was inefficient to collect the logs from each individual computer. The Web form allowed librarians to remove patron information and identify the question type before submitting the log. An examination of this process revealed, however, that only 71% of transactions were submitted by librarians. Following the migration to the single computer staffing model during the Summer of 2006, the automatic logging feature was used to capture statistical data more efficiently. Automatic logging is a common feature among IM clients. This feature saves a transcript of the transaction, including date, time, and patron exchange. Automatically logging allows for both quantitative and qualitative assessment. As discussed above, the IM page includes information on logs and their purpose, and confirms that any personal information is removed.

Such detailed information naturally raises questions about patron privacy. To address this issue, the IM Group developed a process for systematically purging patron information from the transcript. This includes patron IM IDs and any identifying information transmitted during the transaction. The "Find and Replace" function is used to quickly replace the patron's ID with "Patron" and the transcript is scanned to identify and replace any personal information that was exchanged during the transaction, i.e., personal names or student ID numbers. Finally, the question type is determined. All logs are then saved using a standardized labeling process. The date, time, and question type are included in the file label so that basic statistical data can be collected without opening each file. This data is also totaled in an Excel spreadsheet and graphically represented periodically as a report to administration. This process has been done manually, but automation of the process is in the planning stages. As the number of transactions received per month increases, alternative assessment models, such as a sampling schedule, will provide assessment feedback at a more manageable rate.

Data garnered from the logging process is used to determine service hours and staffing structures. It is also used to develop training materials for both librarian and non-librarian staff members

---

Figure 6. Snapshot of the purged files

Patron 01-03-07 10 D.log	Patron 01-30-07 22 R.log	Patron 02-13-07 13 D.log
Patron 01-05-07 09 R.log	Patron 02-01-07 10 R.log	Patron 02-13-07 14 R 1.log
Patron 01-05-07 12 D.log	Patron 02-01-07 18 R.log	Patron 02-13-07 14 R 2.log
Patron 01-05-07 14 D.log	Patron 02-03-07 12 R.log	Patron 02-13-07 14 R.log
Patron 01-09-07 16 R.log	Patron 02-03-07 13 R.log	Patron 02-13-07 19 R.log
Patron 01-10-07 11 D.log	Patron 02-03-07 17 R.log	Patron 02-13-07 20 R.log

covering the service. The purged logs are periodically reviewed to determine how patrons are using the service and what resources are being used in response. Future work by the IM Group will focus on the further development of qualitative assessment measures.

Future Plans

Over the past year, the IM Reference program at GW has grown exponentially, and there are plans for future growth. The service will expand to provide service via all of the major IM chat protocols. Service hours will also expand to include all Reference Desk hours by utilizing student library assistants at Gelman Library as is already the practice at Eckles Library.

Trillian has limited the library's ability to expand the service because it is only compatible with five protocols. This is a concern with the growing popularity of Google Talk. Regular reviews of updated software options will determine if new developments would better meet the library's needs. Unfortunately, changing the IM client would have significant repercussions, including retraining staff members, compatibility with the library's current IM polices and procedures, and implications for end users.

While the IM Group has already expanded to include members from other library departments, thus far the IM service at the Gelman Library has been staffed solely by the Reference Department. In the future, the service will grow into a cooperative venture to include coverage by other departments in accordance with the implementation of an information commons service model. These new staffing structures also require the development of improved assessment tools and cross-training tutorials to address the unique challenges of providing reference service in a virtual environment that is tailored to the equally unique needs of a staff with diverse responsibilities and levels of technological experience. a staff with diverse responsibilities and technological experience.

Finally, IM as a Web 2.0 application is continuing to evolve in exciting ways. Soon the library's IM ID will be added to the library's contact information on students' online library accounts. Future initiatives include embedding an IM chat window into library Web pages, for example the Research Guides pages. Recent developments allow IM to be integrated with social networking applications. Each of these venues represents a point at which a patron is likely to need or seek assistance.

Conclusion

Reference librarians at GW were not the first in the profession to offer IM Reference to their patrons. Yet, as early adopters, we had to consider an array of software, garner support from colleagues, and translate a familiar service to an unfamiliar technology. It was challenging to design a service from the patrons' perspective. The IM reference service was designed anticipating patron need and modified during the pilot in response to patron input. Students continue to use the service in unanticipated ways and this informs planning. For example, GW students studying abroad now easily maintain a relationship with Gelman Library as they ask for assistance and use the resources remotely. Those students are now considered key stakeholders, as the library can serve their information needs more effectively.

IM advertising targeted patrons' point of need, moving reference services and opportunities for contact beyond the library walls. This necessitated coordination and collaboration with other campus departments, student groups, faculty, and the library's outreach committee. Such advertising also raised the profile of the library. As plans for the new service were communicated across the university, other departments, such as the Student Housing Office, began to explore how they could apply this model to their work. Likewise, librarian colleagues beyond Gelman and Eckles Libraries are modifying and delivering reference services to 21st century students and it is gratifying to participate in these new conversations. Our students and patrons are the beneficiaries of these new collaborations and conversations. Join in! For more information IM GelmanInfo or EcklesInfo!

References

Abram, Stephen and Judy Luther. 2004. Born with the chip. Library Journal 29 (May): 34-37.

American Online. 2007. AOL trademark list. http://about.aol.com/aolnetwork/trademarks/

Association of Research Libraries. 2004-2005. ARL statistics questionnaire. http://72.14.205.104/custom?q=cache:8pYFuyXKsJ4J:www.arl.org/bm~doc/06instruct.pdf+reference+transactions&hl=en&ct=clnk&cd=4&gl=us&client=google-coop-np

Comscore. 2006. Europe surpasses North America in instant messenger users, Comscore study reveals. http://www.comscore.com/press/release.asp?id=800.

Foley, Marianne. 2002. Instant messaging reference in an academic library: A case study. College and Research Libraries 63 (January): 36-45.

Houghton, Sarah and Aaron Schmidt. 2005. Web-based chat vs. instant messaging: Who wins? Online 29 (July/August): 26-30.

Lenhart, Amanda, Mary Madden, and Paul Hitlin. 2005. Teens and technology: Youth are leading the transition to a fully wired and mobile nation. Pew/Internet, July 27. http://www.pewinternet.org/pdfs/PIP_Teens_Tech_July2005web.pdf

Lippincott, Joan K. 2005. Net generation students & libraries. In Educating the Net Generation. Oblinger, Diana and James Oblinger, eds. Boulder, CO: Educause.

Maldonado, Laura, Deborah Gaspar and Sarah Palacios-Wilhelm. 2006. Virtual reference, IM chat and beyond: Taking reference services out of the library. Presentation at the 21st Computers in Libraries, Washington D.C.

Schmidt, Aaron and Michael Stephens. 2005. IM me. *Library Journal* 130 (April): 34-35.

Taking the Library to Users: Experimenting with Facebook as an Outreach Tool

Dawn Lawson

Abstract

The author, East Asian studies librarian at New York University (NYU), describes a successful outreach effort using Facebook, a social networking Web site popular among undergraduates. After searching the site for NYU students who had listed East Asian studies as one of their concentrations, the librarian sent messages to them within Facebook, introducing herself and inviting them to make use of library resources. Close to 20 percent of the students replied immediately, several with specific reference questions. In addition to discussing the motivation, methodology, and results of the outreach project, the chapter suggests various possibilities for future expansion of this type of activity.

Introduction

College students in need of library assistance today have many options beyond the traditional one of walking into a physical building in search of a staffed reference desk. At most institutions, they can also search for information themselves on their library's Web site or use links provided there to contact a librarian via e-mail, chat, or instant message. However, these latter options assume that the students visit the library Web site, when in fact studies show that a commercial search engine is their first choice when starting an information search (OCLC 2005).

How can we reach students if they don't come into our physical or even our cyber spaces? One obvious answer is to go into theirs. We know that, in addition to commercial search engines, students are also making substantial use of social networking sites such as Facebook and MySpace (New Media Consortium 2007). In response to these developments, which seem to have happened almost overnight, librarians need to re-imagine their roles and the ways in which they provide services. Despite assertions by some that they would not be welcome in what the students consider to be "their" space (see, for example, "Are We Welcome at the Party," posted on ACRLog by StevenB, February 7, 2006), a number of librarians have established their libraries as "groups" on Facebook. This is a step in the right direction, but it still requires the students to learn of a particular group's existence and join it before they can reap any benefits. What if the librarian were to take a proactive approach, seeking out the students one by one in their own space, so that they need only click Reply to avail themselves of their subject specialist? This chapter describes a successful experiment in doing exactly that.

The first section of this chapter discusses some of the existing literature on the subject of academic libraries and Facebook, as well as Facebook outreach projects by other librarians. Next, I give a brief introduction to Facebook, focusing on the features that played a role in my work. I then describe the motivation behind my project, the methodology used to implement it, and the responses I received from the students contacted. The conclusion outlines my plans to repeat and extend this effort, the results of which I will document on the wiki that supplements this book.

Dawn Lawson, Bobst Library, e-mail: dl80@nyu.edu

Facebook and Academic Libraries: A Brief Review of the Literature

As of June 2007, the most comprehensive article discussing Facebook in the mainstream library and information science literature was "Checking Out Facebook.com: The Impact of a Digital Trend on Academic Libraries," by Laurie Charnigo and Paula Barnett-Ellis, which appeared in the March 2007 issue of *Information Technology and Libraries*. The broad literature review included in the piece encompassed publications on a variety of aspects of online social networks, including privacy issues and usage statistics. The authors reported that, despite the evident interest of librarians in online social networks, "actual literature in the field of library and information science is scarce." They correctly attributed this to the newness of the phenomenon (Charnigo and Barnett-Ellis 2007, 26). The article analyzes the results of their February 2006 survey of 126 academic librarians about their attitudes toward Facebook. The authors found that only "a small group of the respondents... were extremely positive and excited about the possibilities of online social networking" (29).

The situation has changed dramatically in little more than a year. "Librarians and Facebook," a discussion group that Charnigo and Barnett-Ellis founded within Facebook itself, had 1,391 members as of June 2007. This is strong evidence that librarians are embracing this new technology—and quickly. Moreover, "Librarians and Facebook" is not the only such group on the site. Others include "Digital Reference in Facebook," with 260 members; "FacebookAppsForLibraries," with 133 members; and "Learning Communities in Facebook," with 54 members. These membership totals are all as of June 6, 2007; group membership numbers in Facebook tend to increase daily, often dramatically, especially in the first days after a group is formed. While this chapter was being researched and written, a group was started on Facebook to facilitate an in-person gathering of librarians interested in the topic at the 2007 American Library Association Annual Conference in Washington, D.C.

The first librarians to develop a presence for their libraries on Facebook did so by using the site's profile feature, discussed in detail below. However, Facebook eventually prohibited this use of the profile on the grounds that it is intended for use by individuals, not organizations. This move forced these librarians to reinstate their profiles under their own names or establish their libraries as groups. In addition to the disadvantage of requiring users to find it proactively and join, a Facebook group lacks a number of other functionalities that can be useful in library outreach (e.g., friending, the status field, the wall; see the section Beyond Messaging, below). The group presence does have one significant practical advantage, however: once a group is established and has members, any member can send a message to all of them at once. In contrast, an individual can only send messages to other individuals one at a time. As described below, this restriction can make sending messages to large numbers of people in Facebook onerous. For ongoing library outreach communications, it is best to combine the two approaches, that is, to invite the students to join a library group after they have responded positively to being contacted by a librarian with an individual profile in Facebook. This approach makes it possible to send group messages once the students who are open to being contacted have been identified through individual messages and agreed to join a group.

Other than establishing this type of presence on Facebook, to date there appear to have been very few attempts to use the site to reach out to students one by one as potential library users. An early example of such a project, also cited by Charnigo and Barnett-Ellis, was initiated in fall 2005 by Brian Mathews of Georgia Institute of Technology. Shannon Kealey of New York University documented her outreach to science majors in a poster session, "Fishing in a Barrel: Facebook as an Outreach and Marketing Tool," presented at the 2007 ACRL National Conference. On April

29, 2007, Gerry McKiernan, Science and Technology Librarian at Iowa State University, announced on his blog, Friends: Social Networking Sites for Engaged Library Services, (http://onlinesocialnetworks.blogspot.com/) that he would be presenting the results of his summer Facebook outreach initiative at the LITA National Forum 2007.

A recent book, *Social Software in Libraries: Building Collaboration, Communication, and Community Online*, by Meredith Farkas, briefly discusses academic libraries and Facebook in its chapter on social networking, but not surprisingly, most of the "literature" on this topic has appeared on the Internet itself, much of it within groups on the Facebook site. Gerry McKiernan's above-mentioned blog is another venue for discussions of this topic, and the companion Web site to Farkas's book (http://www.sociallibraries.com/) contains a rapidly growing list of links to online resources related to social networking, a number of which concern Facebook.

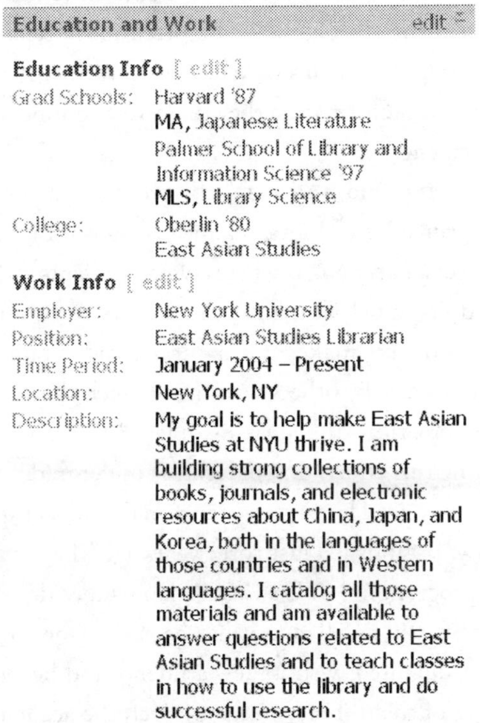

How to Use Facebook

As with other social networking sites, you must register before starting to use Facebook. Facebook originally required a valid .edu e-mail address for registration. While this is no longer the case, the name of the institution in the e-mail address you provide at registration (e.g., the "nyu" in xxxx@nyu.edu) still plays a significant role in your Facebook activities. To do library outreach to students, you must belong to the same "network" that they do. Your network is determined by the institutional name in your registered e-mail address; therefore, the e-mail address you use to register must contain the same institution name as those of the students you will be contacting. Network members can view the profiles of other members and send messages to them if their privacy preferences allow it.

After registering, you create a profile. This is a page of information about yourself. You can only have one profile in Facebook and, as mentioned above, profiles must be associated with a person, not an institution.

Creating a profile is a straightforward process that consists of filling out a series of forms. These forms are categorized under tabs labeled Basic, Contact, Personal, Work, Education, and Courses. The Work tab has a free-text Description field, useful for entering a statement about your role in your library. There is also a tab for adding a photo and one that explains how to drag and drop items in your profile to change the default layout. The amount of information you can provide in the profile, particularly of a personal nature, is considerable. When the profile page is displayed, it does not show the fields you left blank.

Because you will be displaying information about yourself and seeking information about others, it is important to have a basic understanding of Facebook's intricate system of privacy options. The site allows its users a great deal of control over who can see their information. This control is based on two of Facebook's key concepts: networks and friends.

Figure 1: Education and work section of Facebook profile

Education and Work   edit

Education Info [edit]
Grad Schools: Harvard '87
               MA, Japanese Literature
               Palmer School of Library and
               Information Science '97
               MLS, Library Science
College: Oberlin '80
               East Asian Studies

Work Info [edit]
Employer: New York University
Position: East Asian Studies Librarian
Time Period: January 2004 – Present
Location: New York, NY
Description: My goal is to help make East Asian
             Studies at NYU thrive. I am
             building strong collections of
             books, journals, and electronic
             resources about China, Japan, and
             Korea, both in the languages of
             those countries and in Western
             languages. I catalog all those
             materials and am available to
             answer questions related to East
             Asian Studies and to teach classes
             in how to use the library and do
             successful research.

As mentioned earlier, your network is determined by the institution named in your registered e-mail address. For example, my e-mail address ends in @nyu.edu, so I am part of the NYU network. (You can belong to more than one network, in which case you designate one as "primary." For the purpose of library outreach, this discussion assumes that you belong to one network, that of the academic institution with which you and your library are affiliated.) In Facebook, "friends" are people, both inside and outside your network, who have accepted the invitation you issued asking them to be your friend or vice versa. When you attempt to "friend" someone, Facebook sends a message to her or his registered e-mail address, conveying your request and providing a hyperlink to a Facebook page on which the recipient can confirm or reject the request. It is also possible for either party to provide information about how they know the other (from school, work, etc.) and to request confirmation of that information.

The control you have over your information in Facebook begins with who can see your profile. There are three choices: you can make your profile visible to all of your networks and all of your friends, to some of your networks, or to your friends only. Beyond that, you can control who can see certain features of your profile. For example, you can restrict your contact information to one of the three groups just mentioned. Some other parts of your profile can be restricted even more, so that they can be seen by only you or even by no one. You can also mark one or more checkboxes to indicate what types of people in your network can see your profile. In a .edu network, the types of people are listed as "undergrads," "grads," "alumni," "faculty," and "staff." The many other privacy options in Facebook include those related to searching: who can find you and what actions they can take within Facebook when they do. For example, by default anyone in Facebook can send a message to anyone else on the site, but by unchecking a box it is possible to restrict the people who can send messages

to you to only those you have allowed to see your profile. Facebook's privacy options are clearly and thoroughly documented, both under the Privacy link at the top of the user's Facebook home page and under specific topics in the Help index.

The Initiative

In February 2007, I used Facebook to locate East Asian studies majors at NYU and send them messages introducing myself, their subject specialist, and encouraging them to make use of library resources. Several considerations brought about this project. First, it was inspired by the perennial librarian's desire to let as many students as possible know that special expertise and a universe of helpful, often untapped, resources is available to them. Academic librarians have always sought innovative ways to reach out to students, but the need to do this is more pressing today than ever. Not only do students have an unprecedented amount of information available to them—unmediated—via the Internet, but the existence of this perceived wealth of resources has caused significant decreases in in-person visits to the library and the reference desk. This is accompanied by a parallel tendency by students to overlook the often-more-reliable electronic content licensed by their libraries in favor of the free information they find using commercial search engines.

Another motivation for the project was one of the principles of Library 2.0: Taking the Library to Users. Facebook is where college students today are doing much of their communication with one another. This makes it a natural choice as a medium for use by others wanting to reach them.

A practical difficulty also played a role in inspiring this effort, that of locating undergraduates who may need library assistance in my subject specialty. Established just three years ago, the graduate program in NYU's East Asian studies department is still small, and it has been easy for me to get acquainted with its few students and become aware of their library needs. In fact, the academic department maintains an e-mail distribution list of those graduate students, to which it will forward messages from me about the library on request. Graduate students in other departments whose research topics involve East Asia in some way, such as those in history, education, and cinema studies, have managed to find me, or I them. Undergraduates, however, are another matter entirely. The department does not maintain an e-mail list of this more fluid population. Even if one were available, it would include neither minors in the discipline nor those who had not yet declared a major, two groups who might arguably be more in need of research assistance than the majors because of their lesser knowledge of the topic. In addition, the widely noted trend toward interdisciplinarity in all areas of study has reduced the significance of a student's declared major. Because Facebook allows users to list multiple academic concentrations, and because it displays information about the students that they have chosen to disclose, it is an ideal vehicle for seeking out students who might need library assistance in the field.

Methodology

I began by registering my NYU e-mail address with Facebook. I then created my profile, which I filled in with mostly professional information, although I did include some information in the Personal category on favorite books, movies, and so on. For my profile photo, I chose to post a somewhat casual picture of myself rather than one taken in a library setting.

My next step was to use the Advanced Search function to locate East Asian studies majors at NYU. Advanced Search in Facebook is limited to searching one of two realms of people. By default, an Advanced Search encompasses all of one's networks and all of one's friends (as mentioned above, friends can be inside or outside your networks). The other Advanced Search option searches only within your primary network. I searched within the NYU network for users with the concentration East Asian studies (selected from a drop-down list) and with the class years of 2007, 2008, 2009, and 2010. This procedure required four separate searches, one for each year.

Because I began my outreach in February 2007, I decided to send messages to that year's class first. Facebook found more than 50 East Asian studies majors in this category. For each result on the list, the individual's name and photo were displayed. Below each name was a list with items labeled "Networks," (for example, "NYU '07"); "Fields" (for example, East Asian Studies, Economics, etc.) corresponding to the concentration parameter of the search; and "Matches," indicating which search parameters the results matched. Each of my search results listed Class Year and Concentration as "Matches." In

Figure 2. Dawn Lawson's profile page

most cases, the Fields portion of the results listed East Asian studies among the areas of concentration. This assured me that I would not be sending someone an irrelevant message.

In a number of cases, however, Fields was not included in a result, perhaps because of privacy configurations. To ascertain that these students were East Asian studies majors, I clicked on the names of each individual to view their profiles. Whenever I was unable to confirm the major because the profile was not linked to the name (another privacy option), I decided not to include that person in my outreach. The same was true of a student's class year. If the year did not appear on the results list, and if I could not view the profile, I excluded that person from the project.

Sometimes a profile revealed that the individual had already graduated in January 2007. In addition, I discovered that the Advanced Search option does not provide for correlating class year with institution. Because of this limitation, I also had to exclude those who had graduated from another institution in 2007, perhaps a graduate school, but from NYU four or more years ago. I later realized that I could have accommodated for this search function limitation by setting the Advanced Search option School Status to Undergraduate. I conducted these careful checks in order to avoid sending an unsolicited message to someone to whom it would have no value. I recommend this procedure to librarians doing outreach of this kind.

After executing my four searches and applying the above exclusions, I ended up with 140 students to contact. The breakdown by class year was as follows: 46 in 2007, 44 in 2008, 34 in 2009, and 16 in 2010. A Facebook user is not permitted to do mass messaging except to friends or to all members of a group of 1,000 people or fewer to which the user belongs. Therefore, I sent each student an individual message. I accomplished this from the Results list of my search for East Asian Studies concentrators in each class year. This was easy to do because there is a Message button by each name. I composed my initial outreach message in Microsoft Word so that I could copy and paste it each time. The message was as follows:

Hi [First Name of Student],

I'm the East Asian Studies Librarian at NYU. I see that you are studying EAS, so I wanted to introduce myself and let you know that I'm eager to help you take advantage of all the resources and services we offer at Bobst.

If you have any questions about your research or about using the library, or if you want to make suggestions about our collection of books and electronic resources, please feel free to contact me here on Facebook or at dawn.lawson@nyu.edu.

Sincerely,

[my name, title, e-mail address, library address, telephone number]

Facebook's sophisticated spam detection system posed a significant hurdle to my effort. I was aware that there was a limit to the number of messages—even individual ones—that could be sent within a short period of time, but the exact number is not disclosed on the Facebook site. When Brian Mathews conducted his outreach project in the fall of 2005, he was able to send eighty messages in less than twenty minutes. At that time, Facebook's policy was apparently to allow the sending of eighty messages every six hours (Mathews 2006, 306). I sent twelve messages in my first eight minutes of work. After the first few, I received an on-screen warning informing me that what I was doing could be construed as violating the Facebook terms. I paused, but did not stop sending messages because I believed I was operating within the rules. However, when I sent three messages over a period of three minutes one hour later, a message displayed on my Facebook session screen informing me that my account had been disabled. I immediately sent Facebook Customer Support a polite e-mail message, explaining the nature of my project and asking them to consider not blocking me while I carried it out. If that was not possible, I requested that the Facebook representative tell me how many messages one was permitted to send over what period of time. I also pointed out that Facebook users would not be harmed by this use of the system for educational purposes. As additional proof of the legitimacy and safety of my messaging activities, I attached the exemption document I had received from my university's Committee on Activities Involving Human Subjects.

A representative from Facebook Customer Support replied promptly, informing me that my appeal was under review, but the message did not answer my questions about permissible levels of e-mail activity or refer to the information I had provided about the nature of my project. My account was reinstated in less than forty-eight hours. The message informing me of my reinstatement included a stern warning that any future incident could result in termination. It explained that it was a violation of the Facebook terms to "repeatedly send the same message or send the same post." Scouring the Facebook Terms of Use, I was unable to find a reference to this policy (http://www.facebook.com/terms.php).

As a next step, I took measures that I hoped would prevent me from having my account disabled again. I created two additional versions of the outreach message by varying the wording, the paragraph formatting, and the opening and closing salutations. In addition, I began allowing intervals of one minute between messages, and I alternated among the three texts. Even with these precautions in place, I received an on-screen warning soon after I began my messaging activity again. This time I stopped immediately. When

I resumed, I allowed fifteen minutes between the messages, still alternating the texts. This approach was successful.

Results

Watching the clock between each copying, pasting, and sending of a message was tedious at best. But once I received my first positive response from a student—on my second day of activity, when I had sent just 16 messages—the drudgery was no longer an issue. In response to my 140 messages, I received acknowledgments from twenty-four students, or 17.14 percent (some students acknowledged the message in multiple ways, but I am counting them only once). Figure 3 shows the number of acknowledgments received by class year. Of the twenty-four responses, fifteen were messages to me in Facebook from students who thanked me for contacting them about the library and indicating that they would be in touch when the need arose. Four students sent a friending request rather than a message. Three of the students who sent thank-you messages also sent friending requests, and one wrote on my "wall" (see below) in addition to sending a friending request.

Beyond these, and of greatest interest to me, were the five students who responded immediately with reference questions, one of whom sent an additional question some six weeks later. This illustrates that students have library-related questions in mind that they may not make the effort to pose to a librarian by initiating contact either in person or online, but that they will ask immediately upon being contacted directly. Two of the questions were general ones about the library's collection of East Asian materials, while the other three were about resources the students were seeking for papers they were researching and writing.

A Dissenting View

In his blog, The Ubiquitous Librarian (http://theubiquitouslibrarian.typepad.com/), Brian Mathews reflects on the use of Facebook by librarians and on his own outreach project, in which he sent

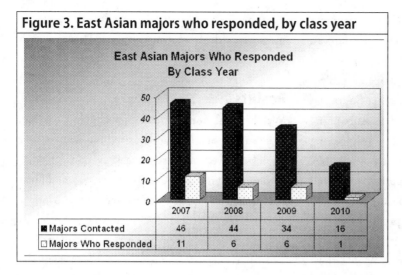

Figure 3. East Asian majors who responded, by class year

East Asian Majors Who Responded
By Class Year

	2007	2008	2009	2010
■ Majors Contacted	46	44	34	16
□ Majors Who Responded	11	6	6	1

individual e-mail messages in Facebook to more than 1,500 graduate and undergraduate mechanical engineering students. On December 6, 2006, he wrote:

> Scratch everything I said in the *CRL News* article. Essentially, it is a direct violation to e-mail a student and advertise a service or event….[H]as my effort paid off? Sure several students "friended" me and many responded to my messages—but none of them have used Facebook to contact me since then about the library or assignments. My objective of *appearing* in their space has ultimately failed. While they don't mind me there, they don't recognize me as librarian. If I offer help they'll take it, but they won't ask for it.

As discussed above, I was temporarily banned from Facebook while attempting to carry out my project. I differ with Mathews' view that this kind of activity is a violation of the Facebook terms for two reasons. First, although making patrons aware of library services is now commonly referred to as marketing, it is better described as an extension of our educational mission. We are not selling anything for profit. In fact, we are urging students to make use of something for which they have already paid in the form of tuition. Second, I described what I was doing to Facebook representatives, and no one ever suggested that my activities constituted a violation of the terms of service because I was actually marketing or selling something.

In addition, I think that Mathews' dismissive view of his experience is overly pessimistic. The disappointment he expresses can be addressed by engaging in persistent use of this new channel and by imaginative extension of activities in Facebook such as I describe below. Despite the tone of his post, Mathews is not abandoning the use of Facebook to reach students. On July 2, 2007, he posted a blog entry describing his participation in the group "Georgia Tech Class of 2011."

I consider the fact that I received a nearly 20 percent positive response rate and no negative feedback to be a strong affirmation of the effectiveness of this type of search-and-contact effort. Librarians contemplating doing this, however, should bear in mind that carrying out an outreach project on a significantly larger scale than mine under the terms that applied in February 2007 would require weeks or months. It is advisable to maintain a spreadsheet or other type of record listing the names of those students already contacted. Particularly when there is a time delay between sending messages, it is easy to forget the identity of the last addressee. While it is possible to refer to Sent Messages for this information, doing so takes you away from the Search Results screen and requires that the search for potential recipients be re-executed.

Beyond Messaging

There are many additional functionalities within Facebook that also can be used to enhance a librarian's visibility on the site. One option is use of the status field and the "wall" to note when you are working at the reference desk or engaged in another library-related activity. The status field allows you to post what you are currently doing, either in the form of canned (is "at home," "in the library," "at work," "out at a party," or "sleeping") or free text. You can also check your friends' current statuses from your profile page. The wall is an area on your profile page on which you and your friends can write publicly viewable messages.

As mentioned above, Shannon Kealey invited the NYU science students who responded to her message to join a group named after her library. She also created an Events page for the group that lists library happenings. She advertises these events with a Facebook flyer, which is an online advertisement that displays only to users in a specific network. Facebook also allows you to import blog entries to your Facebook profile page or Group page. If you maintain a library-related blog, this option provides another avenue for enhancing your library's presence on Facebook. Note, however, that when you post content on Facebook you automatically grant the company

> an irrevocable, perpetual, non-exclusive, transferable, fully paid, worldwide license (with the right to sublicense) to use, copy, publicly perform, publicly display, reformat, translate, excerpt (in whole or in part) and distribute such User Content for any purpose on or in connection with the Site or the promotion thereof, to prepare derivative works of, or incorporate into other works, such User Content, and to grant and authorize sublicenses of the foregoing (http://www.facebook.com/terms.php).

In late May 2007, Facebook introduced Facebook Platform (http://developers.facebook.com/), an Application Programming Interface (API) for building applications that can be integrated into Facebook. This greatly expands the possibilities for use of the site by libraries. David Ward of the University of Illinois, Urbana-Champaign, developed a widget for searching his institution's library catalog and several of its journal databases, for which he posted the code (http://uillinois.facebook.com/apps/application.php?id=2414276217/). Several other libraries immediately adapted it for their use. As this chapter went to press, Ward and the other librarians were experiencing difficulties receiving Facebook's approval of their applications. The reason isn't entirely clear because, according to accounts on the discussion board of the FacebookAppsforLibraries group (http://nyu.facebook.com/topic.php?uid=2469777131&topic=2579/), Facebook representatives have provided differing rationales to several of the librarians.

A number of commercial applications are also beginning to appear. LibGuides, created by SpringShare, Inc., is one of the first applications developed for library use in Facebook. According to the SpringShare Web site (http://www.springshare.com/), LibGuides will recognize Facebook users' school affiliations and give these users seamless access to library resources and services from their Facebook home page.

Future Plans

My future activities in Facebook, which I will report on the wiki that supplements this book, will include both continuing the outreach project I have described here and expanding on it. Each semester I will search Facebook for new East Asian studies majors and send them an introductory message, keeping track of the number and nature of the responses I receive. I will also watch the development of library-related groups on Facebook, compile information on their membership numbers, and summarize any significant new discussion topics. This includes following the dispute between developers of library search applications and Facebook, Inc.

Some of the students volunteered information about themselves that will help me target library services for them in the future. For example, several noted that they were currently studying abroad and that they would check out the library on their return. A student who has spent a year in an Asian country will return with a greatly improved ability to read and speak the language. I intend to send a message to these students when they return, informing them of the library's books in Chinese, Japanese, and Korean. These are resources they may not have known about when they were in the first two years of language study, using an introductory-level textbook. As mentioned above, some of the students to whom I sent messages sent me friend requests, which I accepted. Because Facebook's News Feed function displays information about the Facebook activities of your friends to your Facebook home page, I see news of these students whenever I log in to the site. This allows me to keep an eye out for activities that might be related to library services. I will also seek additional opportunities to provide personalized library assistance by redoing the search for majors, reviewing their profiles for relevant changes, and looking at the courses they have listed in the Education section to determine whether a targeted instruction session for that course might be in order. The NYU network on Facebook has more than 500 groups associated with it. I intend to search these periodically to see if any relate to East Asian studies and whether I might contribute to them in a way that could benefit library users. The site's frequent additions of new applications and expansions of existing functionalities are described in its blog (http://blog.facebook.com/); I will consider the potential of new developments reported there for possible connections to library services. These plans all assume that Facebook will remain the dominant force among undergraduates that it is today, in mid-2007. Future activities must also include keeping a close eye on online trends and standing ready to switch tools whenever circumstances dictate.

Conclusion

This project embodies the Library 2.0 Principle of Taking the Library to Users. It is hoped that this case study will be useful to academic librarians who wish to implement their own Facebook outreach activities.

Given the blindingly fast pace of change in the online world, the fact that our users are on Facebook today is far from a guarantee that they will be there tomorrow. As we are all aware, a meteoric rise in popularity on the Internet is not a guarantee of longevity. Facebook itself did not exist just three years ago. Like all wildly successful online ventures, it is constantly reinventing itself to accommodate other Internet-wide developments and is frequently the object of acquisition offers that could result in significant changes. Far more important, therefore, than the methodology and results of any particular study is the message that librarians must become nimble responders to the changing environments of their users, prepared to go to places unanticipated and unforeseeable. However, as Meredith Farkas has written: "A big difference exists between being where our patrons are and being useful to our patrons where they are" (2007, 122). Just as a physical library is more than a building full of books, Library 2.0 means more than merely showing up in the users' space. Once there, librarians need to anticipate, understand, and fulfill these users' needs effectively. The author would like to express her gratitude to Shannon Kealey, Coles Science Center, New York University, for providing the initial inspiration for this project. Thanks are also due to Paula Barnett-Ellis, Houston Cole Library, Jacksonville State University; Alan Campbell; Laurie Charnigo, Houston Cole Library, Jacksonville State University; Evelyn Ehrlich, New York University Libraries; Diana Greene, New York University Libraries; Gerry McKiernan, Iowa State University Library; and Brian Mathews, Georgia Institute of Technology, for commenting on drafts of this chapter.

References

Charnigo, Laurie and Paula Barnett-Ellis. 2007. Checking out Facebook.com: The impact of a digital trend on academic libraries. *Information Technology and Libraries*, 26 (March): 23-34.

Farkas, Meredith. 2007. *Social Software in Libraries: Building Collaboration, Communication, and Community Online.* Medford, NJ: Information Today.

Kealey, Shannon. 2007. Fishing in a barrel: Facebook as an outreach and marketing tool. Poster presented at the 13th ACRL National Conference, Baltimore.

Mathews, Brian S. 2006. Do you Facebook? Networking with students online. *College and Research Libraries News* 67 (May): 306-307.

New Media Consortium and EduCause Learning Initiative. 2007. *The Horizon Report 2007 Edition.* http://www.nmc.org/pdf/2007_Horizon_Report.pdf.

OCLC Online Computer Library Center. 2005. College Students' Perceptions of Libraries and Information Resources: A Report to the OCLC Membership. http://www.oclc.org/reports/pdfs/studentperceptions.pdf.

http://acrl.ala.org/L2Initiatives/index.php?title=Chapter_11/

YouTube University: Using XML, Web Services, and Online Video Services to Serve University and Library Video Content

Jason A. Clark

Abstract

This chapter looks at popular online video sites and demonstrates how the data infrastructures and active user communities of these sites can be incorporated into digital video library projects. Specifically, the chapter examines how Application Programming Interfaces (API) and XML feeds have enhanced content for Montana State University (MSU) digital library projects. The case study project, "TERRA: The Nature of Our World," is a working digital video library which leverages the user communities of blip.tv, iTunes, and FeedBurner to distribute its content. The site features a robust XML metadata architecture that enables podcasting and syndication of content. It also features social networking functionality with ratings and comments for each episode. The chapter considers: the advantages of leveraging popular online video sites to distribute content; employing the network infrastructure of these sites to serve large video files; how to use common XML formats for pushing content to users and retrieving content from remote Web sites; and finally, the advantages of opening up digital library sites to user communities through commenting, rating, and forum systems. Simple source code examples using Javascript, XML, PHP, and MySQL will be posted on the associated wiki to give readers a head start in implementing some of the projects and widgets described in the chapter.

Introduction

When it comes to online video, Silicon Valley startups and academic library digitization groups are just getting started. The phenomenon of online video is so new that interested parties are still arguing over the exact date when digital videos broke into the mainstream. It could have been December 2005 when the digital short produced by Saturday Night Live cast member Andy Samberg went viral from YouTube and "Lazy Sunday" was a hit (Wikipedia 2007a). Or maybe it was lonelygirl15, the series of bedroom confessionals from an actress pretending to be a teenager published weekly on YouTube since June 2006, that solidified the Web as a viable video entertainment medium (Wikipedia 2007b). Whatever the reason, only recently have Internet users begun to view the Web as a primary medium for video. Widespread broadband, simplified video editing and creation tools, and a perfect storm of people wanting to watch other people being creative on a computer screen have also contributed to the ubiquity of digital videos on the Web.

Ubiquity often breeds scholarly interest and academia has not escaped the siren's call of online video. In my work at the MSU Libraries as the Digital Initiatives Librarian, I have seen a growing interest in creating and preserving digital video formats. MSU is within a stone's throw of Yellowstone National Park, and this proximity has created a burgeoning nature documentary filmmaking community of professionals and students. Digital video is the preferred medium and MSU is actively building a curriculum around new forms of media. I was approached by the Media and Theatre Arts (MTA) Department at MSU to build a

Jason A. Clark, Montana State University Libraries, e-mail: jaclark@montana.edu

Figure 1. A CONTENTdm Results Web page

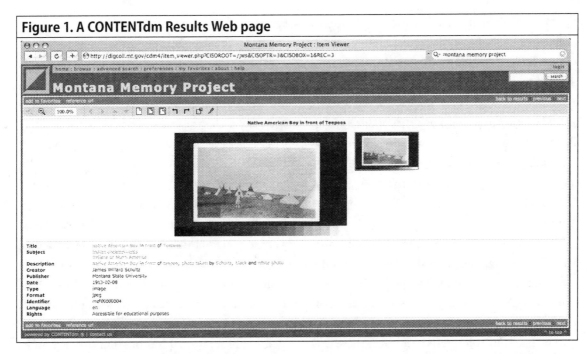

digital video library capable of archiving and distributing the growing number of films produced by the university and other affiliated groups.

As part of my reasoning for creating a digital library for videos, I wanted to explore what academic libraries and interested parties across MSU could do with digital video projects. Could academia follow the YouTube and blip.tv (http://blip.tv/) model? I had been working in digital librar-

ies for about three years and had been struck by the stiff and guarded nature of most of my digital library applications. They did their job by applying controlled vocabularies, adhering to metadata standards, and letting people find content. But in the end, they felt a bit disengaged from the types of Web applications I was seeing and using online. For example, I was creating applications that looked something like figure 1.

Figure 2. A Flickr Web site tagging screen

These traditional digital library applications, such as the CONTENTdm example above, tended to look like the library online catalog. They were characterized by sterile, fixed data and simple text-based designs. The typical display offered a series of fields listing important qualities about an item along with a link to the digital object. While this is useful, expectations with the open Web were starting to change. More interactive Web applications, such as Flickr, were appearing on the scene (figure 2).

These new types of applications were allowing users to tag their items, embed collections as slideshows on any Web page, and upload/organize/share their content with anyone else. They made it simple to browse collections and connect with users who had similar interests. And all of these new applications used XML as a backbone to allow other developers to remix or "mashup" their content in fascinating ways. Library Web applications were missing many, if not all, of these features.

By exploring what Tim O'Reilly has called Web 2.0 principles and their related Library 2.0 ideas, I started to understand more about the types of Web applications I was seeing (O'Reilly 2005a). At the center of Web 2.0 and Library 2.0 is an acceptance of the read/write Web. Current and emerging Web applications are moving away from read-only type sites that offer only static viewing of Web pages and toward read/write sites that allow for user participation, personal storage, and contributions. This is a transformation of the medium from a passive to an active experience. The Web always had this capability and many sites were able to employ it early on. (Think Amazon.com and Ebay.com). What has changed is the user expectation that most sites should work in this way. Users were starting to think in different terms: I should be able to set up an account and personalize a site to my preferences. I should be able to comment on and rate an item. I should be able to upload a file or two and distribute my content through your Web site. Library 2.0 continues in this vein in its push for open standards and innovation in library services.

It was these social and personalized features of the new Web applications which got me thinking that what O'Reilly called Web 2.0 might be applied to digital library projects (O'Reilly 2005b). I started experimenting and built several digital library prototypes with 2.0 features, for example a tagging and folksonomy widget, a Web feeds

Figure 3. An item results view from the "TERRA: The Nature of Our World" Web site

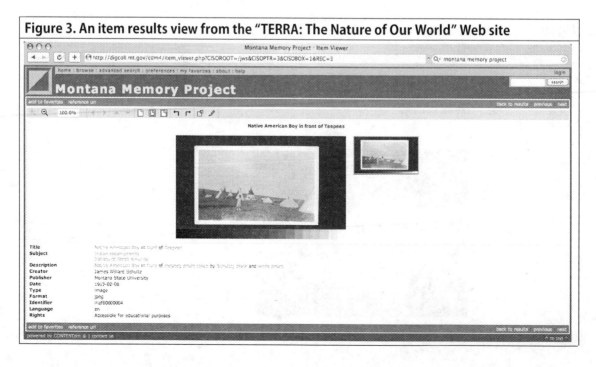

module that created different flavors of XML using a single data source, and a search form that recorded users' search terms and created a recent searches feature linking people to common search results. I was energized by the possibilities and began to wonder, "What would digital libraries 2.0 look like?" If pressed for an answer, my vision for the intersection of Web 2.0 and a digital library would look something like figure 3.

The Initiative

"TERRA: The Nature of Our World" (http://life-onterra.com/) was designed with a nod to the future of digital libraries. It is a digital library of science and natural history videos with commenting, ratings, forums, tags, and multiple subscription/delivery options wrapped up with AJAX (Asynchronous JavaScript and XML) functionality and a Dublin Core metadata backend. AJAX is a programming technique that is able to target pieces of content on a page and run micro-requests behind the scenes to update those pieces of content. On the user end, you see an almost immediate update or page change without the usual full-screen reload. The snappy, instantly responsive interface integral to the user experience of TERRA is made possible with AJAX. On the social networking side of things, TERRA offers a "Related Shows" tab that groups similar videos together (similar to the popular Amazon.com feature "Users who liked this book also liked…") and a rating system allowing users to weigh in on a video's quality or value to the TERRA community. However, even with all these social Web widgets, it is one of the simplest technologies that is the cornerstone of the sociality of TERRA; that simple technology is XML.

Common XML formats, such as RSS and Atom, allow incredible flexibility in how TERRA content can be delivered and recombined. On the delivery side, XML enables TERRA to broadcast to many channels and push our content into the networked research environment. As a user, you can pick your preferred option: iTunes, the Miro video player (http://www.getmiro.com/), a Google personal home page, a standard feed reader, and so on.

Figure 4. The "TERRA: The Nature of Our World" RSS 2.0 podcast feed rendered by FeedBurner in a Safari Web browser

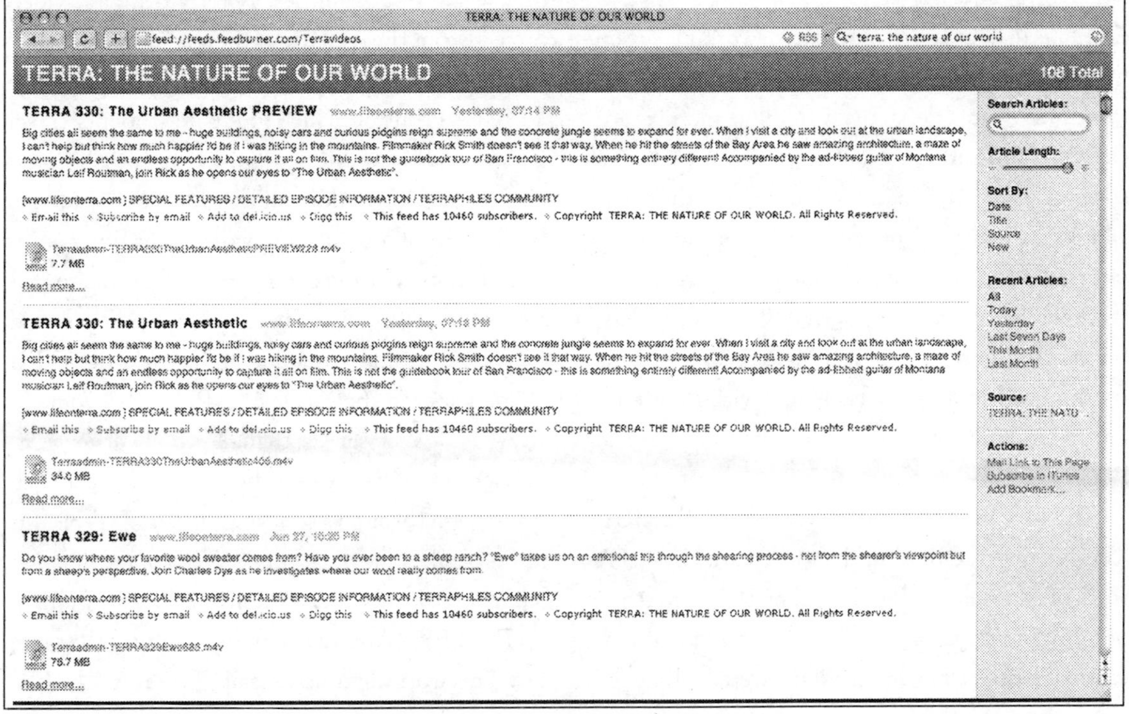

The TERRA group is a partnership between Montana PBS, the MTA Department at MSU, and various independent filmmakers. TERRA films are typically documentary video shorts about science and natural history. Recent episodes include films about the Exxon Valdez oil spill, miracle medicines from the Amazon, and a look at the Mongolian snow leopard. The shorts are produced in conjunction with the MFA program in Science and Natural History Filmmaking at MSU, Filmmakers for Conservation, and Montana PBS. Published weekly via FeedBurner, iTunes, blip.tv, and the TERRA Web site itself, each week provides a short episode "teaser" and also the full episode download in high or low resolution. To date, there are around eighty published videos and the students are readying season three for uploading and distribution.

The TERRA projects brought together several of the above parties, but most of the parties play ancillary roles. The primary relationship that makes TERRA Web projects and content creation happen is the one between MSU Libraries and The TERRA group from MTA. The latter consists of a faculty member and graduate students from the MFA program in Science and Natural History Filmmaking. It is a triangulated working group dependent on close collaboration and communication. MSU Libraries actively develop and manage the Web site and related Web projects. Creation, solicitation, and promotion of new films falls to the MTA graduate student project manager and other interested MTA graduate students. An MTA faculty member oversees the active TERRA projects, but more importantly he seeks and secures outside funding by building relationships with university groups and independent entities such as Montana PBS.

The first iteration of the Web site, "TERRA: The Nature of Our World," was created by MFA students on the Google Blogger platform in October 2005 and was an early adopter of video podcasting. At the time, the students were looking for a simple Web site to promote their work. Almost immediately, the podcasts grew in popularity, demand skyrocketed, and interest in creating and delivering content to a wider audience became a goal. To take the project to the next level, the students needed a Web developer and a digital content strategy. A large part of my job is recognizing when university departments need help in creating access to and preserving their data. This core job duty, along with my interest in moving towards a digital library with Web 2.0 features, made the TERRA opportunity one I couldn't ignore. I was referred to the students and faculty of the TERRA group by a colleague in the Arts and Architecture department who knew of my interest and had seen some of my prototype digital library 2.0 applications. Within a week, I met with the TERRA group and demonstrated some possibilities for the site. The following week, MSU Libraries were brought in to build/program/code the site and to create a content management architecture, including the metadata and data preservation architecture.

The success of MSU Libraries collaboration with the TERRA group has led to further digital library 2.0 opportunities. A related digital video project from the TERRA group is "TERRApod." Currently in beta, this is a pilot project from the TERRA group in which graduate students travel to remote areas of Montana and run workshops on filmmaking for middle and high school students. At the end of a workshop, video recording equipment is provided and an assignment is given to create a topical film. The assigned films are uploaded to YouTube and the data is pulled into the TERRApod site via the YouTube API. In this context, an API is a Web service that allows an authenticated user to remotely access the data stored in a Web application through a scripting language. Typically, the user takes the data from a Web application and repurposes it to create a wholly new application.

The TERRApod site employs many of the same social networking functions of "TERRA: The Na-

Figure 5. "TERRA: The Nature of Our World" as it appears in iTunes

ture of Our World." In the TERRApod forums, students are able to speak with their peers as they create films and consult with graduate student experts when questions arise. When the assignment is finished, all videos are published with associated metadata, given peer and expert comments, and voted on with the top vote-getters appearing on the TERRApod home page. The goal is to create an online community for workshop participants through the various social Web widgets on the site. TERRApod is currently in a true beta testing phase and restricted to a small sample of Montana participants. It may be opened to the public as development continues.

At its core, the TERRA project team is lean, but effective. The team is comprised of an MTA faculty member, an MTA graduate student project manager, an interface designer, and a Web developer (the author). The small size of the group makes for a very efficient and communicative team, limiting the need for committee work and potentially drawn-out group decision-making. TERRA runs on an Apache Web server and uses

MySQL, PHP, Flash, and Javascript to power the dynamic portions of the site. The team used open source options almost exclusively to reduce cost and to tap into a wealth of expertise on the open Web. Initial funding for the TERRA group came from seed money from the MTA department. The team worked with the hope that the final goal of distributing good content would lead to further opportunities. Since the launch in December 2006, several grant funding and private interest funding opportunities are in the works to keep TERRA viable and the outlook is good. In addition, "TERRA: The Nature of Our World" has been honored at several International Web competitions, notably as a finalist at South by Southwest Interactive (http://2007.sxsw. com/interactive/web_awards/finalists/) and as a winner at The Webby Awards (http://www. webbyawards.com/webbys/current.php?media_ id=97&season=11).

Early on in the development of TERRA, it became apparent that the network and storage architectures in place on the MSU campus were not going to be sufficient. At its core, TERRA was a Web application characterized by large streaming files and robust Flash interfaces and would need to take advantage of broadband Internet connections. This wasn't your father's HTML site. The MTA Department at MSU had a single server and a single staff member, while MSU Libraries were engaged in a set of projects that could not be pushed aside to create and maintain a digital media network. The TERRA team realized that it needed to locate outside hosting services to provide the bandwidth intensive distribution functionality that TERRA was going to need. We looked at several video hosting sites and settled on two for distributing the large, rich media files: YouTube and blip.tv. All files are also stored locally on the MSU campus network within a preservation server architecture with regular tape backups.

We also looked at several channels to help in promoting the use of the video files. The team recognized that its content needed to be pushed to users and quickly looked to common XML formats that would enable this service delivery vision. Due to the site's blog beginnings, the team knew that our users were familiar with the benefits of Web feeds. We took this a step further and dynamically generated different versions of XML feeds to broadcast our content. TERRA content is distributed in iTunes RSS, RSS 2.0, Miro Player RSS, and FeedBurner HTML feeds.

As mentioned earlier, the "TERRA: The Nature of Our World" Web site was an opportunity to bring aspects of Web 2.0 and Library 2.0 into the digital library realm. With this in mind, we will take a closer look at the intersection between the TERRA projects and Web 2.0 and Library 2.0. At their core, Web2.0 and Library 2.0 are about Web applications that

+ are social

+ are continuously developed or in "perpetual beta"

+ are built with lightweight programming models

+ are created with open data structures to allow for remixing

+ embrace multiple modes of content distribution

On the social end, TERRA features a community space for comments about its videos. It even allows a rating system to help users judge and navigate to useful resources. The team built these functionalities with the idea that harnessing the collective intelligence of our users would make for a better application. The TERRA team also set up a forum space for users in the community to meet and chat. The site also features filmmaker chats which allow for any "TERRAphile" to converse with directors of the films. The team was interested in creating an active and involved user base and determined that giving users the opportunity to interact with TERRA site content was an essential move. The social Web widgets that allow TERRA users the opportunity to share thoughts with peers and directors, to create access points into the videos, and to rate and comment on the quality of the videos, all work to build a community and to forge a Web site that becomes much more than a few links to some digital objects. Our users are interested and invested because they can see that the site is organic and can participate in making it what it is.

A common theme in the development of 2.0 sites and applications is the notion of "perpetual beta," the idea that software or a system never leaves the development stage of beta (O'Reilly, 2005a). Behind this idea is a kernel of truth: quickly release your application, keep talking with your users via feedback mechanisms on the site, modify the application, rinse, and repeat. The TERRA team applied this idea by engaging users early and often. And no, the team did not engage in usability testing. Rather, we built feedback loops and an agile Web development team into the process. Case in point: my typical digital library development process follows a rigid six month project plan, from scanning and conversion to metadata and quality control and finally to interface and search/retrieval design. TERRA cut this development time in half, and closed those three months with the understanding that tweaking and responding to requests for additional features would be vetted and acted upon. For example, the "Recently Popular on TERRA" feature on the home page was a suggestion from a user who wanted to know what people had been watching lately. One of the challenges of this iterative approach to site design has been answering the wishes of an invested user community in a timely fashion.

The TERRA team is also utilizing lightweight programming models. Rather than build a piece of software with a versioning process, we have adopted open source programs to expedite development. The team has also worked to reuse project code and to rely on scripts developed by the PHP and MySQL programming community. By standing on the expertise of others, we can learn and develop TERRA applications expeditiously. In addition, we are using external network data stores at blip.tv, YouTube, and FeedBurner. Our data is distributed and this enables a nimble application.

Remixing, or "mashing up" content, was not a primary objective for the TERRA projects. To be honest, it was a fateful decision dictated by the campus network infrastructure. However, the move to mash up the Web services of TERRA resulted in numerous benefits. I am using the term "mashup" broadly here to mean the act of using third-party Web services and data sources to create new Web applications. As two examples of TERRA project mashups, we use XML to repurpose TERRA data into various corners of the Web such as iTunes and Google Reader, and we leverage the network infrastructure of YouTube and blip.tv to create a video storage and distribution module for TERRA data.

One of the first benefits that TERRA realized from the move to mash up was the delivery of our content to a broad audience on its own terms. Many visitors get our content in iTunes or their personal feed readers without visiting the site. We monitor

this fact in our server logs. In this new model of distribution, users are in charge and decide when to read and view TERRA videos or even how the videos might be organized to their own tastes.

Second, the scattered pieces of TERRA data can be consumed and reconstituted by other Web developers. With the exception of iTunes, all of our secondary service providers have standardized APIs that allow our data to be queried and rewritten into new Web applications and uses. A brief example: For the TERRApod project, the team is uploading video files onto YouTube and using the service as the storage back-end "database." We then make service calls with a Web scripting language to the YouTube API for XML data. The data is then transformed into a public interface. The whole process of consuming the YouTube Web service requires some technical knowledge and familiarity with a scripting language, but learning the guidelines and protocols is not impossible. A typical library systems department should have at least one worker who could make her or his way through it.

Third, the move to mash up our data created a network infrastructure that did not exist at the time. What is most striking about the TERRApod mashup is how it runs almost entirely within YouTube's public framework. In the end, we had a video upload module, a search interface, and rich media distribution "server" compliments of our leveraging the YouTube network cloud.

Fourth, the data mashup accelerated the pace of innovation at the library by introducing me to the power of Web services and standard open data. I was already aware of the benefits of standardized data in my work with MARC, but witnessing the power of re-purposing TERRA data to create entirely new Web applications was something altogether new. Along these lines, we have a public map view that records (voluntarily) where our users are from. The map application was created using Google Maps, a third-party Web service, which records and displays locations and pictures of our users on a world map (figure 6).

Fifth, and finally, the mashup strategy communicated to the library and university the changing nature of the Web. The remix mentality of "small pieces loosely joined" illustrated how the Web was becoming a platform for Web application development (O'Reilly 2005a). A Web developer could store data remotely and use various Web services to "stitch and weave" the components back together and create a Web application. It was a very liberating realization for a library that had felt tied to the static vision of the Web as a place to load HTML pages and pass around some pdfs.

In terms of content distribution, 2.0, TERRA illustrated to me how new models of pushing content are begging to be used. Consider the following: A NetFlix user downloads a copy of *The Departed* to his PC. A student searches the Apple iTunes store for her favorite song, downloads the file to her iPod, adds it to her playlist, and she is on to the task at hand. A faculty member visits the ABC news Web site, finds the news clip he missed from the night before, and watches the video in his Web browser from his desk over lunch. Increas-

ingly, these new models of content distribution are the norm. Leveraging built systems such as iTunes and standard XML formats such as Atom and RSS allowed the TERRA digital libraries to take advantage of the long tail (Anderson 2004). And we did not forget our old friend, e-mail. TERRA users can subscribe to a weekly e-mail detailing news and the latest video podcast release.

By distributing our content into multiple channels, TERRA was able to increase the demand for our content without having to work through traditional modes of promotion. For example, in the beginning of January 2007, "TERRA: The Nature of Our World" was packaged as a featured podcast in the Miro Player Download. Over the course of the next few weeks, we watched as up to 800 people per week became subscribed Terra users. This is the power of the long tail.

Future Plans

It is a challenge to envision all the features that the team could add. This is in keeping with the notion of perpetual beta. In his concise defini-

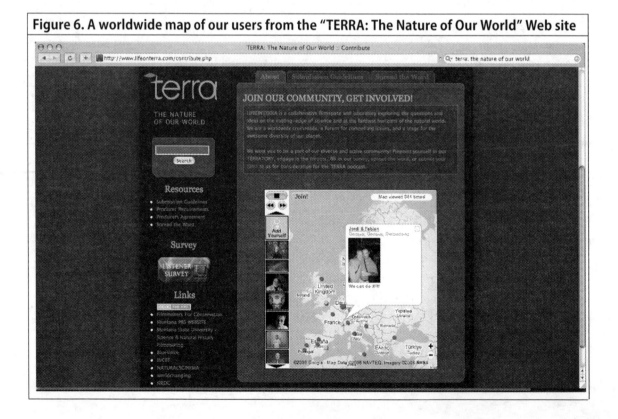

Figure 6. A worldwide map of our users from the "TERRA: The Nature of Our World" Web site

Figure 7. "TERRA: The Nature of Our World" as it appears in Wikipedia

tion of Web 2.0, O'Reilly mentions "delivering software as a continually-updated service that gets better the more people use it" (2005b). The team has embraced this notion of continual updates to the service and has outlined top priority enhancements. One is building into the TERRA platform a means for the general user to contribute films. The team has been looking at creating a module for direct upload of videos using the blip.tv API that would allow for the upload and subsequent rating of user-contributed videos. The plan is to allow some of the highest rated videos into a contest for a chance to produce a podcast for "TERRA: The Nature of Our world."

In addition, the team would like to create a more robust user tagging or folksonomy module for the site and mine the search data to create a search cloud of common queries. The team has also been discussing a means of embedding TERRA videos into blogs and Web pages. Open Archives Initiative (OAI) harvester compliance is also being considered to give the academic digital repositories outside of MSU a chance to col-

lect and preserve TERRA data. Another possible feature is the building of an eCommerce section, specifically a shopping cart application that would sell T-shirts and TERRA merchandise.

Conclusion

Web 2.0 and Library 2.0 have given rise to many challenges and opportunities for libraries. The user experience with the Web is changing. Users are changing the way they consume information. New technology has given rise to desktop-like interfaces in the Web browser. And most importantly, user expectations have changed. To meet these expectations, today's Web applications should be social, iterative, and built with open data structures.

MSU Libraries and TERRA have begun to experiment, and this experiment has informed current and future library applications at the university. In the process, we have learned several lessons.

Lesson one: Trust your users and learn from them. Users are telling us all kinds of things by their actions, contributions, and search queries.

Record this feedback and build it back into your service or application.

Lesson two: Build a community around your services. TERRA has made a point of engaging our viewing community. We have set up viewer surveys, allowed for continuous feedback with comments and rating within the site, and put our viewers in touch with our directors in the site forums. All of these acts have made for a loyal following. In fact, some users have created a Wikipedia entry for the site (Wikipedia 2007c).

Lesson three: Use open source and open data standards. The TERRA team relied on free software and widely supported data structures, such as XML, for the underpinnings of the Web site. This open programming and data foundation gave us a chance to innovate quickly and spread our content widely. Big time applications, such as Flickr, are leading the way by demonstrating how to use such open source software as MySQL and PHP to build large-scale Web applications. If they can use it on an enterprise level, it can certainly work for library applications.

Lesson four: Release early and often. The accelerated development timeline for TERRA was unnerving at times, but it did lead to a responsive and iterative Web application. In focusing on the essential functionality and building feedback loops into your application, you can bring applications to your public quickly and respond to user wishes more effectively.

Lesson five: Find a way to broadcast your content. The days of gatekeeping and shepherding people into a single Web service point are fleeting.

The TERRA projects confirmed for me the advantage of pushing your content into many corners of the Web. Even the aforementioned Wikipedia example is a means to create new access points. Use the networked environment to your advantage and sprinkle your library content around.

And finally, lesson six: Standardize your data for others to use. The TERRA projects embraced RSS as a format for content distribution. Because it is the de facto XML standard for the Web, we watched as our users found new and interesting ways to use and read our data. In effect, users started to create their own TERRA viewing modules and bypassed the site entirely. Digg.com (http://digg.com/) used our XML in this fashion when it syndicated "TERRA: The Nature of Our World" and placed it within the Digg.com Podcast module at

http://digg.com/podcasts/TERRA_THE_ NATURE_OF_OUR_WORLD/.

Suddenly, TERRA was part of the Digg.com phenomenon, but most importantly our data was exposed to a broad audience and repurposed for its specific needs. None of this would have been possible if the team had not standardized our data and allowed others the ability to apply a common format (RSS) to a new means of using TERRA data.

Each of these lessons brings home the fact that libraries can begin to move toward Library 2.0 services. As expectations and uses of the Web change, it is up to libraries to follow suit. Our library Web services and digital library applications can and will change and the TERRA case study only confirms that digital library 2.0 is not far away.

References

Anderson, Chris. 2004. The long tail. *Wired* (October). http://www.wired.com/wired/archive/12.10/tail.html.

Casey, Michael E. and Laura C. Savastinuk. 2006. Library 2.0: Service for the next-generation library. *Library Journal*, September 1. http://www.libraryjournal.com/article/CA6365200.html.

LISWiki. Library 2.0. http://liswiki.org/wiki/Library_2.0.

O'Reilly, Tim. 2005a. What is Web 2.0: Design patterns and business models for the next generation of software.

http://www.oreillynet.com/pub/a/oreilly/tim/news/2005/09/30/what-is-web-20.html.

O'Reilly, Tim. 2005b. Web 2.0: Compact definition? http://radar.oreilly.com/archives/2005/10/web_20_compact_definition.html.

Wikipedia. 2007a. Lazy Sunday. http://en.wikipedia.org/wiki/Lazy_Sunday (accessed June 17, 2007).

Wikipedia. 2007b. lonelygirl15. http://en.wikipedia.org/wiki/LonelyGirl15 (accessed June 17, 2007).

Wikipedia. 2007c. TERRA: The nature of our world. http://en.wikipedia.org/wiki/Terra:_The_Nature_of_Our_World (accessed June 17, 2007).

http://acrl.ala.org/L2Initiatives/index.php?title=Chapter_12/